The Metaphysics of Darkness

ROYAL ROUSSEL

The Metaphysics of Darkness

A STUDY IN THE UNITY AND DEVELOPMENT OF CONRAD'S FICTION

THE JOHNS HOPKINS PRESS
Baltimore and London

To Curley, Moe, and Larry

Copyright © 1971 by The Johns Hopkins Press
All rights reserved
Manufactured in the United States of America
The Johns Hopkins Press, Baltimore, Maryland 21218
The Johns Hopkins Press Ltd., London
Library of Congress Catalog Card Number 74-146458
ISBN 0-8018-1187-2

Contents

Preface

This book is an attempt to discover the unity of Conrad's fiction. It tries to demonstrate, in one context at least, a coherence underlying the apparent diversity of his novels and to trace the logic which dictates their order.

In this attempt I have juxtaposed two distinct perspectives on the landscape of Conrad's work. The opening chapter treats Conrad's writings—fiction and nonfiction—as one completed whole. This chapter has, in fact, two purposes. First, by considering Conrad's writings as a single linguistic gesture I have tried to isolate a fundamental vision at the center of all his fiction. I have tried, in other words, to show that a perception of the self's alienation from the source of its own existence delineates a world whose boundaries include, and unite, works as different as *Nostromo* and *A Personal Record*.

For Conrad, however, this central perception does more than generate a world. If his major characters are all engaged in voyages which are ultimately attempts to achieve a stable identity, then it is clear that the shape of Conrad's world will in turn determine the directions these voyages will take. From this point of view, the possible ways in which Conrad's characters try to define themselves and, in fact, the ways in which Conrad thought of the act of writing as defining himself, are dictated by the nature of this fundamental vision. The second half of the opening chapter describes this range of alternatives.

The chapters which follow take a different approach. They trace the chronological development of this vision as it is defined within the context of successive works. These chapters treat the novels as explorations in which the causes of consciousness' isolation gradually become explicit and the alternative methods of transcending this isolation are evaluated. Although I have given full readings of some novels, my real interest has been in the dramatic relation among them, in discovering the way in which the situation at the end of one novel implies the starting point of the next.

It is clear from even this brief description that the two sections of this study exist on radically different levels. The first chapter intentionally ignores the chronological order of the novels. Precisely because in its opening pages I am trying to define a vision common to all his writings, I bring together passages from as widely separated contexts as possible in order to isolate what is common to all of them. Again, in the latter half of this chapter I am dealing with a tension between an active commitment to life and an attitude of ironic detachment as this tension defines the spectrum of possible stances allowed by Conrad's world. I am dealing with it not as a contrast between two stages in Conrad's career, however, but as a dialectical opposition which is a part of his seminal perception of the world and which is implicit, therefore, in each moment of his work.

Obviously the movement from the abstractions of the opening pages to the explications of individual works which follow is at least potentially confusing, but I think it offers one valuable way of understanding the development of Conrad's fiction. Framed in the context of the first chapter, the progression of Conrad's novels reveals a certain internal logic. The sequence of the novels appears not as the result of a series of arbitrary choices but rather as the progressive working out of possibilities which are inherent in the perception from which all the fiction flows. In this sense, Conrad's central vision can be said to contain the order of the novels in the same way that a certain assumption can be said to contain a set of theorems which derive from it. It is the discovery of this logical order in the temporal progress of Conrad's novels which is the specific rationale for what might seem to be a perplexing mixture of critical foci.

Rather than the explication of individual works, the real subject of this study is clearly the continuity and development of a consciousness. This is not, of course, what might be called the biographical consciousness of Conrad himself. Instead, it is the consciousness immanent in the language of the literary work, the source from which the novels flow and of which the characters, descriptions, action and dialogue are expressions. The Conrad of the first chapter is defined by those qualities of vision which, persisting throughout the novels, make each recognizably Conradian. While this literary awareness is obviously a reflection of the actual Conrad, the precise angle of this reflection can never be measured and when I have referred to the narrator of a novel as "Conrad" or spoken of "Conrad's world" it is with the distinction always in mind.

In view of Conrad's productivity, any attempt to come to terms with the whole of his fiction inevitably must involve a choice of novels. I have chosen those which seem to me to mark important transitions in Conrad's development or to give a particularly clear access to a specific area of his world, but my choice is meant in no way to imply a qualitative evaluation or to suggest that only these novels are worth study. In fact where critical comment has been particularly full, as in the case of "Heart of Darkness" and *The Nigger of the "Narcissus,"* or where there exists a reading close to my own, as in the case of *The Secret Agent,* I have assumed these readings and only tried to indicate briefly the place of these novels in my tracing of the curve of Conrad's development. While I have assumed this material for the most part implicitly in order to devote most of my attention to Conrad himself, I am anxious here to express my debt to all of the students of Conrad who have attempted to map the often obscure and perplexing boundaries of his world.

The ultimate test of any critical approach is not in its complexity or its internal, logical consistency but in the quality of insight it allows into the literature itself. The abstractions of this

Preface and of the pages which follow are justified only if they permit the reader to return to Conrad's novels with a new vision. I did not intend in this book to reduce Conrad to a series of logical propositions, but to convey some of my own excitement in tracing his attempts to come to terms with his strange and terrible vision of the darkness. It is on the success of this project, and this alone, that the study must stand or fall.

Acknowledgments

During my work on the several forms of this study I have incurred a number of obligations. The greatest of these is to J. Hillis Miller. Professor Miller's influence on this manuscript will be apparent to anyone familiar with his work. It is responsible for whatever virtues this study might possess and I am grateful to be able to acknowledge it. But more than this he has taught me that literary criticism can be an honest and enjoyable activity, and this is a debt less easily discharged in a note.

I am grateful, too, for the company of Joe Riddel and Ed Dryden, my colleagues at the State University of New York at Buffalo. Their criticism saved me numerous embarrassments and at times their encouragement kept me from burning this manuscript.

I wish also to thank the staff of the Milton S. Eisenhower library of Johns Hopkins University, particularly Miss Martha Hubbard, and the library of the University of California at Santa Barbara, which provided me with facilities during the past two summers.

A Note on References

For Conrad's novels I have used the Canterbury Edition (Garden City, N.Y.: Doubleday, 1924). The Roman numerals refer to the following works:

I	*The Arrow of Gold*	XIII	*The Secret Agent*
II	*Chance*	XIV	*An Outcast of the Islands*
III	*Notes on Life and Letters*		
		XV	*Victory*
IV	*The Mirror of the Sea*	XVI	*Youth*
		XVII	*The Shadow Line*
V	*The Inheritors*	XVIII	*A Set of Six*
VI	*A Personal Record*	XIX	*'Twixt Land and Sea*
VII	*Romance*	XX	*Typhoon*
VIII	*Tales of Unrest*	XXI	*Lord Jim*
IX	*Nostromo*	XXII	*The Rescue*
X	*Within the Tides*	XXIII	*The Nigger of the "Narcissus"*
XI	*Almayer's Folly*		
XII	*The Rescue*	XXIV	*The Rover*

Where I have cited *Last Essays* (LE) I have used the Dent edition (London, J. M. Dent and Sons, 1955). "The Sisters" was published in *The Bookman*, LXVI (January, 1928), 481–95.

CHAPTER I

The World of Conrad

> *The novel is the form of adventure of the proper value of inwardness; its content is the history of the soul as it voyages in search of itself, seeking adventures in order to test itself and, through these adventures, finding its own essence.*[1]

All Conrad's major characters are, in a fundamental sense, orphans. For some, like Razumov in *Under Western Eyes*, their actual parentage is a question mark, but even those who have and know families feel a curious estrangement from them. To men like Marlow and Jim, their parents offer them no predestined place in an ordered world, or, if such a place exists, they do not feel it is a real alternative for them. Consequently they find themselves, like Razumov or like Pip in *Great Expectations*, existing in an open-ended world. The meaning of their lives is cast in the future tense. It lies in neither the past nor the here-and-now but is before them as a dream on the horizon.

It is this lack of an innate sense of a place in the world, of an identity, which is behind the restlessness which possesses characters as diverse as Razumov and Gould. Because they are not

[1] George Lukacs, *Theorie des Romans* (Darmstadt: Druck- und Verlags-Gesellschaft, 1965), p. 89. "Der Roman ist die Form des Abenteuers des Eigenwertes der Innerlichkeit; sein Inhalt ist die Geschichte der Seele, die da auszeiht, um sich kennenzulernen, die die Abenteuer aufsucht, um an ihnen geprüft zu werden, um an ihnen sich bewährend ihre eigene Wesenheit zu finden."

given such a place and such an identity, they discover they must turn outward to the world and win them. In this way Jim must search for some opportunity to realize his dreams of heroism in order to become truly a seaman and take his place in the community Marlow defines by the phrase "one of us" (XXI, 106). Until the opportunity is seized, Jim's existence is only potential, he has only "ability in the abstract" (XXI, 4), and as long as this ability is not made concrete he must remain as insubstantial as the shifting mists which continually obscure him from Marlow's view. This necessity to bring the dream to life applies equally to Gould's ambitions for a just government in Costaguana, Lingard's project to restore Hassim to his throne and Almayer's hopes for a life of wealth and ease in Amsterdam. Each of these men is engaged in an expedition, an adventure in Lukacs's words, to realize their vision and thereby escape the tentativeness of the dream.

Conrad's fiction is concerned with the various directions and forms this adventure may take, but although each novel may investigate a different alternative through which the self attempts to give itself solidity, the conditions which underlie the initial instability of all his characters remain constant throughout the body of his fiction. For Conrad, these conditions, conditions which measure the dimensions of his world, ultimately are neither political nor psychological. They flow instead from a more fundamental vision of the nature of all reality and of man's place in this reality, and it is with this unifying vision that we begin.[2]

The secret of the universe is in the existence of horizontal waves whose varied vibrations are at the bottom of all states of consciousness. If the waves were vertical the universe would be different.... Therefore it follows that two universes may exist in the same place and in the same time.... if by universe we mean a set of states of consciousness. And, note, *all* (the universes) composed of the same matter, matter, *all matter* being only that thing of inconceivable tenuity through which the vari-

[2] Again, this is not to imply that studies of Conrad's work from psychological or political points of view are less valid. I mean only that Conrad's work does imply a basic idea of the nature of creation and that, on one conceptual level, it is this idea which determines the structure of his world.

ous vibrations of waves (electricity, heat, sound, light, etc.) are propagated, thus giving birth to our sensations—then emotions—then thought. Is that so?

These things I said to the Dr while Neil Munro stood in front of a Röntgen machine and on the screen behind we contemplated his backbone and ribs. The rest of that promising youth was too diaphanous to be visible. It was so—said the Doctor—and there is no space, time, matter, mind as vulgarly understood, there is only the eternal something that waves and an eternal force that causes the waves...and by virtue of these two eternities exist that Corot and that Whistler...and Munro's here writings and your Nigger and Graham's politics and Paderewski's playing (in the phonograph) and what more do you want?[3]

Like many nineteenth-century writers Conrad was fascinated by theories of evolution and the picture they presented of a world of forms and men developing from undifferentiated matter. The ultimate reality in Conrad's world, the truth which underlies the "diaphanous" structures of all possible universes and all possible states of consciousness is just such inert matter. This "eternal something that waves" is dark like "the darkness before creation" (XVII, 113). It is "another night seen through the starry night of the earth—the starless night of the immensities beyond the created universe" (XX, 29). Because it precedes the creation of any form, it is itself formless. When the narrator of *The Shadow Line* steps into this darkness, he discovers that "every form was gone...spar, sail, fittings, rails; everything blotted out in the dreadful smoothness of that absolute night" (XVII, 113). This primal darkness transcends even the most basic categories of time and space. Like the silver of *Nostromo* which shares in the "majesty of inorganic nature, of matter that never dies" (XIII, 14), it is "incorruptible" (IX, 333) by time; like the plains and skies of Russia which so impress the young Stephan in "The Sisters" it seems to extend "through infinite space into an infinity of time" (TS, 484).

Conrad's primal darkness should not be associated in a simple and direct way with the everyday materiality of things. "There is," remarks Conrad, "no...matter...as vulgarly understood." This "unearthly substance" (XVII, 108) not only transcends time

[3] Edward Garnett, *Letters from Joseph Conrad* (New York: Bobbs-Merrill, 1962), pp. 143–44.

and space; it is also free of all characteristics of weight and mass which objects possess. Although this darkness is material, Conrad insists on the ephemeral nature of its materiality. It is, we recall, "a thing of inconceivable tenuity" which he describes in a letter to Cunninghame-Graham as "une ombre sinistre et fuyante dont il est impossible de fixer l'image."[4] To encounter this fundamental reality is not to meet a brick wall but to confront something "less palpable than a cloud" (XII, 247). It is to reach a point where all things are on the verge of "dissolving in a watery atmosphere" (XIII, 100). This darkness, it seems, is like "a wet London night, which is composed of soot and drops of water" (XIII, 150), but soot and water rarefied to the nth degree. The darkness from which all being comes is an image of matter stripped of all attributes but existence. It *is*, but nothing more can be said about it; it has no accessory qualities. For Conrad, this materiality is prior even to the "eternal force which causes the waves." Ultimately, it is something inconceivably still and quiet. It is "perfect silence joined to perfect immobility" (XVII, 115), an "indefinite immensity still as death" (XXI, 114), a "sinister immobility" (XII, 247).

Although it is itself without weight or dimension, this darkness lies behind all the distinct forms of creation. In his personal myth, the evolution of the cosmos seems to have been marked for Conrad by a series of stages in which this matter inexplicably took on more and more complex characteristics. In *An Outcast of the Islands* the narrator's description of the "smooth darkness" becoming "blotchy with ill-defined shapes, as if a new universe were being evolved out of a sombre chaos" (XIV, 236) suggests how the formless night comes to take on elementary qualities of weight and dimension. It is this "universe of drops of fire and clods of mud"[5] which, in turn, has given birth to the mechanical order of our world.

There is a—let us say—a machine. It evolved itself (I am severely scientific) out of a chaos of scraps of iron and behold!—it knits. . . . And the most withering thought is that the infamous thing has made itself; made itself without thought, without conscience, without foresight,

4 C. T. Watts, ed., *Joseph Conrad's Letters to R. B. Cunninghame-Graham* (Cambridge: Cambridge University Press, 1969), p. 117.
5 *Ibid.*, p. 65.

without eyes, without heart. It is a tragic accident—and it has happened. You can't interfere with it. The last drop of bitterness is the suspicion that you can't even smash it.[6]

As this passage indicates, Conrad does not believe that this creation took place in accordance with any coherent principle. The reason for his emphasis on its accidental quality is clear. The concept of evolution itself seems to have embodied for Conrad a fundamental contradiction. It seems, to him, to suggest that something can produce a creation which, if not its opposite, is at least totally foreign to its own nature. Thus the development of the knitting machine is absurd because the mechanical order of this machine is no more dormant in the "chaos of scraps of iron" than the weight and dimension of these scraps is implicit in the tenuosity of the darkness. Each stage of creation does not develop from the preceding stage according to some inherent principle in the way that an embryo, for example, gradually takes on human form. Such a concept would give Conrad's world an order and coherence which it does not possess. Instead, Conrad presents us with a universe which is progressively born from a ground opposed to its own being. The characteristics of the various stages of existence simply appear, and their appearance is as inexplicable and ridiculous as would be the birth of an elephant out of a rock. For Conrad, the universe has come into being through a series of such births in which absurdity has been piled upon absurdity.

It is important to see, moreover, that the emergence of each stage does not effect a complete transformation of the previous stage. The "immoderate wrath" (xx, 207) of the storm which attacks the *Nan-Shan* with a "senseless, destructive fury" (xx, 44) and the sea which appears to the crew of the *Narcissus* "as mischievous and discomposing as a madman with an axe" (xxiii, 104) suggests how some chaotic and irrational principle remains behind the order of the surface. In the same way, when Peyrol, in *The Rover*, is struck by the manner in which the "grey vapour, drifting high up, seemed to . . . add to the vastness of a shadowless world . . . all softened in the contours of its masses and in the faint line of its horizon, as if ready to dissolve into the immensity

---

[6] *Ibid.*, p. 56.

of the Infinite" (XXIV, 139), his perception testifies to the continued existence, behind even this chaos, of the tenuous darkness from which all has proceeded. Thus Conrad can describe a deserted street in *The Secret Agent* as "in its breadth, emptiness, and extent [having] the majesty of . . . matter" (XIII, 14), where the basic quality of materiality seems to be extension without content.

These primitive levels of existence do not remain present in the structure of our world as vestigial reminders of a departed past. Each is the essential foundation of the succeeding levels of creation. The trees of the jungle in *Almayer's Folly* and *An Outcast of the Islands* "struggle toward the life-giving sunshine above" (XI, 71) in a way that suggests the development of all creation toward higher forms of existence. This struggle does not free them from the darkness which gave them birth, however, and they still remain rooted in the "death and decay from which they sprang" (XI, 71), the "mud, soft and black, hiding fever, rottenness and evil under its level and glazed surface" (XIV, 325–26). In this, they are an image of the whole of creation, for Conrad's discussion of "the secret of the universe" implies not only that the origin of this world of Corots and Whistlers and phonographs lies in the "eternal something" but that it is "by virtue" of this medium that they continue to exist.

It is this birth of form from formlessness which gives Conrad's world its pervading tonality. If this is true, then it seems to him that all the created world is rooted in its own negation. The ordered surface of life, the seeming stability of nature which Jim sees mirrored in the "eternal peace" (XXI, 13) of the Eastern skies not only contains the "chaos of scraps of iron" but is in some way dependent on this chaos for its continued existence. This disordered universe made of "drops of fire and clods of mud" is related to the order of the knitting machine not only as a first cause but as a sustaining cause. Yet it is a sustaining cause whose essential, chaotic quality negates the mechanical stability which characterizes its creation. Such a situation renders this order and stability accidental in the sense that they do not have a ground in the nature of the source which produced them. There seems no logical way in which chaos can give birth to, and support, an ordered world.

6

Yet, as we have seen, this chaos is itself only an intermediate step. Grounded in the diaphanous materiality of the "eternal something," the seemingly immutable qualities of mass and dimension which characterize this universe of "clods of mud" and "scraps of iron" are themselves accidental. In developing his image of the world as knitting machine, Conrad, after stressing its indestructible nature, suddenly remarks to Cunninghame-Graham that "the machine is thinner than air and as evanescent as a flash of lightning,"[7] and the apparent contradiction here expresses clearly the way in which the essential characteristics of this machine are undercut or negated by the tenuous nature of the darkness which produced it. In the same way, Conrad's reduction of all the qualities which we think of as fundamental in existence—the body of Neil Munro, which turns out on investigation to be "too diaphanous to be visible," even "space and time as vulgarly understood"—to mere vibrations reflects this sense of the instability of a world grounded in a source which denies the very nature of its creation. This same sense of the ultimate tenuousness of matter underlies as well the otherwise puzzling disappearance of the Captain of the *Patna* in *Lord Jim*. This captain is described throughout the opening chapters in ways which emphasize his size and weight. He is "the fattest man in the whole blessed tropical belt" (xxi, 36), "a mass of panting flesh" (xxi, 24) who reminds one of "a trained baby elephant walking on hind legs" (xxi, 37). Yet when he leaves in a pony cart, it is as if this mass has suddenly evaporated. "A snorting pony snatched him to ewigkeit in the twinkling of an eye," remarks Marlow, "and I never saw him again; and what's more I don't know of anybody who ever had a glimpse of him after he departed. . . . He departed, disappeared, vanished. . . . He had flown into space like a witch on a broomstick" (xxi, 47). If nothing can be predicated of the original darkness other than the simple fact that it *is*, then, by the logic of Conrad's world, it can support nothing more complicated than simple, unqualified being. Any form of existence more sophisticated than this can have no real support in fundamental reality. It is clear, in this sense, that the greatest absurdity for Conrad is not the genesis of the world, but its continued

7 *Ibid.*, p. 65.

existence. The presence of the darkness at the source of all things is a constant reminder for Conrad of the insubstantiality of creation, of the ephemeral nature of what we accept as reality.

Conrad's discussion of the secret of the universe makes it clear that the vibrations in the "eternal something that waves" produce not only the forms of the physical world, but, even more absurdly, they are the source of the immaterial forms of "all possible sets of consciousness." His remark that these vibrations give birth first "to our sensations—then emotions—then thought" suggests that for him the appearance and development of human awareness has been simply the extension of the process which has brought about the existence of the physical cosmos. In the same way that the order of this cosmos has been born from chaos, so the material world, a world "without thought . . . without eyes, without heart,"[8] has produced the bare awareness of sensation and this primitive awareness has in turn produced progressively more complex modes of consciousness.

In the story of Taminah and Dain in *Almayer's Folly* Conrad has given us a description of this process of evolution. Before Dain's arrival Taminah exists precisely on that first and most primitive level of sensory awareness. It is not simply that she does not have the power of rational thought; she lacks even the most rudimentary emotional consciousness as well. Like the life of the jungle around her which struggles blindly for the sun, Taminah's existence is defined initially by a simple, instinctive reaction to external sensation. "She lived," the narrator tells us, "like the tall palms . . . seeking the light, desiring the sunshine, fearing the storm, unconscious of either. The slave had no hope and knew no change. . . . She had no wish, no hope, no love, no fear except of a blow. . . . The absence of pain and hunger was her happiness and when she felt unhappy she was simply tired" (xi, 112–13).

When the "full consciousness of life" (xi, 115) does come to Taminah, it does not arrive with a sudden flash. As Conrad's remarks indicate, awareness for him does not appear in such an abrupt fashion. Taminah's beginning self-consciousness is emo-

8 *Ibid.*, p. 56.

tional, not rational, and like the knitting machine it is not a creation ab ovo but proceeds from a more primitive level in her unconscious sensitivity to sensation. Conrad is very clear on this point; her awakening flows not simply from Dain's arrival. More specifically it has its beginnings in her first sight of him "walking erect . . . in the flash of rich dress, with a tinkle of gold ornaments" (XI, 114). It is this sight, not any explicit exchange of thoughts or feelings between them, which throws her into a "wild tumult of newly aroused feelings of joy and hope and fear" (XI, 114). In a similar manner, her rational consciousness is grounded in both the sensory and emotional levels of her experience. Taminah's love for Dain carries her eventually to a point where, "in the preoccupation of intense thinking" (XI, 112), she contemplates an image of him which has become less a physical impression than "the faint and vague image of the ideal" (XI, 116). This movement from a world of emotion into a world of thought, however, is one which Conrad is careful to point out has taken place "with the help of the senses" and which has "found its beginnings in the physical promptings of the savage nature" (XI, 116).

Like the levels of creation in the physical world, moreover, each stage of consciousness is not only born from a more primitive stage; it must retain its relation to this stage in order to continue its existence. Neither emotional nor rational consciousness develops into an independent entity. Even man's apparently self-contained reason must maintain its roots in emotion and sensation in order to survive. Again, Conrad is explicit on this point. While Taminah finds that Dain's approach arouses a "wild tumult" of emotions, she discovers as well that this tumult "died away with Dain's retreating figure" (XI, 114–15). When Dain leaves Sambir altogether, Taminah's "full consciousness" departs with him: "Dain disappeared, and Taminah's heart . . . forgot its joys and its sufferings when deprived of the help of the senses. Her half-formed savage mind, the slave of her body . . . forgot the faint and vague image of the ideal that had found its beginnings in the physical promptings of her savage nature. She dropped back into the torpor of her former life" (XI, 116). The peace which comes to her at this point, a peace which "was like the dreary tranquillity of the desert, where there is peace only be-

9

cause there is no life" (xi, 116), is an eloquent testimony to the essential connection which exists for Conrad between our most basic sensory experience of the world and the very existence of emotional and rational self-awareness.

The story of Taminah is, in this context, a revelation of mind's bondage to the laws which govern all creation. Human awareness, for Conrad, has no more independence than any other aspect of the world. It does not arise from an isolated moment of recognition when mind, abstracted from all around it, becomes alive to its own nature. Such a version of the Cartesian *cogito* with its implications of an independent consciousness is not possible here. The way in which Taminah's self-awareness is dependent for its existence on the presence of Dain before her is an example of how this self-awareness never transcends the content of its experience. Because it must always retain its foundation in sensation, it must always remain "the slave of her body."

For Conrad, then, consciousness must always turn outside itself to find the source of its existence in some ground which does not share its own nature. On the most fundamental level the orphaned quality which stigmatizes his characters flows from this position of consciousness in the world. The explanation of this lies in the very nature of what it means to be an orphan. When a child is born into a family, he is presented immediately with a name and an identity which this name symbolizes. Although this name and this identity do derive ultimately from something outside himself, from his family, they are made present to him in such a way that this derivative quality is minimized. Because they are presented to him continuously from the first moment of his awareness, the child assumes both to be innate elements of his existence. He assumes as a matter of course that he is continuous with the reality around him, and in this way, comes to possess a sense of solidity and self-contained being. To such children their names and selves have, in the words of one critic, "the dignity of an essence."[9]

[9] Jean Starobinski, "Truth in Masquerade," reprinted in *Twentieth Century Views: Stendhal* (Englewood Cliffs, N.J.: Prentice-Hall, 1962), p. 15.

10

Because his origins are not, by definition, present to him in such a way that he comes naturally to assume he shares in their reality, an orphan is denied this sense of solidity. On the contrary, his experience of these origins is an experience of something unknown, alien. Instead of assuring his identity, the orphan's relation to his source serves only to cast this identity in the form of a question. It is for this reason that the situation of the orphan has such a fundamental role in Conrad's thought, for it corresponds precisely to what is, for him, the initial standing place of consciousness. Like Pip in the opening chapter of *Great Expectations*, mind in Conrad always awakens to confront a world which has somehow given it birth but which paradoxically offers it no positive assurance of its existence. For this reason, mind's basic experience of itself, the experience which determines the whole quality of its self-awareness, is inevitably a negative one. Mind becomes aware of itself through the experience of what it is not in the same way that Pip becomes self-conscious in the recognition of the hostility of the moors and the alien tombstones of his parents. Such a negative experience, however, can never confer a positive identity. To discover what you are not obviously does not correspond to finding what you are. In fact, the negative experience only makes the absence of a concrete sense of self more acute. Again, this is the real meaning of the narrator's comment that Jim has only ability in the abstract, for to exist abstractly in this way is to exist only as a potential. It is to exist as an empty space which can be filled with any number of things, which can take any number of forms, but which, until then, *is* nothing.

The recognition of what for Conrad is the inevitable position of consciousness in the world allows us to understand not only the most basic cause of his heroes' restlessness but also the real object of their adventures. As is the case with Pip, the very fact that they experience themselves as abstract in this way forces them to voyage into the world which has given them birth and win from it the key to their selves. Like Pip, all are attempting to find the hidden source of their life and, by grounding themselves in it or by mastering it, to find the completeness of being which others are given at birth. But this parallel serves only to remind us of essential differences between a character like Pip and one like Lord Jim. Pip searches for this source in the world of men and discovers it in his symbolic father Magwitch. For Conrad's characters, however, the search has a deeper goal. Conrad is concerned with man's need to find a social or intersubjective ground for his self. The ideal of solidarity describes a world where such a ground is readily available and the same theme is implicit in Jim's desire to belong to the brotherhood of the sea and in Razumov's confession to Natalia Haldin. But in Conrad's world this search never takes place entirely on the human level. It always occurs within the context of the fundamental alienation of consciousness from its metaphysical source. Consequently, for most of his adventurers the voyage is not directed toward the discovery of a human parent but toward the ultimate origin of consciousness itself. The reward of success is not just an identity grounded in a social reality but rather the more basic independence which would result from mind assimilating and controlling its own source. Because they struggle toward a goal which transcends the human world, the adventures of many of Conrad's heroes suggest travels into the distant past toward the fount of life itself. Gould's return to the primitive world of Costaguana, Kurtz's and Marlow's journey up the Congo "to the earliest beginnings of the world" (XVI, 92), all suggest the attempt to descend through the intermediate levels of creation to confront the primal ground of existence.

The direction of this voyage suggests the disturbing truth which awaits these adventurers. Because the process which has given birth to mind is an extension of that which lies behind the structure of the physical world, consciousness is also subject to the same absurd paradox which decrees that the forms of existence should be born from a force which denies their essential nature. In the same way that the ordered surface of life is both produced by and yet threatened by the chaos of scraps of iron which lie beneath it, so mind discovers that it has been born from a force which is hostile to its very nature.

This paradoxical truth is at the center of Lord Jim's experience on the deck of the *Patna*. As we have seen, it is precisely the levels of sensation and emotion which have given birth to reason, which lift Taminah from an awareness which does not differ essentially from the tropical vegetation around her to a "full consciousness of life." For Conrad the essential nature of this consciousness is its sense of freedom and the ability to will which is traditionally associated with reason. This sense of freedom expresses itself on one level in Jim's dreams of heroism and in the feeling of limitless possibility which characterizes not only his attitude but that of all Conrad's youthful adventurers. More specifically, man's general sense of freedom and potentiality is symbolized for Conrad by our ability to move. The power of consciously directed movement seems to him the clearest proof of the reality of our freedom and, therefore, a necessary element in man's attempt to control the source of his existence. "To move," Conrad writes Garnett, "is vital—it's salvation."[10]

Although emotion has given birth to rational consciousness and its sense of free movement, it is just this "vital" characteristic which is destroyed by Jim's fear after the collision. In his description of the conditions surrounding Jim's jump, Conrad goes to great lengths to emphasize the way in which it was not a free action. The effect of Jim's fear is not to render him unconscious but rather to rob him of the ability to act on his thoughts. He discovers that, although there is "a hot dance of thoughts in his head," his terror has "turned him into cold stone from the soles of his feet to the nape of his neck" (xxi, 96–97). These thoughts are like a "dance of lame, blind, mute . . . a whirl of awful cripples" (xxi, 97) precisely because they cannot express themselves in action. For this reason, the jump itself appears to be something which Jim undergoes passively. As Marlow tells us, "something had started him off at last, but of the exact moment, of the cause that tore him out of his immobility, he knows no more than the uprooted tree knows of the wind that laid it low" (xxi, 109). From this point of view, the sense of passivity which infuses Jim's narrative, the impression he gives that "he had not acted but had suffered himself to be handled" (xxi, 108) is not, as Marlow implies, an illusion. It is a revelation of the hostility of emotion to the essential characteristic of its own creation.

The destruction of the dream of reason by the irrational is not, however, the final revelation which comes to Conrad's characters. Emotional and sensory awareness are themselves intermediate

10 Garnett, *Letters*, p. 109.

stages of creation and, consequently, they themselves flow from sources which absurdly deny their nature. Sensation and emotion are, after all, modes of consciousness, however primitive, and the final truth at which Conrad's characters arrive is one which denies not only rational awareness but awareness itself. All awareness flows from the vibrations in the "eternal something that waves" which are the source of "sensations—then emotion—then thought." When these characters confront the darkness in its most primitive form, however, they find to their horror that these fundamental vibrations are not inherent in the basic nature of the "eternal something." Instead they discover "perfect silence joined to perfect immobility" (xvii, 115).

To see this "deadly stillness" (xvii, 95) lying behind the vibrations of the eternal something is, again, to see the forms of creation rooted in a source which denies them. Because the darkness in its ultimate form negates the ground of any awareness, Conrad's characters experience this darkness not as a sensation but as the absence of sensation, an absence which is like "a foretaste of annihilation" (xvii, 108) precisely because it deprives consciousness of its foundation in sensory experience. The most obvious instance of such a deprivation of sense is that of Martin Decoud. Decoud's one last belief in the "truth of his own sensations" (ix, 229) is destroyed when he voyages from "sights and sounds" (ix, 152) of the shore into the "enormous stillness, without light or sound" (ix, 262) which enshrouds the Golfo Placido. It is implicit also in Jim's experience in the *Patna* incident. His leap into the darkness carries him into a world where "the silence of the sea, of the sky merged into one indefinite immensity still as death" (xxi, 114), where "there was nothing to see and nothing to hear. Not a glimmer, not a shape, not a sound" (xxi, 114). It is this death-like stillness, rather than his irrational fears, which is the final threat of the darkness. It promises not paralysis, but complete extinction. Marlow himself explicates this threat in a passage which summarizes the relation between sensation and consciousness. "His saved life was over for want of a ground under his feet, for want of sights for his eyes, for want of voices in his ears. Annihilation—hay!" (xxi, 117). One of Conrad's important images for this experience of impending annihilation is that of falling. Willems, in the grip of those feelings for Aissa which result eventually in his death, is "like one who, falling down a smooth and rapid declivity that ends in a precipice, digs his finger nails into the yielding surface and feels himself slipping helplessly into inevitable destruction" (xiv, 78). Willems's experience is essentially similar to that of Kurtz's fall into the abyss after he has "kicked himself loose from the earth" (xvi, 114), or Jim's experience when sea and sky "merged into one indefinite immensity" (xxi, 114) and the boat "seemed to be falling through it" (xxi, 125). In each instance, the image captures the sense of groundlessness and lack of support which comes over these characters when they discover that the darkness denies the very essence of their life.

This sense of groundlessness, and the annihilation which it promises, is a revelation of the infinitely precarious place of mind in the world. Although mind has been produced by the same force which has formed the physical world, its appearance is even more absurd, since by their very nature as physical objects, the forms of the material world have a solidity of being which is denied to consciousness. Even though these objects can be stripped of all accidental qualities of size, shape, and color, they cannot be stripped of that one attribute of bare existence which is the single characteristic of the eternal something. For this reason, the silver of *Nostromo* retains through all its superficial transformations from ore to ingot a certain continuity of existence. At its core, its material essence, it is something which is outside of time, something whose basic existence cannot be tampered with. "Matter," Conrad remarks, "never dies" (xiii, 14), and for this reason material objects possess a certain smugness in Conrad's world—they can be altered but not annihilated.

Because mind is not essentially material, however, it is denied such a firm ground. Consciousness is, for Conrad, one of the accidental properties which, like size, weight, and color, appear in material bodies at various stages in their evolution. To strip these bodies to their center of bare existence is, therefore, to annihilate mind entirely. The death of Stevie Verloc in *The Secret Agent* is an image of this radical disparity between mind and matter. The explosion does not destroy Stevie's body. Although it is reduced to formless bits and pieces, it remains in some sense indestructible. But there is no trace of his consciousness.

The knowledge of a hostile, annihilating force at the center of existence brings to Conrad's characters a constant sense of their personal vulnerability. Before this revelation, they were orphans in search of a ground for their lives, but they never doubted their ability to discover such a ground. Marlow in "Youth," Lord Jim, Razumov, all are like the narrator of *The Shadow Line*, who initially sees his life's road laid before him like a line on a chart and supposes that the difficulties which he will meet are predictable and easily dismissed. With the discovery that this assurance of a realized self is an illusion, however, the initial restlessness of Conrad's heroes is transformed into something much more destructive and difficult to contend with. Condemned men, they are forced to live in the contemplation of the immediate possibility of their death, and like a tightrope walker whose casual glance down destroys his equilibrium, the knowledge of possible destruction becomes itself the first step toward this destruction. The full realization of their danger appears in a nervous sensitivity to self, a persistent, subliminal fear which undermines any sense of rational control in the same way that the tightrope walker's awareness of the emptiness beneath him robs him of his ability to balance. In this way, Lord Jim's confident march toward heroism is transformed into his frightened retreat toward the East.

For most of Conrad's characters, the experience of vulnerability marks the real beginning of their voyage. Conrad's novels are attempts to come to terms with this experience, to work out ways of living with or overcoming this knowledge, for only if some such way can be found can man ever attain a stable identity. How is this possible? What are the directions this search can take? In Conrad's world there are two general alternatives open to man.

Perhaps mind can confront the darkness directly and master it. Although this darkness is in its essence something alien to mind, if mind can assert its control over this force, if it can give it rational form and substance and thus fix the image of the "ombre sinistre et fuyante"[11] the darkness will be robbed of its destructive potential. By assimilating its sources in this way, it might still be possible for man to achieve self-sufficiency. While he will not have found a father, found some source which naturally confers its reality upon him, man will have made one.

For most of Conrad's characters, the initial thrust of their attempt to assert sovereignty over the ground of their existence is directed toward its immediate source in the irrational. Jim's search for another opportunity for heroism is a search for some way to vindicate the code of the sea, and this code implies just this ability of the conscious will to control the irrational. The code of the sea, Marlow tells us, is "a precious notion of a convention ... with its assumption of unlimited power over natural instincts" (XXI, 81). On a larger scale, Charles Gould's visions of rational justice in Costaguana are an effort to assert mind's power over the "natural instincts" of greed, hatred and fear which have been responsible for the country's fifty years of misrule.

Ultimately, however, man's efforts to control the darkness must lead him beyond the irrational. He must come to grips with the tenuous material of the darkness whose vibrations give rise to all levels of consciousness if his efforts to master his own being are to be successful. For this reason, Conrad's heroes are not contemplatives. Although most are obsessed by the dream and by their habit of "idealizing every simple feeling" (IX, 214), their object is not, at least initially, to create a fantasy world in which mind exists unto itself. Like the dreams of Don Quixote, these visions express the desire of consciousness itself to mould the world around it to its own image. In the final analysis, the aim of these characters is always to perform some concrete action in the world, an action which will bring the dream to reality. Some, like Lord Jim or Captain Anthony, are driven by the "need for embodying in their conduct [their] dreams ... passion ... impulses" (II, 328); others, like Charles Gould, work on a larger canvas. All, however, are concerned with this act of incarnation through which the physical world is moulded to a spiritual vision.

[11] C. T. Watts, *Letters*, p. 117.

To perform this act successfully is to transform matter into mind, to make it something which is no longer alien and hostile but which shares the nature of consciousness. It is just such a transformation which Emma Gould at least momentarily accomplishes in *Nostromo*. When she lays her hand on the first bar of silver from the San Tomé mine, "by her imaginative estimate of its power she endowed that lump of metal with a justificative conception, as though it were not a mere fact but something far-reaching and impalpable, like the true expression of an emotion or the emergence of a principle" (IX, 107). If man can succeed in spiritualizing matter in this way, if he can transform lumps of metal into incarnations of his dreams, then the world around him will no longer turn a hostile face toward him. It will, instead, reflect his own nature. When this occurs, man will have succeeded in assimilating his own source to himself and, in doing so, have founded his inner world in external reality. For this reason, men like Gould and Jim are constantly searching for the moment when they will have achieved such a true incarnation and their rootless lives will be transformed by the "marvellousness of an accomplished fact fulfilling an audacious desire" (IX, 105).

It is not absurd for men to hope to master the darkness in this way. In Conrad's private mythology there was a time during the golden age of sail when men were able to control their world, a time when they had no destructive sense of a hostile force at the center of creation and were able to live in a fellowship with it which approached the medieval concept of the unity of man and nature in God. Conrad praises James Fenimore Cooper for capturing just this aspect of the world of sail. "In his sea tales," Conrad writes, "the sea inter-penetrates with life . . . it is always in touch with the men who . . . traverse its immense solitudes" (III, 55). In parts of *The Nigger of the "Narcissus"* and in *The Mirror of the Sea*, Conrad himself tries to re-create the sense of a time when man and nature interpenetrated. To such men, the sea "is not a navigable element, but an intimate companion" (IV, 71) and, as such, shares a fundamentally human quality. The crew of the *Narcissus* begin their voyage in a world governed not by the negative principle of the darkness but by a benevolent providence which sends storms "paternally, to chasten a simple heart" (XXIII, 31) and breezes which stir the "tumbled hair" of the crew "with a touch passing and light like an indulgent caress" (XXIII, 32).

These men lack as well the more personal sense of the darkness at the source of their own being. In the same way as they accept unquestioningly the surface of the world around them, they accept their own sense of conscious control of themselves and their environment. Protected by the "blessed forgetfulness of sailors, that forgetfulness natural and invincible, which resembles innocence in so far that it prevents self-examination" (XIX, 82), they have no awareness of the force which, on the deck of the *Patna*, robs Jim of just this control. Since they are blessed with a sense of the inviolate integrity of their will, all problems are practical ones. Characters such as Lingard approach life with an instinctive optimism because the question for them is never whether they have the power to achieve some end but rather how it is to be accomplished. When they contemplate the world around them they contemplate only "the visible surface of life open in the sun to the conquering tread of an unfettered will" (XII, 210). For them, the step from vision to reality, from the dream to its successful incarnation, is a short one. Lingard's relation to his bark, *Flash*, is a symbol of his early ability to realize the dream in this way, to bring the external world under the control of consciousness and subdue its alien and hostile nature. "He," we are told, "was the inspirer of that thing that to him seemed the most perfect of its kind. His will was its will, his thought was its impulse, his breath was the breath of its existence" (XII, 11).

Because the men of this time have a natural control of themselves and of their environment, they are able to live in harmony with one another as well, and, in the Preface to *The Nigger of the "Narcissus,"* Conrad speaks directly of the "latent feeling of fellowship" (XXIII, xiii) which, more than uniting "all mankind to the visible world," in addition "binds men to each other" (XXIII, xvi). The harmony and fellowship appear specifically in the openness which exists among men who live the life of the sea. They share a true interworld in which each has access to the thoughts and heart of those around him. When they look to the other members of their world, they find that their nature is

19

understood, accepted and, in this sense, confirmed by these others. When he assumes his first command, the narrator of *The Shadow Line* finds himself, alone and frightened, staring at his reflection in the cabin mirror, but he is saved from this isolation by his sudden discovery that the nature he sees reflected is one whose validity is grounded in its relation to a whole community:

It struck me that this quietly staring man whom I was watching, both as if he were myself and somebody else, was not exactly a lonely figure. He had his place in a line of men whom he did not know, of whom he had never heard; but who were fashioned by the same influences, whose souls in relation to their humble life's work had no secrets for him. (XVII, 53)

Conrad gives no single explanation for the disappearance of this sense of stability from man's life. At times he suggests that the modern mind's "intense consciousness of itself" (LE, 48) results from the inevitable development of human awareness from primitive to more sophisticated levels; at times it results from some specific event, such as the First World War. It is clear that for Conrad the knowledge of the darkness is close to the surface of modern life and that even the initial, naive restlessness of his heroes implies some vague awareness of their vulnerability which would be foreign to Singleton and the men of his generation. The London commuters who scatter "in all directions, walking away fast from one another with the hurried air of men fleeing from something compromising . . . like truth or pestilence" (VIII, 119) are different only in degree from Jim fleeing the memory of his cowardice, and, by the same token, the disintegrating effects of this awareness touch not only the lives of individual adventurers but attack the very fabric of society. It is because the knowledge of the darkness lies just beneath the surface of the modern consciousness that civilization has become for Conrad something "essentiellement criminelle."[12] Increasingly trapped in the constricting circle of their own fear, men are no longer able to commit themselves to any principle or person in an unselfish way. Now, Conrad remarks, "fraternity means nothing unless the Cain-Abel business."[13] In such a world, it is not possible for a

[12] *Ibid.*, p. 47.
[13] *Ibid.*, p. 117.

real society to exist. Men no longer live with one another in mutual openness but turn on others "the same stare, concentrated and empty" (VIII, 119) and present to those around them the blank and hostile wall of their egoism.

Man's gathering sense of the darkness thus robs him not only of a sense of ontological security. It destroys any subsidiary foundation he might find in his relation to other men and, in this, we can see how, for Conrad, man's position in society is always related to the fundamental situation of consciousness in the world. It would be a mistake, however, to see his image of the world of the sea as simply a point of reference from which he can measure man's fall from innocence—for one side of Conrad, and for one set of his characters, it is a positive goal. Charles Gould's ambition to bring order to Costaguana by controlling the power of the silver or Jim's effort to validate the ideal of the brotherhood of the sea in one heroic action are both attempts to reassert man's power over the darkness and, by doing so, to re-create the condition of stability which allowed man's former, happy state to exist.

Perhaps, however, the attempt to control the darkness is an act of madness. The presence of an annihilating darkness at the source of creation suggests that in the "contest of man interlocked with matter"[14] man will achieve at best a temporary victory. Since mind must draw its strength from the very force which contests its domination, it would seem that it would be impossible for mind ever to defeat this source. It would always lose in such a contest. If this is true, then to attempt to subjugate this source is to invite inevitable destruction. To follow such a course is for man to bring himself willingly into contact with his own negation.

Conrad himself casts doubts on the possibility of re-creating the world of Singleton in a modern context. On the one hand, there is no doubt concerning the continued appeal of these values for Conrad, and at many points during his career he returns to express his belief in the simple virtues of this time.

[14] Garnett, *Letters*, p. 84.

The passage from the Preface to *A Personal Record* affirming his conviction that "the world, the temporal world, rests on a very few simple ideas; so simple that they must be as old as the hills. It rests, notably, among others on the idea of Fidelity" (VI, xxi) is only the most often quoted. The pervasive emotional tone of works such as *The Mirror of the Sea* and *The Nigger of the "Narcissus"* testifies to the depth of this belief.

At the same time, many of his comments suggest not only that the security of the men of Singleton's world was an illusion but that it is impossible for men today to re-create this illusion. Thus, while he refers to *The Mirror of the Sea* as "the soul of my life,"[15] he casts doubts on his ability to participate once again in its unique outlook. "It was another life," he wrote Huneker, "which I remember with misty tenderness, as a transmigrated soul might be supposed to remember its previous envelope."[16] Again, writing to Henry James on *The Nigger of the "Narcissus,"* he stresses the illusory nature of this world, a world which seems irretrievably lost:

Il est, sans doute, mauvais, rien de si facile comme de recounter un rêve, mais il est impossible de pénétrer l'âme de ceux qui écoutent par la force de son amerturme et de sa doceur. On ne communique pas la realité poignante des illusions.[17]

Conrad's scepticism concerning any attempt to master the darkness and thus retrieve the peace of man's youth appears particularly clearly in his correspondence with Robert Cunninghame-Graham. Cunninghame-Graham was, for a time, a liberal member of Parliament and remained throughout his life a political radical devoted to reform. The arguments which Conrad directs against his friend are not, however, those of a simple political conservatism, and he is not concerned with advancing another, alternative political philosophy. Conrad's objections are more fundamental in that they raise the question of the validity and efficacy of *any* political movement and, in this sense, testify to the depth of Conrad's commitment to what is basically a metaphysi-

15 R. L. Megroz, *A Talk with Joseph Conrad* (London: Faber, 1926), p. 53.
16 Arnold T. Schwab, "Joseph Conrad's American Friend: Correspondence with James Huneker," *Modern Philology*, LII (May, 1955), 222–32.
17 Joseph Conrad, *Lettres Françaises*, ed. Georges Jean-Aubry (Paris: Gallimard, 1930), p. 34.

cal vision. Conrad undercuts Cunninghame-Graham's optimism by arguing that man's awareness of the negating force at the center of his existence and the irrational sense of vulnerability which follows this discovery are unavoidable and that, for this very reason, any rational political movement is impossible. Against Cunninghame-Graham's belief in man's power to consciously mould his world, Conrad opposes the vision of a mankind which, like Jim on the deck of the *Patna*, has been inevitably reduced to cowardice by its knowledge of the darkness.

You with your ideals of sincerity, courage and truth are strangely out of place in this epoch of material preoccupations. What does it bring? What's the profit? What do we get by it? These questions are at the root of every moral, intellectual, or political movement.... Every cause is tainted: and you reject this one, espouse that one as if one were evil and the other good, while the same evil you hate is in both, but disguised in different words.... Alas! what you want to reform are not institutions—it is human nature. Your faith will never move that mountain.[18]

In a world where men are obsessed by their own safety and well-being, a community such as existed among the men of Singleton's generation is impossible. Conrad can remark to Cunninghame-Graham that "la société est essentiellement criminelle"[19] precisely because men have become "fourbes, lâches, menteurs, voleurs"[20] who, like criminals, are in their fear devoted to their own selves at the expense of those around them. If this is the inevitable condition of mankind, then politics is in truth a pointless game. In another letter to Cunninghame-Graham, Conrad calls into question not only the validity of political movements, but of any positive commitment to the world.

"Put the tongue out" why not? One ought to really. And the machine will run on all the same.... The attitude of cold unconcern is the only reasonable one. Of course reason is hateful—but why? Because it demonstrates (to those of us who have the courage) that we, living, are out of life,—utterly out of it. The mysteries of a universe made of drops of fire and clods of mud do not concern us in the least. The fate of a humanity condemned ultimately to perish from cold is not worth troubling about. If you take it to heart it becomes an unendurable

[18] C. T. Watts, *Letters*, p. 68.
[19] *Ibid.*, p. 117.
[20] *Ibid.*, p. 84.

tragedy. If you believe in improvement you must weep, for the attained perfection must end in cold, darkness and silence. In a dispassionate view the ardour for reform, improvement for virtue, for knowledge, and even for beauty is only a vain sticking up for appearances, as though you were anxious about the cut of one's clothes in a community of blind men.[21]

These passages from Conrad's letters define another side of Conrad, a side radically opposed to the image of a conservative ex-ship's captain committed to the preservation of the simple virtues of the past. Although Conrad in his more optimistic moments can write to H. G. Wells that "the future is of our own making—and (for me) the most striking characteristic of the century is just that development, that maturing of our consciousness which should open our eyes to that truth" there is always an element which leads him, even then, to qualify "that truth" with the phrase "or that illusion."[22] Early critics of Conrad give a perplexing vision of a man who was split in this way between light and dark. On the one hand M. C. Bradbrook pictures him as a writer whose triumph consists in "reducing the complex to the simple."[23] On the other, Arthur Symons calls him one of "the most sinister and somber personalities of our time"[24] and gives a diametrically opposed analysis of the temperament behind his works:

Conrad created by some inexplicable, by some mysterious, by some occult form of mesmerism, worlds unknown, unimaginable, monstrous and most perilous; and, having created and judged them, I imagine him, squatting like some Satanical spider in his web, in some corner; stealthily hidden away from view, throwing out ... tentacles into the darkness. At the center of his web sits an elemental sarcasm discussing human affairs with a cynical ferocity; behind that sarcasm crouches some powerful devil, insidious, poisonous, irresistible, spawning evil for its own delight.[25]

[21] Ibid., p. 65.
[22] Gérard Jean-Aubry, Joseph Conrad: Life and Letters (Garden City, N.Y.: Doubleday, 1927), I, 323.
[23] M. C. Bradbrook, Joseph Conrad: Poland's English Genius (Cambridge: Cambridge University Press, 1941), p. 77.
[24] Arthur Symons, Notes on Joseph Conrad with Some Unpublished Letters (London: Myers, 1925), p. 7.
[25] Ibid., pp. 7–8.

The correspondence with Cunninghame-Graham does more, however, than simply define one, generally unemphasized, aspect of Conrad's personality. Within the conceptual framework of Conrad's thought, these letters suggest another method of coming to terms with the darkness. The second approach begins, too, with an awareness of the negative force at the center of existence. "Aussi, souvent," he writes to Cunninghame-Graham, "je n'y pense pas. Tout disparaît. Il ne reste que la vérité,—une ombre sinistre et fuyante dont il est impossible de fixer l'image."[26] But instead of reacting to this intuition with an attempt to subdue the darkness and bring it under the control of consciousness, Conrad here points in an opposite direction. He implies that man can escape destruction by accepting the fact that it does invalidate existence. For characters such as Jim or Nostromo, this perception gives birth to an irrational sense of danger which ultimately destroys them, but the fact that they do react in this way is evidence of their emotional commitment to their own existence. If one has the courage to face rationally the fact that "we, the living, are out of life" and to take this to its logical conclusion then even this final commitment to self vanishes. "C'est un égoïsme rationnel et féroce que j'exerce envers moi-même" continues Conrad, and this allows him finally to achieve the proper attitude of "cold unconcern." "Je ne regrette rien— je n'espère rien car je m'aperçois que ni le regret ni l'espérance signifient rien à ma personnalité."[27] If one is able to detach one-self from all ties to the world, to distinguish his "personnalité" from all positive involvement in existence, then he is impervious to any destructive sense of vulnerability precisely because the negation of life no longer means anything to him. Once this point has been reached, his life comes to possess a certain stability.

If one looks at life in its true aspect then everything loses much of its unpleasant importance and the atmosphere becomes cleared of what are only unimportant mists that drift past in imposing shapes. When once the truth is grasped that one's own personality is only a ridiculous and

---

[26] C. T. Watts, *Letters*, p. 117.
[27] *Ibid.*, p. 117.

aimless masquerade of something hopelessly unknown, the attainment of serenity is not very far off.[28]

It is this detachment which lies behind the ironical stance of Decoud in *Nostromo* and of the narrators of the first four chapters of *Lord Jim* and *Nostromo*. In this context, their attitude appears not as the expression of an arbitrary mood but something which functions on a more important level. A certain detachment is implicit in irony because irony implies a dual perception. It is the expression of an awareness of the tension between two levels of existence or meaning, one of which undercuts the other. The ironic point of view is never completely committed to the literal level of experience in the same way that the ironic character is never completely committed to the activity in which he is engaged. In both cases, their vision always extends beyond to encompass a wider context which qualifies in some way this primary level.

For Conrad's ironic characters and narrators, this tension exists between their initial commitment to the world of men and action and their awareness of a darkness which nullifies the validity of this world. Commenting on the characters in Alphonse Daudet's fiction, Conrad writes that "inevitably they *marchent à la mort*—and they are very near the truth of our common destiny: their fate is poignant; it is intensely interesting, and of not the slightest consequence" (III, 24). The dynamics of this passage is an image of the dynamics which informs the consciousness of all of Conrad's ironic characters. On the one hand there is a primary commitment and sympathy with a mankind which is "poignant" and "interesting." Then this involvement is immediately and deliberately undercut by a nihilism which destroys this commitment by trivializing it, by making its object something "of not the slightest consequence," in the same way that Conrad, in his letter to Garnett, advises him to attain serenity by recognizing that "one's own personality is only a ridiculous and aimless masquerade."

From their initial encounter with the darkness, then, there emerge two possibilities for Conrad's characters. They can return to commit themselves to the world and the men who inhabit it. To do this is to affirm at least the possibility that the dream can be realized: that man, through his own will can master the darkness and win for himself a stable identity. Alternatively, they can accept the darkness as final and, by doing so, come to terms with the ephemerality of their own selves. To do so is to reconcile themselves to being orphans who can never transcend their initial, tentative state of existence.

This polarity between a commitment to the dream and an acceptance of the darkness determines the limits of the whole spectrum of Conrad's characters, from Lord Jim and his visions of heroism to Martin Decoud's ironic murmurs. It also delineates as we shall see a range of aesthetic alternatives, moving from the realism of *Almayer's Folly* to the ironic narrator of *The Secret Agent*. Defining as it does the modes both of confronting the darkness and of writing about it, this polarity can be said to mark the limits of Conrad's fictional world.

Yet, to view Conrad's fiction in this way as a series of alternative stances deployed logically around a central perception is to view his work as a static, completed whole. It is to stand where the reader stands after the completion of a novel: at that point where he reflects and assembles into one perspective vistas which have opened to him one by one. Such a perspective allows us to capture the internal logic of Conrad's fiction, but its sense of comprehensiveness is, on one level at least, misleading. Just as the experience of reading is defined not only by our final perspective of a work but also by the limited horizons opened by each succeeding page, so the essence of Conrad's work lies not only in a last, all-encompassing definition of his world but in the developing perspectives which each novel affords. If Conrad's work does indeed define a world, a world implicit in the first and last novel, it is one which, like all new worlds, must be explored gradually. To the reader, and, in a sense, to Conrad himself in the course of writing his novels, it appears first as the East does to Jim, a vague, seemingly infinite horizon whose limits, dangers and promises are realized only in the act of voyaging to it. The following chapters are concerned with this voyage. They attempt to trace Conrad's gradual definition of his world and his investigation of the alternative ways in which men can live in it.

27

CHAPTER II

Almayer's Folly: *The Voyage to the Source of Life*

The development of Conrad's fiction from *Almayer's Folly* through the early versions of *The Rescue* is the record of his discovery of the darkness. For Conrad, this discovery is a gradual one. It does not come as a sudden revelation of the destructive truth at the center of existence but flows from a preliminary and more limited awareness of the corruption of modern society. In the beginning, it seems, Conrad does not recognize the nature of this truth nor does he understand its effects on the men around him. Coming from years in the communal life of the sea, he appears to have been struck most forcefully by the barren landscape of the city in which men exist rootless and isolated, cut off from all life outside themselves. Consequently, despite its primitive setting the Malayan trilogy is not begun as a deliberate exposition of the darkness. The novels are initially concerned with explaining how the egoism and materialism of a world in which "each must button himself together, and take no thought ... of his neighbour"[1] are on the point of destroying

[1] The line is from Carlyle, quoted in James Anthony Froude, *Thomas Carlyle: A History of the First Forty Years of His Life in London* (London,

society. It is only in the course of this analysis, and through the subsequent search for a way to purge man of these qualities, that he discovers the true nature of the force behind creation.

Both Almayer in *Almayer's Folly* and Willems in *An Outcast of the Islands* are representative of this corrupt world, and both exhibit those qualities which Conrad sees as the fundamental causes of its disintegration. Almayer leaves home fired with dreams of "great piles of shining guilders . . . all the possibilities of an opulent existence . . . the indolent ease of life—for which he felt himself so well fitted" (xi, 10). In the same way, Willems jumps ship to make his fortune and his first words to Lingard are, "Get money here; home no good" (xiv, 15). Willems in particular is characterized by that egocentricity which, for Conrad, goes hand in hand with the profit motive. "There is always some one thing which the ignorant man knows," remarks the narrator of *An Outcast of the Islands*, "and that thing is the only thing worth knowing; it fills the ignorant man's universe. Willems knew all about himself" (xiv, 6).

Because these two characters are so directly the products of the dominant forces in European civilization, the worlds which Almayer and Willems build for themselves in Malaya are in effect microcosms which reflect the conditions existing on a larger scale in London and Amsterdam. It is these microcosms which are the real subject, the real starting point, of the novels. They allow Conrad to focus in detail on the relationship between the individual and others which is the foundation of society and to capture the particular quality of this relation in a world governed by selfishness and greed. For Conrad, it is only by grasping the special coloration of the egoist's attitude to those around him that we can understand the nature of the threat these forces pose to civilization.

The key to this explanation lies in the paradoxical nature of Willems's and Almayer's dependence on others. On the one hand,

---

1884), p. 207, but it suggests how the starting point for Conrad is a characteristically Victorian perception of the failure of society which he shares with novelists such as Dickens and Trollope.

it is clear that their egoism does not free them from that law of Conrad's world which dictates that consciousness must look outside itself for some stable ground. On the surface it might appear that their selfishness would give these characters a certain independence; because they are committed only to themselves, it would seem that they could exist without thought for anything beyond themselves. But, for Conrad, egoism does not confer any such sense of a stable, independent identity. Both Almayer and Willems show, if anything, more than ordinary concern with those around them. Even at the peak of his self-satisfaction Willems retains an almost obsessive need to be recognized by others. The power and position which he enjoys as Hudig's assistant and which define for him the meaning of his life are real to Willems only if he achieves a continuing affirmation of their reality. It is not enough that he himself is confident of his success; he must be constantly surrounded by an audience in which he can see it reflected. Willems's nightly billiard games, for example, are ritual performances in which "for their own good and for his greater glory" (xiv, 6) he expounds the secret of his success. His wife and family perform this same function: "That family's admiration was the great luxury of his life. It rounded and completed his existence in a perpetual assurance of unquestionable superiority" (xiv, 3–4).

It would be a mistake to underestimate the importance of his audience to Willems. His role as poseur is not an affectation. On the contrary, his need for an audience exhibits a compulsive quality which can only be understood if we realize how his audience provides the external ground necessary to establish his identity.[2] It is because his relation to his audience does lie at the center of his life that Willems's obsession with himself appears most clearly in his extreme sensitivity to the impression he makes on those around him. Willems is at least partially aware that the

---

[2] Conrad's letters from this period to Cunninghame-Graham and Garnett testify to his own sense of the necessity of a relation to someone outside himself. He writes to Garnett, for example, that Garnett is "for me . . . the reality outside, the expressed thought, the living voice! And without you I would think myself alone in an empty universe" (Edward Garnett, *Letters from Joseph Conrad* [New York: Bobbs-Merrill, 1962], p. 97). Or again he remarks, "All of you stand by me so nobly that I must exist" (*ibid.*, p. 161).

existence and strength of his personality are tied to the strength of this impression. Consequently, he will go to any lengths to maintain its force, and when he returns from billiards with the uneasy feeling that "he had not done himself justice over there in the hotel . . . he had not impressed his hearers enough" (XIV, 8), he does not hesitate to seek confirmation elsewhere.

> Now he would go home and make his wife get up and listen to him . . . and listen patiently. . . . If he wanted he could make all the DaSouza family get up. He had only to say a word and they would all come and sit silently in their night vestments on the hard, cold ground of his compound and listen, as long as he wished to go on explaining to them from the top of the stairs, how great and good he was. They would. However his wife would do—for to-night. (XIV, 8–9)

If this passage confirms the dependence of Willems on his audience, it reveals as well the particular quality which his egoism gives to this relationship. Although Willems looks to those around him for the confirmation of his identity, he looks in a very narrow way. He looks only to see himself. In this sense, it is appropriate to speak of his "audience." Like the traditionally egocentric actor, his concern for his audience is a concern only for the effect he can produce on them. Willems has no interest in the DaSouza family as individuals and it does not even matter to him that they are "a half-caste, lazy lot," "a numerous and an unclean crowd" (XIV, 4). He uses them only as a mirror in which he can admire the reflection of his own power and glory, but he does not open himself to them. He sees them only as tools, as extensions of his own self.

The relationship between Willems and the DaSouza family reveals why, for Conrad, egoism destroys the foundations of society. A genuine society is characterized by an openness among men such as exists among the members of the world of the sea. In such a world, men have a real access to one another, and, because mutual understanding exists, each individual is not only grounded in the hearts of those around him but serves himself as their foundation. The primary effect of Willems's egoism is to destroy this mutual relationship. His blindness to others denies them any ground in his own self. To ignore others in the way Willems does is to reduce them to the level of objects without a consciousness of their own; it is to condemn them to a living death. Conrad emphasizes this by continually pointing to the way in which Willems has reduced his wife's family to the status of slaves. His financial support has robbed them of "the little aptitude and strength for work they might have had" (xiv, 5). It is because "they lived now by the grace of his will" (xiv, 5) that Willems can keep them "singing his praises in the midst of their laziness" (xiv, 4) and revel in the "feeling of enormously remote superiority" (xiv, 5) which comes from the knowledge that "should he close his hand, all those admiring human beings would starve" (xiv, 5).

Willems's attempt to assert himself over others and turn them into mirrors of his success not only robs them of their identity; it is the source of his own failure, because the same egocentricity which blinds him to the human reality of others denies him a positive ground in this reality. Willems is able to obtain a super-ficial accession to his self-esteem, but an identity founded in such an accession is itself superficial and has no firm foundation in the consciousness behind this surface. Thus although he is able to force the DaSouzas to pay him lip service, he never comes to terms with, in fact never recognizes, the thoughts which lie behind this façade.

When Willems returns from the fateful interview with Hudig which marks the end of his dreams, he is amazed at "the mystery of anger and revolt in the head of his wife" (xiv, 27). This amazement, marking as it does his failure to recognize the world of the other's consciousness, is the final sign of the ultimately self-defeating quality of Willems's egocentricity. The egoism of modern society it seems consigns men to one of two roles: actor or audience. In the one case he embraces isolation; in the other he has it thrust upon him. But in both instances he lives in a solipsistic world which makes an authentic life impossible. Before man can hope to transcend that initial, tentative state of existence which is the starting point for all Conrad's characters, he must find some way to escape the prison of his own ego. Both *Almayer's Folly* and *An Outcast* accept this picture of a world of men trapped within themselves. Both are concerned with the search for some way to free them.

Conrad offers a clear explanation of the terms and direction of this search in his early story "The Return." Like *Almayer's Folly* and *An Outcast,* "The Return" begins with the description of a society in which each member is motivated by a "recklessly picturesque desire to get promptly something for himself only" (VIII, 153). A man "whose connections, education and intelligence were on a par with those with whom he did business or amused himself" (VIII, 119), Alvan Hervey moves easily and naturally in this world where "noble sentiments are cultivated in sufficient profusion to conceal the pitiless materialism of thoughts and aspirations" (VIII, 121). His marriage is also a paradigm of the kinds of relation which exist among the members of such a society. Although neither Hervey nor his wife is a poseur in the obvious way that Willems is, Conrad makes it clear that their attitudes are equally self-centered. Hervey, we are told, desired his wife "for various reasons; but principally for the satisfaction of having his own way" (VIII, 120). For her, in turn, Hervey is only a means "to get away from under the paternal roof ... to assert her individuality, to move in her own set (so much smarter than the paternal one); to have ... her own share of the world's respect, envy and applause" (VIII, 123). Because they are both "unable to look at a fact, a sentiment, a principle, or a belief otherwise than in the light of their own dignity, of their own glorification" (VIII, 123) they exist in that isolation which is the inevitable result of egoism. Their marriage is a lie which conceals the fact that they are "no more capable of real intimacy than two animals feeding at the same manger" (VIII, 122).

In "The Return," Conrad emphasizes the close relation between the Herveys' egoism and their repression of any strong emotion. Hervey's belief that "any excess of feeling was unhealthy" (VIII, 172) is more than lip service he pays to a world which hides "the shameful impulse of passion" (VIII, 132) behind "the correct silence of walls, of closed doors, of curtained windows" (VIII, 136). His entire existence is founded in this repression. Early in his courtship, his "dull and solemn" (VIII, 120) declarations of love serve "no earthly reason, unless to conceal his feelings" (VIII, 120) and his subsequent marriage is based on the continuation of their concealment. The Herveys, the narrator remarks, "skimmed over the surface of life hand in hand, in a pure and frosty atmosphere—like two skillful skaters cutting figures on thick ice for the admiration of the beholders, and disdainfully ignoring the hidden stream, the stream restless and dark; the stream of life profound and unfrozen" (VIII, 123).

In this story, the world of passion is opposed to the world of egoism because the experience of emotion negates the consciousness of a discrete and independent identity which is the foundation of egoism. The irrational is a threat to Hervey precisely because it attacks the distinct and overriding awareness of self which is the center of his life. What shocks Hervey in his wife's infidelity is not the crime itself but the way her passion seems to have destroyed her stable ego and replaced it with a "sinful self-forgetfulness" (VIII, 172). In the same way, his feelings at the discovery of her desertion appear to him as a direct threat to his self. They are something "disintegrating, tormenting, sapping to the very core of life" (VIII, 172); he experiences a "loathsome rush of emotion breaking through all the reserves that guarded his manhood" (VIII, 130). Hervey constantly refers to her infidelity as a "filthy fact" (VIII, 132) and something "loathsome" (VIII, 130) which overcomes him with a sense of "physical disgust" (VIII, 167). The way in which he constantly returns to this theme underlines how it, like our experience of anything obscene, is associated in his mind with an uneasiness which threatens self-possession.

The key to Conrad's initial explanation of the state of modern society lies in this association of egoism and repression. The explanation has two sides. First, "The Return" seems to imply that the force behind the development of civilization is itself responsible for Hervey. The logic of this is clear: the development of civilization reflects for Conrad the growth of mind from its birth in an undifferentiated awareness of sensation and emotion to more and more differentiated states of consciousness, in which the self becomes increasingly particularized and sensitive to its individuality. If this is true, then the egocentricity of Hervey appears to be the result of such a growth. The excessive self-consciousness which gives even Willems a certain effete quality suggests that this development has continued too far and too fast and that, as a result, mind has been cut off from its own source. Second, Hervey's fear that even his lukewarm marriage was a danger because "it was too much in the nature of giving yourself away, of wearing . . . your heart on your sleeve" (VIII, 129), indicates that there is something intentional in his egoism. The egocentricity of Willems and Hervey seems at times a result of mind's attempt to declare its independence of all outside support and to demonstrate this independence by dominating everything in its field of consciousness. In this way Hervey insists on his ability to cut himself off from the levels of emotion and sensation which have given birth to awareness, while Willems, although he looks to others for his confirmation, does so in a way which turns them into slaves.

If this is true, and the egoism of the world is only a matter of misguided evolution allied with misguided choice, then the answer is simple. Man has only to abandon his independence and return to the world which gave him birth. This is the lesson Alvan Hervey comes to understand in the closing pages of "The Return." Like Willems, Hervey has concerned himself only with surfaces. He has assumed that the "imposing, unthinking stillness" of his wife's features has "mirrored . . . the tranquil dignity of a soul of which he had thought himself . . . the inexpungable possessor" (VIII, 171). With the blindness of all Conrad's egoists, he has ignored the world behind this façade. Now, with the revelation of her illicit love which has existed beneath the mask, he is struck by a sudden and horrible perception of his isolation. Seized by the fear that his wife is "impossible to know" (VIII, 172), he feels trapped within himself "like a prisoner in chains" (VIII, 168) assailed by "a heart-probing, fiery sense of dangerous loneliness" (VIII, 173).

Yet despite its pain, Hervey's new awareness is the way to a more positive knowledge. It brings, first, an understanding that the self cannot remain independent of those around it. By the end of his confrontation with his wife, he comes to realize that "there can be no life without faith and love—faith in a human heart, love of a human being" (VIII, 177). His discovery that only this faith and love gives to a man the "certitude immaterial and precious" which raises him above "all the meaningless accidents of existence" (VIII, 177) is an implicit acknowledgment that the only true ground of individual identity lies in the thoughts and heart of another. The last half of the story is concerned with

Hervey's effort to obtain such a place. This section of "The Return" portrays, in a way which is difficult to summarize, the struggle of two people attempting to come to grips with one another in the face of their newly discovered strangeness.

The answer to Hervey's problem of how "to see, to penetrate, to understand (VIII, 146) his wife comes with the realization that he does, in fact, love her. At this point, he discovers that his only escape from his old life is in committing himself to this love. To do so is to submit the self to the destructive effects of passion. But this might well be the only way, while the violence of emotion ruptures the integrity and self-possession which are at the root of egocentricity. Perhaps it is only by such a deliberate sacrifice of his ego that a Willems or a Hervey can transcend his isolation. The other is an enigma, and, Hervey realizes, "the enigma is only made clear by sacrifice" (VIII, 176). The meaning of "The Return" lies in this realization and in Hervey's final vision of the "certitude immaterial and precious" which is open to man, for they imply that if a man and a woman are willing to give themselves to their love in this way they will perhaps achieve the openness which for Conrad is one key to true identity. Conrad's image for such an existence in which each occupies a firm place in the thoughts and heart of the other is one of life in a transcendent realm permeated by a "great tenderness, deep as the ocean, serene and eternal, like the infinite peace of space above the short tempests of the earth" (VIII, 178). "The Return" indicates clearly the only possible entrance to this world; it is gained only by descending into the dark river of passion and making the "awful sacrifice" of casting "all one's life into the flame" (VIII, 184).

This is the starting point of Conrad's early novels. As in the later works, the central character of "The Return" is faced with the problem of securing a stable self. Implicit in Hervey's appetite for "the admiration of the beholders" (VIII, 123) and his desire to "grasp [the world] solidly, to get as much gratification as he could out of it" (VIII, 153), we can see the same initial instability which defines all of Conrad's orphans. But in Hervey's case the isolation of the orphaned state is not seen as the inevitable position of consciousness in the world. Instead it appears to be the result of social factors. Willems and Hervey are the products not of nature but of a culture which mistakenly encourages such self-assertion, and both are examples of the way this self-assertion, by cutting them off from the source of life and from others, makes a valid identity impossible.

Thus like Lord Jim, Hervey's initial efforts to establish his identity are frustrated by the intrusion of a dark and alien force —but here the parallel ends. At this time, it does not seem to Conrad that the dark force of passion is totally hostile to consciousness since it is, after all, "the stream of life" and the source of awareness. Presumably if it gave birth to life it contains some positive principle of being, and it could be that its violence is therefore directed only at what is false and unauthentic. If this is true, then it should be possible to embrace this force and, by doing so, found the self in this positive principle. The vision of life in a world of infinite peace and certainty which Hervey glimpses at the end of "The Return" is an image, as we have seen, of a life truly grounded in the other. But it draws its ultimate validity from the fact that this intersubjective relationship is one which is born from and which continues to exist in close harmony with those levels of sensation and emotion which are "the stream of life."

Because Conrad believes initially that the darkness might offer such a positive ground of being, Hervey's situation is the exact reversal of Jim's moment of truth on the deck of the *Patna*. Jim's failure comes because he cannot control the irrational, Hervey's because he can. This is the paradoxical message of Conrad's early fiction. It begins as an attack on a world in which men have mistakenly built their lives on self-assertion and suggests that the key to identity lies not in such assertion but in an act of sacrifice. *Almayer's Folly* and *An Outcast of the Islands* are both investigations of this possibility. Both are examinations of the ability of man to discover a more authentic world by returning to the primitive source of life.

The key to this theme in *Almayer's Folly* lies in the emphasis which Conrad places on Nina's dual nature. Her personality is an image of that unhappy mating of the civilized and the primitive which characterizes her parents' marriage. When she returns to Sambir, she returns a woman "with great sad eyes, where the startled expression common to Malay womankind was modified by a thoughtful tinge inherited from her European ancestry" (XI, 29). Throughout the novel she stands at the focus of this tension between European and Malayan. *Almayer's Folly* is the story of Almayer's ultimate disillusionment, but it is a disillusionment which results from Nina's final choice between these two sides of her nature. To understand the logic of his fall, then, is to understand the rationale of her choice between the forces represented, on the one hand, by her father and the world of Singapore and, on the other, by her mother and Dain.

Nina's choice is between two kinds of society: between a world, like that of the Herveys, characterized by isolation and egoism, and a world in which, for all its apparent savagery, people are able to establish a real communion. The analogy between the conditions which govern the Herveys' marriage and those which control Nina's relationships to the representatives of the civilized world is suggested by the references to her interlude in Singapore. Here Nina encounters a society which, like that of the London of "The Return," is founded on the repression of emotions. She finds herself wrapped by Mrs. Vink in "the narrow mantle of civilized morality" (XI, 42) and refers to this period later as "her days of restraint, of sorrow, and of anger" (XI, 72).

If the occasional references to Nina's stay in Singapore suggest the general outlines of the civilization which produced Willems, Almayer's attitude toward his daughter is in a more specific way a redaction of the relation between Willems and his wife. As in the case of Willems, Almayer's relationship to Nina suggests not only the crucial act by which Conrad's characters look outside themselves to ground their identity but also the way their egoism robs this act of any authenticity. On the one hand, Almayer from the beginning invests his entire life in Nina. In *An Outcast*, he is described standing "before the curtained cot looking at his daughter . . . at that part of himself, at that small and unconscious particle of humanity that seemed to him to contain all his soul" (XIV, 320). As it is portrayed in *Almayer's Folly*, his whole existence after her return from Singapore is governed by his belief that "his faith in her had been the foundation of his hopes, the motive of his courage, of his determination to live and struggle, and to be victorious for her sake" (xi, 191–92).

Yet it is clear from these passages that Almayer does not open himself to Nina but merely absorbs her into his life as an extension of himself. When he tells Nina that he "wanted to see white men bowing low before the power of your beauty and your wealth" (xi, 101), it is an obvious echo of his own dreams of success, and this echo is significant because it indicates how Almayer sees Nina only as an instrument through which he can achieve the vicarious fulfillment of his ambitions. Because Almayer's eyes are "dimmed by self-pity" (xi, 103) and can see things only in the light of his own concerns, Nina finds herself trapped in the isolation to which the egoist condemns all his victims. She can only dream "dreams of her own with the persistent absorption of a captive thinking of liberty within the walls of his prison cell" (xi, 151–52).

While Almayer speaks of the civilized and restrained world of the West, Dain appeals to the latent savagery Nina inherits from her mother. He gives the impression "of a being half-savage, untamed, perhaps cruel" (xi, 55), and "the mysterious consciousness of her identity" (xi, 64) with Dain is founded in the "subtle breath of mutual understanding passing between their two savage natures" (xi, 63). More than this Dain offers an alternative to her isolated existence with Almayer. He offers her a life founded in the kind of openness which will allow them to live in a common world. At the crucial point of the novel, Nina herself comes to recognize this and, in a passage which summarizes the theme of the early fiction, she contrasts for Almayer her two alternatives:

You told me yesterday ... that I could not understand or see your love for me: it is so. How can I? No two human beings understand each other. They can understand but their own voices. You wanted me to dream your dreams, to see your own visions.... But while you spoke I listened to the voice of my own self; then this man came, and all was still; there was only the murmur of his love.... In time ... both our voices, that man's and mine, spoke together in a sweetness that was intelligible to our ears only. You were speaking of gold then, but our ears were filled with the song of our love.... Then I found that we could see through each other's eyes: that he saw things nobody but he and myself could see. We entered a land where no one could follow us.... Then I began to live. (XI, 179)

As the logic of "The Return" suggests, Dain can offer Nina this common world because he can give himself to his love in a way which is completely foreign to Almayer. He lives "with all the unrestrained enthusiasm of a man totally untrammelled by any influence of civilized self-discipline" (XI, 64) and consequently his nature is one which can easily give itself up "without restraint to an overmastering passion" (XI, 69). As in "The Return," the surrender to love is seen as a loss of self, but such a loss does not frighten Dain. The moment when he feels himself "carried away helpless by a great wave of supreme emotion" (XI, 68) does not mark the destructive intrusion into his life of an alien force, but is simply one more expression of the quality of irrationality which pervades his entire life. For this reason he is able to perform easily and naturally the act of sacrifice which is so terrifying to the Herveys, and Conrad makes clear that the new existence which he offers to Nina is grounded in his ability to make this sacrifice. "I have delivered my soul into your hands for ever"; he tells her, "I breathe with your breath, I see with your eyes, I think with your mind, and I take you into my heart for ever" (XI, 178).

Dain's words are a clear expression of what it means to speak of an individual's life grounded in another. To take someone into your heart in this way is to make yourself the incarnation of his subjective world—in Dain's phrase, to see with his eyes. To do this is to give it a reality it did not have before. No longer a dream, it has concreteness and, because this is "for ever," the permanence which assures a stable identity. Yet even this explanation distorts because it retains the concept of individuality. The common world of Dain and Nina is defined by their mutual surrender and, in such a relationship, it makes no sense to talk of discrete personalities. Because each offers himself as the ground of the other, their world cannot be identified with either but is the unique product of the relation between them. *Almayer's Folly* seems to promise that through this mutual surrender two people can achieve such a miraculous continuity and enter an

existence in which any distinction between self and other disappears.

The dramatic center of *Almayer's Folly* comes with Nina's
decision to enter this world, to accept the counsel of the darkness
which "seemed to be full of menacing voices calling upon her to
rush headlong into the unknown; to be true to her own impulses
to give herself up to the passion which she had evoked and
shared" (xi, 147). By doing so, she throws away "her past with all
its . . . faint affections, now withered and dead in contact with her
fierce passion" (xi, 152) and by this is "born . . . to the knowledge
of a new existence" (xi, 64). Again, Conrad's image for this existence is one of a safe, secure, and self-contained world. When the
narrator of *Almayer's Folly* describes Dain and Nina drifting in
their canoe "as if nothing existed . . . outside the gunwales of the
narrow craft," and remarks "it was their world, filled with their
intense and all-absorbing love" (xi, 69), he is not simply engaging
in hyperbole. The sense of a self-contained existence is insisted
upon here because it is symbolic of a mode of life which is based
on the "certainty immaterial and precious" which comes with
being taken into another's heart forever. Yet at the same time
theirs is a life which, for all its circumscription, is rooted in a
force which transcends them both. Their life together is permeated by the forces of emotion and sensation which not only
make it possible for them to achieve this openness but allow
them to sustain it. The world of Dain and Nina is the expression
of this primitive source of life, of the "seeding life and movement of tropical nature" which seems "concentrated in the ardent
eyes, in the tumultuously beating hearts of the two beings" (xi,
69–70).[3]

In this sense *Almayer's Folly* affirms both aspects of Hervey's
final vision in "The Return." It at once validates the possibility
of achieving such openness with another and assures us that the
irrational forces of sensation and emotion do in fact provide a
real foundation for life. Because the force of darkness is such a
positive principle, Nina's choice of Dain over her father, of the
primitive over the civilized, is in fact a choice of life over death,

[3] For another discussion of the symbolic implications of the jungle in these
novels, see Thomas Moser, *Joseph Conrad: Achievement and Decline* (Cambridge: Harvard University Press, 1957), pp. 53–54.

and the child who is born to them after their flight from Sambir seems the final imprimatur on Nina's decision. This is the implication as well of the choice which is offered to Almayer in the closing pages of the novel. For a brief moment, he considers following Nina and Dain:

What if he should suddenly take her to his heart, forget his shame, and pain, and anger, and—follow her! What if he changed his heart if not his skin and made her life easier between the two loves that would guard her from any mischance! His heart yearned for her. What if he should say that his love was greater than . . . . (xɪ, 192)

This passage suggests that if Almayer had yielded, as did Nina, to his heart he too would have had his share of happiness. His rejection of Nina from what he considers "his idea of duty to himself—to his race—to his respectable connections" (xɪ, 192) seems a deliberate choice of the fraudulent world of civilization.

More than this, it is a kind of suicide. The effect of Almayer's rejection of his daughter and of his subsequent attempt to forget her completely demonstrates the necessity of this external ground to the very existence of the individual consciousness. Almayer's "folly" refers not only to the house into which he sank his last hopes and assets but also his resolve "in the undying folly of his heart" (xɪ, 201) to forget Nina. His descent into increasingly pronounced stages of unconsciousness—from the expressionless face "without a sign of emotion, feeling, reason, or even knowledge of itself" (xɪ, 190) which characterized him immediately after Nina's departure, through the period when his pet monkey "seemed to have taken complete charge of its master" (xɪ, 203), to his opium-drugged death—is dictated by the logic of that process by which Conrad's characters establish their identity. Having made Nina "the foundation of his hopes, the motive of his courage, of his determination to live and struggle" (xɪ, 191–92), his efforts to sever this tie are in reality efforts to cut himself off from the ground of his own being. Almayer does achieve a kind of peace at the end, but like the peace which descends on Taminah after Dain's departure, it is "like the dreary tranquillity of a desert, where there is peace only because there is no life" (xɪ, 116).

Conrad's first novel is the record of Nina's journey from the isolation imposed on her by an unauthentic society to her discovery of a ground for her self in the positive source of all life. But if this movement from a state of isolated self-consciousness toward a pre-existing reality defines the first direction taken by Conrad's adventurers we should recognize that it reflects as well the initial thrust of his own art. Conrad's use of amphibian figures such as Marlow, or, for example, his comparison in *A Personal Record* of his first voyage and his first book suggests that he recognized a certain compatibility between his two careers and that, in his eyes at least, his life was not as discontinuous as it might appear. Nor is this compatibility simply a superficial pattern imposed by Conrad to achieve a biographical coherence. There is a more fundamental meaning at the center of his comparison of his two lives, for this comparison implies that the second is in some way an extension of the first and that writing and sailing are simply two versions of that project which dominates the lives of Conrad's characters. It implies, in other words, that they are both modes of the adventure, both quests to establish the self.

It is this parallel between the theme of the adventure in Conrad's fiction and his own attitude toward writing which allows us to understand his early attitude toward his art. From the beginning, Conrad, in outlining the intellectual foundations of his work, shows the same urge to voyage outward and to involve himself with the reality of the men and things around him which underlies the dramatic development of Nina in *Almayer's Folly*. Throughout his career he rejects an art in which the consciousness of the artist takes itself as the subject of the work. Such an art would tend to re-create in an aesthetic dimension the same egoistical, self-reflexive world which a character like Willems builds for himself. His desire to have his work transcend his own consciousness and not to be simply "an endless analysis of affected sentiments"[4] appears particularly clearly in his introductory comments on *The Shadow Line*. This work is autobiographical enough to be subtitled "A Confession"; yet Conrad

[4] William Blackburn, ed., *Joseph Conrad: Letters to William Blackwood and David S. Meldrum* (Durham, N.C.: University of North Carolina Press, 1958), p. 156.

43

feels called upon to deny, in a somewhat paradoxical statement, that the primary concern of his confession is with his own sub-jectivity. "I call it 'A Confession' on the title page," he writes, "for, from a certain point of view, it is that—and essentially as sincere as any confession can be. The more perfectly so, perhaps, because its object is not the usual one of self-revelation."[5]

Instead of his own self, the proper subject of his novels, Con-rad tells us, is the world of things and men. In the Preface to *The Nigger of the "Narcissus"* he insists continually on the real-istic core of his work and on his attention to grasping "a passing phase of life" (XXIII, xiv) and drawing our attention to "the sur-rounding vision of form and colour, of sunshine and shadows" (XXIII, xvi). In its essence, he writes elsewhere, his art is con-cerned with "action . . . action of human beings that will bleed to a prick and are moving in a visible world."[6] Or, again, he remarks that "the aim of the novelist has been . . . to present humanity in action on the background of the changing aspects of nature and a series of acted scenes exhibiting part of life."[7]

Conrad's desire to capture the reality of the "visible world" leads him to insist on what he calls the "fundamental condition of visuality"[8] of his writings, and this need to "rendre fidèlement le mond visible, tel qu'on le voit"[9] determines his whole attitude toward the nature of language. It is, we recall, "by the power of the written word" (XXIII, xiv) that Conrad hopes to attain this visuality, and his hope is based on the assumption that words contain in some way the essential nature of the reality which

[5] Gérard Jean-Aubry, *Joseph Conrad: Life and Letters* (Garden City, N.Y.: Doubleday, 1927), II, 184. Conrad's suspicion of a subjective language appears particularly clearly in his essay "Outside Literature." Here he contrasts the notices to mariners with their "ideal of perfect accuracy" (LE, 40), with imaginative literature which, he remarks, is prose "I never learned to trust" (LE, 43).

[6] Blackburn, *Letters*, p. 156.

[7] The text for this talk is contained in Arnold T. Schwab's "Conrad's American Speeches and His Reading from *Victory*," *Modern Philology*, LII (May, 1955), 345–47.

[8] *Ibid.*, p. 345.

[9] Joseph Conrad, *Lettres Françaises*, ed. Georges Jean-Aubry (Paris: Gal-limard, 1930), p. 61.

they denote. In a long letter of advice to Sir Hugh Clifford, Conrad urges him to remember that "words, groups of words, words standing alone, are symbols of life, have the power in their sound or their aspect to present the very thing you wish to hold up before the mental vision of your readers. The things 'as they are' exist in words; therefore words should be handled with care lest the picture, the image of truth abiding in facts, should become distorted—or blurred."[10] Much of Conrad's early discussions with Ford were concerned with developing their power to discover the truth at the center of the word. As Hugh Kenner points out, "Ford and Conrad . . . undertook to clean up English prose as it existed at the opening of the present century—the forms of language utterly out of touch with any conceivable perception. . . . Verbal manifestations were scrutinized and revised from a standpoint of multi-lingual erudition, to bring them into the closest possible contact with situations as really intuited, and with things as seen, heard, smelt, and touched."[11]

We have to understand, however, that his concern with addressing himself to the world around him does not lead Conrad to a simple idea of realism. He insists just as strongly on the active presence of the artist in his work. The novel, he says, "is born from introspection and bears the impress of one temperament,"[12] and when he discusses *The Nigger of the "Narcissus"* as a "consciously planned attempt to render the truth of a phase of life" he is careful to add that this truth will inevitably appear "in terms of my own temperament" (LE, 138). It is only that for him the essential action of the artist's temperament is not one in which it reflects on itself but rather one in which it turns outward to move into the world. Rather than being either the picture of a consciousness in isolation or of the external world alone, the novel is the product of their interaction. Underlying the existence of a novel, we might say, is for Conrad an act in which the mind of the artist transcends the bounds of its self-

---

[10] Jean-Aubry, *Life and Letters*, I, 280.

[11] Hugh Kenner, *The Poetry of Ezra Pound* (New York: Faber and Faber, 1958), p. 266.

[12] Schwab, "Conrad's American Speeches," p. 346.

awareness to grasp an aspect of the visible world and, through the catalytic action of its temperament, reveals the essential nature of this world. It is the movement of mind into the world which is the real center of Conrad's definition of his art in the Preface to *The Nigger of the "Narcissus."* The novelist, he writes, should "snatch ... from the remorseless rush of time, a passing phase of life." But this "is only the beginning of the task." It is not enough that the writer should simply record this moment. He must "hold up ... the rescued fragment before all eyes in the light of a sincere mood," for it is only by the agency of this mood that the artist is able to "show its vibration, its colour, its form; and ... reveal the substance of its truth" (xxiii, xiv).

The fusion which Conrad hopes to achieve in his work between a factual, realistic center and the temperamental coloring of the author's consciousness is defined for him by the phrase "the truth of my own sensations."[13] The fact that Conrad would use the term "my sensations" implies the existence for him of an individual consciousness which is engaged in the act of sensing and which gives to the act its own unique quality. Yet the phrase as a whole suggests, too, that because language does contain "things as they are" there is an objective truth here which transcends the limits of individual awareness. It implies, in other words, that the writer is able to evoke a level of immediate, sensory experience which, because it corresponds to the reality of the external world, brings us into contact with this world "as seen, heard, smelt and touched." In a letter to Edward Garnett, Conrad praises him for his "gift of the 'mot juste,' of those sentences that are like a flash of limelight on the facade of a cathedral or lightning on a landscape when the whole scene of all the details leap up before the eye in a moment and are irresistibly impressed on

[13] Francis Warrington Dawson, *The Crimson Pall: A Novel with Letters Exchanged on "Critical Novelists" by Joseph Conrad and the Author* (Chicago: Bernard, 1927), p. 24. The phrase is used frequently by Conrad to describe the foundation of his art. He remarks to Blackwood, for example, that his writing is "nothing but action—observed, felt and interpreted with an absolute truth to my sensations (which are the basis of art in literature)" (Blackburn, *Letters*, p. 156). See also Jean-Aubry, *Lettres Françaises*, p. 61.

memory by their sudden vividness."[14] It is his faith in his own ability to capture the reality of a world in this way which leads Conrad to remark, concerning the stories which make up *Within the Tides*, that "the mere fact of dealing with matters outside the general run of everyday experience laid me under the obligation of a more scrupulous fidelity to the truth of my own sensations. The problem was to make unfamiliar things credible. To do that I had to create for them ... to envelop them in their proper atmosphere of actuality" (x, viii).

The work which results from such an interaction of mind and world will be an essential blend of subjective and objective. It is this interpenetration of the writer's consciousness and the reality of the visible world which at this point is the goal of Conrad's art.[15] Because his language does allow the writer to capture the objective, sensory foundation of experience, the act of writing gives him access to the levels of feeling and sensation which are the source of consciousness. In this way he achieves through language the same ground in the source of life which Nina reaches

---

[14] Garnett, *Letters*, p. 32.

[15] This ideal blend of subjective and objective suggests why Conrad might have been attracted to that idea of impressionism which, according to Ford Maddox Ford, Conrad shared with him. Impressionist painting has something of this same dual quality. On the one hand, the Impressionists were attempting to capture the objective content of experience, the "donnés purs de sens" (Pierre Francastel, *L'Impressionnisme*, Publications de la Faculté des lettres de Strasbourg, 2d series, vol. XVI (Paris: 1937), p. 24). Yet this content is always understood to be framed by the consciousness of the artist, and therefore Francastel can say of Monet's work, "Cette peinture a le caractère de la continuité des états intérieurs, elle est un déroulement et substitue les lois de l'expérience subjective à celles de l'expérience objective" (*ibid.*, pp. 93–94). In this sense impressionism is, as Arnold Hauser remarks, "the reproduction of the subjective act ... of seeing" (*The Social History of Art* [New York: Random House, 1958], IV, 70–71), in which both mind and world enter as equal terms. Ford, in his discussion of his literary impressionism, suggests it is characterized by the same synthesis of subject and object. "We [he and Conrad] accepted ... the stigma 'Impressionists' ... because ... we saw that life did not narrate, but made impressions on our brains. We in turn, saw if we wished to produce on you an effect of life, must not narrate but render impressions" (*Joseph Conrad: A Personal Remembrance* [Boston: Little Brown, 1924], p. 194). On the other hand, he remarks that "Impressionism is a frank expression of personality" (*Critical Writings of Ford Maddox Ford*, ed. Frank MacShane [Lincoln: University of Nebraska Press, 1964], p. 36) or

through her relation to Dain. Conrad's description of the "seething life and movement of tropical nature" concentrated in "the ardent eyes, in the tumultuously beating hearts" (XI, 69–70) of Dain and Nina in a curious way images the relationship which he wants to achieve between the consciousness of the writer and the truth of the world he evokes. For Dain and Nina also it is a question neither of their creating a world for themselves apart from reality nor of their losing themselves in this reality. Instead, precisely because this reality is the positive source of consciousness, they become most themselves and are most alive when they immerse themselves in it.

One foundation of Conrad's art, then, lies in the re-creation on the most basic level of the sensory reality of our world in an act which enables consciousness to ground itself, and come to share, in the positive reality of the physical world. This incarnatory movement of the author's consciousness, however, is not limited to the physical world alone. Dain and Nina find themselves not only in a general relation to the "stream of life" but also in their relation to one another, and, if the Preface to the *Nigger* suggests that the artist in an equivalent way should participate in "that feeling of unavoidable solidarity" which unites "all mankind to the visible world," he should remember, too, that this same fellowship binds "men to each other" (XXIII, xiv). The Preface defines, in this way, not only the ideal relation between the artist and the "visible world" but also between the artist and "the human beings who will bleed to a prick" that move in this world.

The Preface indicates, in other words, that in Conrad's initial attitude toward his art, the relationship between the narrator and

---

that while "the Impressionist author is sedulous to avoid letting his personality appear in the course of his book . . . his whole book, his whole poem is merely an expression of his personality" (*ibid.*, p. 43). The best discussion of Conrad's impressionism from this point of view is Ramon Fernandez's essay "The Art of Conrad" in his *Messages*, trans. Montgomery Belgion (New York: Kennikat Press, 1927). Fernandez notes that while Conrad attempts to replace "the recital with the immediate evocation of sensible reality" (*ibid.*, p. 140), it is also true that "Conrad's world always assumes a presence, that of a subject upon the body of whom this world is unrolled and reflected" (*ibid.*, p. 150).

his characters should be defined by the same sympathetic openness and mutual identification which underlies the solidarity of the men of the sea or, on a more intense level, Nina's relation to Dain. In this it provides an explicit rationale for the method behind *Almayer's Folly*, for *Almayer's Folly* has its genesis in Conrad's acceptance of this solidarity. In *A Personal Record*, he recounts the way in which his feeling of kinship for the characters of this novel is the real foundation on which it was built.

> Unknown to my respectable landlady, it was my practice directly after my breakfast to hold animated receptions of Malays, Arabs and half-casts. They did not clamour aloud for my attention. They came with silent and irresistible appeal—and the appeal, I affirm here, was not to my self-love or my vanity. It seems now to have had a moral character, for why should the memory of these beings, seen in their obscure sun-bathed existence, demand to express itself in the shape of a novel, except on the ground of that mysterious fellowship which unites in a community of hopes and fears all the dwellers on this earth? (VI, 9)

The strongest characteristic of the narrating consciousness of *Almayer's Folly* is its unselfish acceptance of what Conrad refers to in the Author's Note as the "bond between us and that humanity so far away" (XI, x). *Almayer's Folly* is, on this level, the record of a series of acts of identification through which the narrator gains access to the minds of the characters. In the opening scene, Almayer, watching a log drifting out to sea, finds his thoughts drawn back to his early days in Macassar: "Almayer's quickened fancy distanced the tree in its imaginary voyage, but his memory lagging behind some twenty years or more in point of time saw a young and slim Almayer ... landing from the Dutch mail-boat on the dusty jetty of Macassar, coming to woo fortune in the go-downs of old Hudig" (XI, 4–5). Extending and amplifying this movement, the awareness of the narrator moves with Almayer's, summarizing the events which have brought Almayer to the bank of the river. What is important here is not simply the way in which the narrator brings us the rhythm of Almayer's consciousness, but the sympathetic identification, apparent in the parallel movement of author's and character's awareness, which allows the former his access to Almayer's world.

49

This intimacy is present in the narrator's relationship to all of the characters in the novel. He has equal insight into their minds, regardless of their level of awareness, and is able to move with facility from Nina to Taminah to Almayer despite the differences which separate one from another. In this ability, the narrator exhibits that same openness which Dain and Nina achieve through their love and which allows them to live in the same world with one another. And while the narrator's openness is not, obviously, an act of love in the same sense that Dain and Nina love one another, it is a testament to an emotional involvement and commitment which is present in the whole tone of the narration. Perhaps more important, it is predicated on the narrator's ability through his participation in this sympathetic bond to transcend the narrow walls of the egoism which surrounds Willems and Hervey, and, hence, Conrad's insistence that the book is not a product of his self-love or vanity.

CHAPTER III

From The Rescue *through* "*Heart of Darkness*": *The Destruction of the Visible Surface*

On both an aesthetic and a thematic level, *Almayer's Folly* reflects an optimistic belief that there exists beyond man a positive force in which he can ground his self. This optimism defines the initial tone of Conrad's fiction and it is important to understand the vision behind *Almayer's Folly* because this vision is the first fictional statement of certain constants in—to use Conrad's word—his temperament. The necessity Nina feels to transcend her initial state of isolation by finding a ground both in an authentic and close relation to another person and in some more general principle of reality remains at the center of his novels, and the persistence with which his characters search for this ground is perhaps best understood against Conrad's early belief in its availability.

Yet there are suggestions even in *Almayer's Folly* that the search is not so easy and that Conrad's later adventurers will have a longer and more dangerous road to travel. On the night Dain and Nina leave Sambir, Mrs. Almayer seems to warn Nina that the secure world which she and Dain share is, if not illusory, at least impermanent. "There will be other women," Mrs. Almayer tells Nina. "Hide your anger, and do not let him see on your face the pain that will eat your heart" (XI, 153). In a similar way, Dain, at the close of the novel, is struck by a sudden feeling that "something invisible . . . stood between them, something that would let him approach her [Nina] so far, but no farther" (XI, 187). This suggestion that "no desire, no longing, no effort of the will or length of life could destroy this vague feeling of their difference" (XI, 187) casts a shadow over the otherwise positive tone of the novel.

The fate of Willems and Aissa in Conrad's next novel, *An Outcast of the Islands*, is the confirmation of all Dain's and Mrs. Almayer's fears. On the surface, Willems's love for Aissa appears to be an echo of that between Nina and Dain. Willems, "who had lived all his life with no preoccupation but that of his own career, contemptuously indifferent to all feminine influence" (XIV, 77), discovers his former existence destroyed by his first encounter with Aissa. At this moment, he finds himself "tingling with that feeling which begins like a caress and ends in a blow, in that sudden hurt of a new emotion making its way into a human heart, with the brusque stirring of sleeping sensations awakening suddenly to the rush of new hopes, new fears, new desires—and to the flight of one's old self" (XIV, 69). Like Nina's encounter with Dain, the passion awakened in this moment brings to Willems a new life, a life which is defined not by his old ambitions of wealth but by his relation to Aissa. Surrendering to this passion, Willems, like Dain before him, is carried into a timeless existence in which he and Aissa appear to live insulated from the cares and accidents of the world. While he is with Aissa, there is "nothing in the whole world . . . but her look and her smile. Nothing in the past, nothing in the future; and in the present only the luminous fact of her existence" (XIV, 76–77). In these moments, it seems to him as if his former life was "an infamous nightmare" and that "true life was this: this dreamy immobility with his head against her heart that beat so steadily" (XIV, 146).

In *An Outcast*, however, the possibility of this world is never indulged and there is no aura of young love triumphant, as there is in *Almayer's Folly,* to counter the sinister implications of Willems's surrender. In the latter novel, while the suggestion that the force of Nina and Dain's desire to be one is qualified by projecting it as an illusion with a future, there is no doubt from the first moment that the timeless world of Willems and Aissa is simply an illusion covering their real isolation from one another. When Aissa appears in native dress, she strikes Willems as "an animated package of cheap cotton goods" (xiv, 128), and this appears to him "another sign of their hopeless diversity" (xiv, 128). For Willems, the moment of surrender is almost simultaneous with this moment of recognition of their underlying isolation from one another. Looking at Aissa soon after they met, "it struck him suddenly that they had nothing in common—not a thought, not a feeling; he could not make clear to her the simplest motive of any act of his" (xiv, 128).

The isolation which surrounds Aissa and Willems at the end of *An Outcast* is a terrifying inversion of the common world which Dain and Nina shared. While *Almayer's Folly* and "The Return" had promised a solitude which reflected the "certitude immaterial and precious" (viii, 177) which two people could share, Willems and Aissa live in the physical isolation of a forest clearing, hemmed in by "thick undergrowth; great, solid trees, looking sombre, severe, and malevolently stolid" (xiv, 329). Rather than the expression of their mutual understanding, their existence here is the result of their failure to achieve such a union. It reflects the fact that they do not see with one another's eyes as Dain and Nina did but are "surrounded each by the impenetrable wall of their aspirations . . . hopelessly alone, out of sight, out of earshot of each other; each the center of dissimilar and distant horizons; standing each on a different earth, under a different sky" (xiv, 333–34).

But Willems's and Aissa's imprisonment in this isolated world is not only evidence of their failure to reach one another through love; it has a more profound meaning for the relation between all life and the force which has given birth to it. Initially the validity of Hervey's and Nina's approach rests, as we have seen, in the fact that their surrender to love marks a return to the primitive but authentic source of life. Nina's choice of Dain over her father is founded on the assumption that this source is a positive principle of being and that, consequently, an individual can live an authentic life by living in accord with it. The image of Dain's and Nina's common world, a world which is at once the expression of their love and a manifestation of the "teeming life" of the jungle, is an image of a human relationship which draws its ultimate sanction from a source beyond the human, from the fact that it is grounded in "the stream of life."

The failure of Willems and Aissa leads Conrad to realize for the first time that no such positive stream exists, and to formulate in its stead that terrible paradox which is at the center of his conception of the darkness. Willems's final vision is a statement of this paradox, a revelation that the force at the center of life is one which is hostile to this life. In the clearing, Willems is surrounded by the same jungle which encompasses Dain and Nina. Just as they are surrounded by "the intense work of tropical nature" (xi, 71), Willems is aware that "the world was full of life. All the things, all the men he knew, existed, moved, breathed. . . . Round him, ceaselessly, there went on without a sound the mad turmoil of tropical life" (xiv, 331). The air of the forest is "full of sweet scent . . . like the impulse of love . . . odorous with the breath of life" (xiv, 337). But when he looks closely at this scene it suddenly occurs to Willems that this force of life is terrifyingly destructive, that it is in reality a "merciless and mysterious purpose, perpetuating strife and death through the march of ages" (xiv, 337).

He saw death looking at him from everywhere; from the bushes, from the clouds—he heard her speaking to him in the murmur of the river, filling the space, touching his heart, his brain with a cold hand. . . . It poisoned all he saw, all he did. . . . He saw the horrible form among the big trees, in the network of creepers, in the fantastic outlines of leaves. . . (xiv, 330–31).

Willems's vision of the force of death at the center of the life of the jungle reveals the ultimate folly of the strategy suggested by *Almayer's Folly* and "The Return." If death does lie at the source of life, then to attempt to escape the world of the Herveys by returning to this source is in fact a form of suicide. Because of this, Willems's commitment to Aissa is pictured throughout the novel not as a rise to some region above the tempests of the earth but as a fall into a bottomless chasm. It is a fall which culminates in the final scene of the novel, when Willems looks "down into the deeper gloom of the courtyard. And, all at once, it seemed to him that he was peering into a sombre hollow, into a deep black hole full of decay and of whitened bones; into an immense and inevitable grave full of corruption where sooner or later he must, unavoidably, fall" (xiv, 339). Here Willems's perception of the death around him is, specifically, an intuition of the darkness which lies behind the "bright promise" (xi, 76) of love, a revelation that the force of this love, like the life of the jungle with which it is associated, "seems to be all grace of colour and form, all brilliance, all smiles, but is only the blossoming of the dead; whose mystery holds the promise of joy and beauty, yet contains nothing but poison and decay" (xiv, 70).

The last scenes of *An Outcast* are thus more than a statement of the failure of Willems's and Aissa's love. They seem to imply that this failure results from the hostility of the darkness to the whole of creation and that, consequently, the belief in a positive source of life which informs *Almayer's Folly* is a mistaken one. At this point, however, the full meaning of Willems's final moments is apparently, for Conrad, still unclear. Although the darkness destroyed Willems, he was, as we have seen, an exemplum of all that is weak in men and his capitulation to Aissa and betrayal of Lingard are related directly to his weakness. Perhaps, however, the darkness would not be threatening to someone stronger. Or even if it remained hostile, perhaps his strength would be enough to protect him. If this were true, then Willems's defeat would not be final. Even if man could not find a ground in a positive source of life, he could create his own by bringing the darkness under his control.

Conrad's formulation of the possibility, and his movement from the tentative perceptions of *An Outcast* to the full vision of the darkness which informs *Lord Jim* turns around his third novel, *The Rescue*. Although it was not completed and published until 1919, *The Rescue* is clearly in conception a product of Conrad's early years as an author. It was begun in 1896 as the final novel in the Malayan trilogy, and Conrad worked on it intermittently, and unsuccessfully, for the next three years.[1] During this period, it occupied a major portion of his time and, perhaps even more, of his energy. The very persistence of his attempts to finish the novel, and the fact that he returned to it years later to complete and publish it, testify to *The Rescue*'s importance to him. It is only by grasping this importance that we can perceive the logic which transforms the aesthetic realism and romantic primitivism of *Almayer's Folly* into the ironic vision of Conrad's middle novels.

Thematically, *The Rescue* is an investigation of the most obvious alternative to Willems's last vision. It examines the possibility that men can create and sustain a world of their own values and, in this intention, we can see the logic which transforms the pattern of *Almayer's Folly* and *An Outcast* into the paradigm of a novel like *Lord Jim* or *Nostromo*. Like the earlier works, *The Rescue* deals with the relationship between the Western consciousness and the primitive. Unlike these works, however, now that Conrad suspects the hostility of the darkness, the orientation of the hero's voyage from Western society into the East changes. The first two novels presented us with characters who were the products of an unauthentic society. The egoism and willfulness of Almayer and Willems, and, implicitly, the attempt by mind to assert its independence of and control over all that enters its field, were qualities which were imposed upon them by this society.

In *The Rescue*, however, this focus changes. The picture of the society of Almayer and Hervey is still there in the figure of Edith Travers's husband, but Lingard comes from the sea not the shore, and his commitment is not to himself but to the values of his world. Consequently his egoism takes on an entirely different quality. The independence and willfulness of his character appear as the fundamental qualities which allow man to dedi-

[1] John D. Gordan, *Joseph Conrad: The Making of a Novelist* (Cambridge: Harvard University Press, 1940), pp. 175–268, deals with the chronology of the early novels. Thomas Moser deals specifically with the development of *The Rescue* both in " 'The Rescuer' Manuscript: A Key to Conrad's Development and Decline," *Harvard Library Bulletin*, X (1956), 325–55, and in *Joseph Conrad: Achievement and Decline* (Cambridge: Harvard University Press, 1957), pp. 62–81.

cate himself to an idea and carry this idea through to realization. The sense of mastery which defines him in all he does is not something to be transcended in a rush of passion. Since the will is the agency by which the mind shapes the world to its own ideals, its strength along with its integrity becomes the central issue in his life. From being the curse which cuts man off from the source of true being, will becomes itself the possible source of such an existence.

It is this logic which determines the development of Lingard's character through the Malayan trilogy. In *Almayer's Folly* he had appeared briefly as an old man obsessed with visions of a lost treasure, scarcely different from Almayer himself. In *An Outcast* Conrad makes him a member of Singleton's generation and uses him as a foil for Willems. Lingard is, the narrator tells us, one of the "strong men with childlike hearts" (xiv, 12) who were content to live and die by the grace of the sea. By *The Rescue*, however, this simplicity has been fused with an idealism which anticipates Kurtz and Gould. In the opening chapters of the novel, Lingard is compared to the English adventurer James Brooke who founded a native state in Malaya. Lingard, like Brooke, is interested not in plundering the East but in civilizing it. Brooke was "a true adventurer in his devotion to his impulse —a man of high mind and of pure heart" who laid "the foundation of a flourishing state on the ideas of pity and justice" (xii, 4). In the same way, Lingard's commitment to restore Hassim to his throne flows from just these ideas.[2]

[2] Gordan, *Joseph Conrad*, pp. 44–73, discusses the sources for Lingard's character and draws the obvious conclusion that Lingard is most Brookean in *The Rescue*. See also Gordan's "The Raja Brooke and Joseph Conrad," *Studies in Philology*, XXXV (October, 1938), 613–34. For a discussion of Conrad's attitudes toward Brooke, see Avrom H. Fleishman, *Conrad's Politics: Community and Anarchy in the Fiction of Joseph Conrad* (Baltimore: Johns Hopkins Press, 1967), pp. 99–105. Fleishman suggests that, for Conrad, Brooke was an example of the true colonist as opposed to those who, like the manager of the Central Station in "Heart of Darkness," want only to exploit the wilderness. As both Fleishman and Gordan observe, Lord Jim falls into this same idealistic category and his career in Patusan owes much to Conrad's knowledge of Brooke's adventure. The close connections in source and theme which exist among *Almayer's Folly, An Outcast of the Islands, The Rescue,* and *Lord Jim* suggest the importance of *The Rescue* to the development of Conrad's thought during this period.

> When at the conclusion of some long talk with Hassim . . . he lifted his big arm and shaking his fist above his head, shouted: "We will stir them up. We will wake up the country!" he was, without knowing it in the least, making a complete confession of the idealism hidden under the simplicity of his strength. He would wake up the country! That was the fundamental and unconscious emotion on which were engrafted his need of action, the primitive sense of what was due to justice, to gratitude, to friendship. . . . (XII, 106)

In *An Outcast* Lingard was an old man, the image of the virtues of a departed past. In *The Rescue* he appears in his youth, and for Conrad the change has an obvious significance for he is now the promise of the future. Trapped between his vow to Hassim on the one hand and his newly discovered passion for Edith Travers on the other, Lingard is a test case for man's ability to withstand the negating effect of the darkness and, through the power and effectiveness of his will, to establish and maintain his own values.

This is a test which Lingard fails. Just as Willems awakens to the "horror of bewildered life . . . where he could guide, control, comprehend nothing and no one—not even himself" (XIV, 149), Lingard loses his "sense of mastery" (XII, 329) in an all-encompassing feeling that "he did not know his mind himself" (XII, 210). As in the case of Willems, moreover, the first stage in Lingard's destruction is marked by his encounter with a world of emotion which robs rational consciousness of that vital quality of freedom. Like Jim on the deck of the *Patna*, Lingard experiences the negation of reason by emotion as an alienation of the will from consciousness, so that he is no longer able to choose its object or to determine his own action. Willems had discovered that under the influence of Aissa he had become as powerless as a leaf "spinning and turning before the breath of the perfumed breeze, driven helplessly into the dark night" (XIV, 108). In a similar manner Lingard, under the influence of Mrs. Travers, has "the sensation of being whirled high in the midst of an uproar and as powerless as a feather in a hurricane" (XII, 179).

But Lingard's first experience of the darkness as the destruction of conscious will by emotion is not a final one. Willems was led from his initial meeting with Aissa, and with the irrational, to his wider vision, in the forest clearing, of a destructive force

58

which lies not only at the source of mind but at the source of all life. In a similar manner, Lingard moves from a preliminary confrontation with the immediate source of mind in emotion to confront the infinite stillness of the "eternal something" which lies behind, and negates, both mind and world. Such a movement from the surface to the source of creation is implied in Conrad's description of the journey which Lingard and Edith Travers make from the brig to the mainland in Part III of *The Rescue*. In this journey Lingard turns his back on the *Flash* and the "visible surface" with which his ship is associated, and turns into a night which is explicitly identified with the darkness. Their journey is one into "an obscurity that seemed without limit in space and time" and which "had submerged the universe like a destroying flood" (xii, 241). When they looked about them, "their glances plunged infinitely deep into a lightless void" (xii, 241). In this context, the experience of an infinite and eternal peace which overcomes both Edith Travers and Lingard appears as the experience of the infinitude and eternality which are the essential qualities of the darkness. The equation of these two nights is particularly clear in the description of Edith Travers's sense of the motion of their small boat:

Puffs of wind blew about her head and expired; the sail collapsed, shivered audibly, stood full and still in turn; and again the sensation of vertiginous speed and of absolute immobility succeeding each other with increasing swiftness merged at last into a bizarre state of headlong motion and profound peace. The darkness enfolded her like the enervating caress of a sombre universe. It was gentle and destructive. Its languor seduced the soul into surrender. Nothing existed and even all her memories vanished into space. She was content that nothing should exist. (xii, 244–45)

The swift alternation of motion and rest leads Mrs. Travers to a point at which the two blend, and she experiences motion as a kind of stasis, a "profound peace." For Conrad, this experience is not illusory. It is a perception of the true relationship between the surface of creation and the darkness. The explanation of this is simple. Our experience of motion is the experience of movement in time through space. Movement, therefore, implies at least the conditional validity of the concepts of measurable time and space, concepts which are implied as well in the whole struc-

THE METAPHYSICS OF DARKNESS

ture of discrete, limited forms which make up the created world. It is just these concepts, however, which are undercut by Mrs. Travers's experience of the infinite and eternal void. Just as infinity does not refer to the longest distance but involves the negation, or at least the inapplicability of the idea of measurable distance, so eternity does not refer to the longest time but involves the negation of measurable time. One way to understand the hostility of the darkness for that universe of forms and days to which it has given birth is to see this hostility expressed in the tension between the concepts of space and time on the one hand and those of eternity and infinity on the other.

Mrs. Travers's paradoxical sense of the coalescence of motion and rest is not simply an experience of a force hostile to life. Here, the somewhat allegorical contest of life and death which informed Willems's last vision of the jungle becomes, in fact, a full statement of Conrad's idea of the darkness. To see the darkness "without limit in space and time" lying behind the created world is to realize that the opposition of the surface and the depths is not an opposition of two independent principles. Instead it is to recognize that the world of the surface is threatened by its own source, that all aspects of the visible surface of life rest in their own negation in the same way that the idea of infinity "negates" the concept of measurable time by rendering it meaningless and absurd.

It is this discovery of the true nature of the darkness, a discovery embodied in Mrs. Travers's intuition that "nothing existed," which marks the final threat to man's will. The experience of the irrational, Lingard's passion for Mrs. Travers or Jim's fear on the deck of the *Patna,* undercuts the ability of consciousness to will effectively by violently wrenching the will from the control of consciousness and directing it toward some object which mind has not chosen. Mrs. Travers's perception that all existence is "less palpable than a cloud" (xii, 247) attacks the will in precisely the opposite way. Instead of directing the will uncontrollably toward one object, it destroys the whole orientation of mind toward willing by undermining any sense of a reality toward which the mind can move. If there is no positive being whose concreteness and stability mind can appropriate through its action, then action itself is useless and the crucial act of incarnation toward which so many of Conrad's characters struggle is robbed of any possible validity. Faced with the ephemerality of existence, mind can only resign itself to an equivalent ephemerality. Mrs. Travers experiences the "black stillness" (xɪɪ, 241) of that night as an "enervating caress" which reduces her to the barest level of self-awareness. Her state of dreamlike languor is characterized by the almost total passivity, a withdrawal of consciousness even from sensation. For Conrad, Mrs. Travers's surrender to this dreamlike passivity in which she is "content that nothing should exist" (xɪɪ, 245) is directly related to her discovery that there is no positive object for the will, that in her words, there is "nothing for the hand to grasp" (xɪɪ, 241).

The dissolution of the will in the discovery of the tenuosity of the created world is, in the completed version of *The Rescue*, the real cause of Lingard's betrayal of Hassim. The turning point for Lingard is not the moment when he leaves his brig under the influence of his love for Mrs. Travers, but rather his own experience of this infinite and eternal darkness which makes "every thought of action . . . odious" (xɪɪ, 246). It is this sense of peaceful annihilation which reasserts itself during the night he spends at Mrs. Travers's feet in the camp of Belarab.

He looked around him, dazedly; he was still drunk with the deep draught of oblivion. . . . He looked down at the woman on the bench. She moved not. She had remained like that, still for hours, giving him a waking dream of rest without end, an infinity of happiness without sound and movement, without thought, without joy; but with an infinite ease of content, like a world-embracing reverie breathing the air of sadness and scented with love. (xɪɪ, 431)

Here the qualities of Lingard's "waking dream" correspond to his earlier experience of the darkness during his journey with Mrs. Travers. Again, he encounters a world "without end, an infinity of happiness without sound or movement" in which consciousness, deprived of any content, is replaced by "a divine emptiness of mind" (xɪɪ, 432). Once more, this awareness of the "eternal something" behind the surface of creation destroys the orientation of mind toward action in the world by destroying its fundamental commitment to the reality of things. Lingard wakes to find himself in accord with a "blind and soundless peace" (xɪɪ, 437), a peace which expresses itself in "this profound indifference, this strange contempt for what his eyes could see, this distaste for words, this unbelief in the importance of things and men" (XII, 431–32). Under the pressure of this experience, Lingard finds that "the fierce power of his personality seemed to have turned into a dream" (XII, 435). "With the sublime indifference of a man who has had a glimpse through the open doors of Paradise" (XII, 433) he is no longer concerned with "the mere life of men" (XII, 436).

Lingard's defeat comes with his failure to recommit himself to life, to will himself back to a world of things and men. On waking, he tries to escape an existence "without speech, without movement" (XII, 432) and to "regain possession of himself, of his old self which had things to do, words to speak as well as to hear" (XII, 432). His failure to involve himself in that adventure which "made him in his own sight exactly what he was" (XII, 219) is the source of his infidelity to Hassim. It is not a question of his willfully ignoring the meaning of the ring which is the symbol of his commitment to Hassim, for Mrs. Travers never gives it to him. Lingard himself realizes that this is irrelevant when he tells Jaffir, "If she had given the ring to me it would have been to one that was dumb, deaf, and robbed of all courage" (XII, 450). Lingard does not choose another course of action. His fall consists precisely in the fact that, robbed of his belief in the validity of things, he is unable to choose at all. He is reduced, like Mrs. Travers, to almost total passivity.

Taken together, the novels of the Malayan trilogy lead inevitably to a nihilistic vision, a vision which seems to force man to accept the fact of his own insubstantiality and resign himself to perpetual orphanage. *Almayer's Folly* had investigated the possibility of man discovering an identity by abandoning himself to the primitive force of creation, and had discarded this possibility with Willems's discovery of the hostility of this force. *The Rescue*, it seems, destroys the other alternative. With the realization that this force is not simply a hostile but a negating one, man must accept the fact that there exists no substantial being which he might appropriate to himself by an act of the will. Because he can neither embrace some positive principle nor, through his action, create such a principle, he is reduced to impotence. There is, it would appear, no act by which man can assure himself a positive existence.

*The Nigger of the "Narcissus," "Heart of Darkness," and *Lord Jim*,* the most important of the fiction Conrad produced during the years he struggled with *The Rescue,* are all, on one level, redactions of this completed vision of the darkness. Each novel is centered on some figure, the crew of the *Narcissus,* Kurtz, Jim, who like Lingard is symbolic of the power of men to shape and control their world. Each novel, in recording the defeat of this symbolic figure, confirms the inability of men to create through an act of will the ground of their own lives.

Yet as the parallel in Conrad's world between the adventurer and the writer would suggest, *The Rescue* has implications which bear more directly on his role as artist. If the voyage of the adventurer into the world images the movement of the author's consciousness to involve itself in the reality of things and men, then the failure of the former will inevitably call into question the validity of the latter. After such a discovery, neither a voyage nor a novel can be begun with quite the same "sense of mastery" (XII, 329) as before. And it is not surprising then that *The Rescue* does, in fact, mark the beginning of a time when Conrad's attitude toward his work was becoming more difficult and complex.

Conrad had written *Almayer's Folly* with comparative ease despite what must have been inevitable difficulties with the language, and he encountered trouble only with the closing chapters of *An Outcast.* With *The Rescue,* however, he is tormented for the first time by what he refers to as "les stérilités des écrivains nerveux"[3] and any attempt to write is enough to bring on an almost suicidal mood. "I have long fits of depression," he writes, "that in a lunatic asylum would be called madness. I do not know what it is. It springs from nothing. It is ghastly. It lasts an hour or a day; and when it departs it leaves a fear."[4] The persistence and intensity of his despair led Conrad to look back

[3] Gérard Jean-Aubry, *Joseph Conrad: Life and Letters* (Garden City, N.Y.: Doubleday, 1927), II, 14. The phrase is Baudelaire's.
[4] Edward Garnett, *Letters from Joseph Conrad* (New York: Bobbs-Merrill, 1962), p. 56.

longingly to the time of *Almayer's Folly* as if it were a pre-lapsarian time of innocence and simplicity. "The more I go," he remarks to Sanderson, "the less confidence in myself I feel. . . . Gone are, alas! those fine days of *Alm: Folly* when I wrote with the serene audacity of an unsophisticated fool. I am getting more sophisticated from day to day. And more uncertain!"[5]

From this point of view it is clear that *The Rescue* marked for Conrad a radical disruption in his initial relationship to his work, and the history of his attempts to finish this novel gives some insight into the nature of this disruption. Since an outline of the novel's plot existed as early as 1897, it seems unlikely that Conrad's troubles were with the over all shape of the action,[6] nor does it seem that they were the result of matters of style in any abstract sense. When, for example, Conrad changed the subject of Part II from Lingard's meeting with the Traverses to an account of his early relations with Hassim these troubles evaporated and he wrote enthusiastically to Cunninghame-Graham that he was "busy about his [Lingard's] youth—a gorgeous romance."[7]

This incident implies that Conrad's technical difficulties were related directly to matters of content and theme and, particu-

---

[5] Jean-Aubry, *Life and Letters*, I, 196.

[6] In September of 1897 Conrad wrote to Blackwood outlining the plot as follows: "The human interest of the tale is in the contact of Lingard, the simple, masterful, imaginative adventurer with a type of civilized woman—a complex type. He is a man tenacious of purpose, enthusiastic in undertaking, faithful in friendship. He jeopardises the success of his plans first to assure her safety and then absolutely sacrifices them to what he believes the necessary conditions of her happiness. He is throughout mistrusted by the white whom he wishes to save; he is unwillingly forced into a contest with his Malay friends. Then when the rescue, for which he has sacrificed all the interests of his life, is accomplished, he has to face his reward—an inevitable separation. This episode in his life lifts him out of himself" (William Blackburn, ed., *Joseph Conrad: Letters to William Blackwood and David S. Meldrum* [Durham, N.C.: University of North Carolina Press, 1958], pp. 9–10). This passage suggests that in its final form *The Rescue* does represent the fulfillment of Conrad's original intention. In the same way, the imagistic continuity between Conrad's letters from the late 1890's and Lingard's voyage into the night "without limit in space and time" (XII, 241) suggests that the latter, although written when the novel was completed, represents an accurate reflection of Conrad's experience during the original period of composition.

[7] C. T. Watts, ed., *Joseph Conrad's Letters to R. B. Cunninghame-Graham* (Cambridge: Cambridge University Press, 1969), p. 60.

larly, to the overtones of Lingard's meeting with Mrs. Travers and the fatal events which follow. Conrad was never able to develop the novel past the crucial point when Lingard and Mrs. Travers begin their voyage from the brig into the night "without limit in space and time" (XII, 241). According to Moser "the yacht people were the rock upon which 'The Rescuer' foundered" and from 1899 to 1916 Conrad abandoned the manuscript, leaving his story somewhere between the time Edith Travers moves to Lingard's brig and the moment when they leave the mainland.[8] For Conrad, clearly, the process of recording Lingard's encounter with the darkness held dangers that were not present in the earlier novels, and the real source of his frustration seems to lie in the implications of Lingard's experience. The history of *The Rescue* suggests, in other words, that Conrad in some sense understood Lingard's failure as involving his own, and that the ramifications of this failure undermined his role as writer as surely as it did Lingard's as Raja Laut.

Conrad's letters from this period support this conclusion, for they reveal that his depressions are closely related to an experience of the darkness which he himself understands as a product of his involvement with *The Rescue*. "The more I write the less substance do I see in my work," he remarks to Garnett. "It is tolerably awful. And I face it, I face it but the fright is growing on me. My fortitude is shaken by the view of the monster. It does not move; its eyes are baleful; it is as still as death itself—and it will devour me."[9] This feeling that "all is darkness"[10] or that he has "come blundering in the dark"[11] manifests itself, moreover, in a failure of the will which echoes that of Lingard. Conrad speaks in his correspondence of "the horror of that powerlessness I must face through a day of vain efforts"[12] and of a "lack of strength, of power, of an uplifting belief in oneself"[13] which has destroyed his self-confidence in the same way that Lingard's failure to "regain possession of . . . his old self which had things to do, words to speak" (XII, 432) destroys his sense of identity.

[8] Moser, *Joseph Conrad*, p. 64.
[9] Garnett, *Letters*, p. 153.
[10] *Ibid.*, p. 141.
[11] *Ibid.*, p. 142.
[12] *Ibid.*, p. 135.
[13] Jean-Aubry, *Life and Letters*, I, 282.

Whatever other reason we may assign, it is this sense of impotence which for Conrad is primarily responsible for his inability to complete *The Rescue*.

> What wonder that during the long blank hours the doubt creeps into my mind and I ask myself whether I am fitted for that work. The worst is that while I am thus powerless to produce my imagination is extremely active: whole paragraphs, whole pages, whole chapters pass through my mind. Everything is there: descriptions, dialogue, reflexion —everything but the belief, the conviction, the only thing needed to make me put pen to paper.[14]

These letters, moreover, show precisely how Conrad's experience of the darkness eroded his art by destroying his belief in the objectives toward which the act of writing was directed. On the one hand, it makes impossible any simple commitment to an art which intends to capture the objective surface of life, because an awareness of the darkness robs one of any belief in the validity of this surface. The sense of impotence which Conrad shares with Lingard and Mrs. Travers suggests that for Conrad himself the failure of the will was related to a loss of belief in a positive reality toward which the will can move in the same way: for example, Mrs. Travers's languor follows from her realization in the darkness that there is "nothing for the hand to grasp" (XII, 241).

Conrad's correspondence implies just such a discovery, and it reveals for the first time his sense of the tenuousness of the created world which appears so clearly in his discussion of the "eternal something that waves." "I am like a man who has lost his gods," he remarks to Garnett, "My efforts seem unrelated to anything in heaven and everything under heaven is impalpable to the touch like shapes of mist." And, he continues, "even writing to a friend—to a person one has heard, touched, drank with, quarrelled with—does not give me a sense of reality. All is illusion—the words written, the mind at which they are aimed, the truth they are intended to express, the hands that will hold the paper, the eyes that will glance at the lines. Every image floats vaguely in a sea of doubt—and the doubt itself is lost in an unexplored universe of uncertainties."[15] Conrad's own awareness

14 Blackburn, *Letters*, p. 26.
15 Garnett, *Letters*, p. 155.

here of the way in which his growing sense of the dissolution of the physical world undermines his art allows us to see the real relevance of his comment to Blackwood that although he can conceive "whole paragraphs, whole pages, whole chapters . . . descriptions, dialogue, reflexion" he lacks "the belief, the conviction, the only thing needed to make me put pen to paper."

It is in the context of this loss of conviction in the surface of existence that we should place his repeated complaints about his loss of style. As this letter to his publisher Blackwood reveals, his loss of style did not involve a basic failure of linguistic ability, since it is clear that he could still compose "whole paragraphs, whole pages." But for Conrad, as we have seen, style is never a thing unto itself. Language for him draws its ultimate justification from its relationship to the real world, from the fact that it corresponds to "things as they are," and the letter implies that it is the validity of this fundamental ground in things which has been called into question. Because he can no longer accept the solidity of this visible surface of life, Conrad seems to feel he can no longer commit himself to a style which is designed to capture and re-create the surface.

The way in which Conrad's style seems to him to have been crippled by this loss of a ground in an assured reality appears nowhere more clearly than in his despair over what he feels to be the failure of the visual quality in his writing. Outlining the novel to Blackwood in September of 1897, he writes, in a manner which foreshadows the Preface to *The Nigger of the "Narcissus"* that "I aim at stimulating vision in the reader: if after reading part 1st you don't see my man then I've absolutely failed,"[16] and later remarks about the same section that he "did try for the visual effect."[17] Yet his complaints point to the fact that it is just this visibility—a quality which seemed so easy to grasp in *Almayer's Folly*—that evades him when he tries to complete *The Rescue*. "Alas," he writes "no one can help me. In the matter of *Rescue* I have lost all sense of form and I can't see *images*."[18]

[16] Blackburn, *Letters*, p. 11.
[17] Garnett, *Letters*, p. 141.
[18] Jean-Aubry, *Life and Letters*, I, 237. Conrad's sense of the way in which his new awareness of the darkness empties physical reality of its solidity is suggested also by his remark to Garnett, "I have had some impressions, some

THE METAPHYSICS OF DARKNESS

The artist who experiences the darkness becomes like Jörgenson, in *The Rescue*. His eyes are no longer fixed exclusively on
the visible surface but now see "beyond . . . into the void" (XII,
251) where they confront a truth which denies this surface. More
than this, however, this new truth robs the act of writing of its
power to confer a solid identity. For Conrad, as we have seen,
writing was one way to define the self because it was an act of
incarnation in which the consciousness of the artist, his temperament, was through the medium of language fused with the reality
of "things as they are." But if these things have no positive
ground in the source of being, then ultimately this world of the
surface has no more validity than a fiction or a dream. It is just
as arbitrary, just as rootless. In such a universe, it is impossible
to write a "realistic" novel in the way in which Conrad initially
wants to, and, for this reason, it is impossible for the act of writing to confer a "real" identity. To incarnate oneself in a ground-
less fiction is to become a fiction oneself. "It is strange," remarks
Conrad about one of his attempts to finish *The Rescue*, "the
unreality of it seems to enter one's real life, penetrate into the
bones, make the very heartbeats pulsate illusions through the
arteries. One's will becomes the slave of hallucinations, responds
only to shadowy impulses, waits on imagination alone. A strange
state, a trying experience, a kind of fiery trial of untruthful-
ness."[19]

To write in this way is to lie. It is to present a world as real
which is not, and to define the self in a way which gives it only a
fictional reality. "I am writing," Conrad tells Garnett, "—it is
true—but this is only piling crime upon crime: every line is
odious like a bad action."[20] This danger of bad faith is not the
only peril of the act of writing. This act initially, for Conrad,
grounded the self not only in the solidity of things but also in
the solidarity of the human community. The openness of the
writer was directed not only toward the physical world but also
to the world of other men, and the knowledge of the darkness

sensations—in my time:—impressions and sensations of common things. And
it's all faded . . . faded and thin like the ghost of a blond and sentimental
woman, haunting romantic ruins pervaded by rats" (Garnett, *Letters*, p. 59).

[19] *Ibid.*, I, 283.
[20] Garnett, *Letters*, p. 155.

destroys this intersubjective ground as well. The key to this lies in the relationship between Lingard and Edith Travers.

Critics who have concentrated on the sexual attraction between these two have done so at the expense of a more complete understanding of the issues involved in their relationship. Conrad's first two novels are concerned with the possibility that love can allow a man and a woman entrance to a common world grounded in the source of life and with the discovery that surrender to this love is a way into the darkness. But while *The Rescue* in some sense continues this theme, it places it in a slightly different context. In *Almayer's Folly* Dain's love for Nina was the expression of his primitive mode of thought and in *An Outcast* Willems's feeling for Aissa was his moral weakness. In Lingard's case, however, it has another source. It is grounded in the openness to others, the capacity for sympathetic identification, which is the foundation of the solidarity that unites the brotherhood of the sea.

In the Lingard of *The Rescue* this openness appears in a particular form. It appears in his unconscious acceptance of responsibility for the lives of those around him, and in his acknowledgment of any trust reposed in him whether explicit or not. In a larger sense, it is this form of openness that underlies his involvement both with Hassim and with the yacht people. Standing on the deck immediately after he has rescued Hassim and Immada, Lingard discovers that "what appealed to him most was the silent, the complete, unquestioning, and apparently uncurious trust of these people. . . . This amazing unconcern seemed to put him under a heavy load of obligation" (xii, 88). From this point, Lingard's life becomes, as he explains to Jörgenson, an assertion of the validity of this claim.

"Look here," said Lingard, "I took these people off when they were in their last ditch. That means something. I ought not to have meddled and it would have been all over in a few hours. I must have meant something when I interfered, whether I knew it or not. . . . When you save people from death you take a share in their life. That's how I look at it." (xii, 102)

As the quotation suggests, it is this same receptivity which underlies his efforts to save Travers's yacht. The yacht, like

Hassim and Immada, is delivered into his hands, and, again, Lingard reacts to "the unconscious demand of these people's presence" (xii, 121), and he finds that he has a share in their lives as well. His involvement with Hassim is thus balanced by the faces of the seamen on Travers's yacht, faces suggesting "old days —his youth—other seas—the distant shores of early memories" (xii, 129). The initial dilemma in which Lingard finds himself, in other words, is not one in which, like Nina, he is caught between civilized and primitive modes of thought, or, like Willems, between ethical and unethical courses of action. The contradictory demands made on him flow from the same source in his character, a source which, moreover, defines precisely what is most admirable in him. The fact that Lingard is unable to resolve these contradictory and equally valid demands suggests that *The Rescue* is concerned with the inadequacy of the ethos of the world of the sea to accommodate any world more complex than the deck of a merchant ship.

It is not, however, the external complexities of the situation which defeat Lingard. He is destroyed by a perception of the darkness, a perception which results from his relationship to Mrs. Travers, and it is important to see that his feeling for her is initially an extension of his feelings of responsibility for the whole yacht party. He is attracted to her because she alone of all the passengers responds to his offer of trust. On her part, Edith Travers is drawn to him precisely because he is open to others, because she can see "the workings of a human soul, simple and violent . . . laid bare before her" (xii, 165). In this sense, their love for one another is not the agency by which they achieve a common world and understanding. Instead, a common understanding, one which is essentially similar to the solidarity which binds together the men of the sea, is the foundation of their passion.

In this context, the fate of Lingard and Mrs. Travers is much more than a condemnation of the kind of romantic love which existed between Willems and Aissa. Their love had been set in opposition to Willems's moral obligations to Lingard; but the feeling of Lingard and Mrs. Travers for one another grows out of that openness to others which in his case is fundamental to his commitment to the ideal, which, in turn, suggests that in the world

70

of *The Rescue* not only love but any sympathetic relationship with another poses a danger. If, as *An Outcast* has shown, the darkness is at the center of any consciousness, then to obtain access to this consciousness, whether through the love of a man for a woman or through the fellowship which unites men in a community, is equally suicidal. To attempt to ground one's life in another person by whatever means is to ground oneself in the darkness.

The Rescue undercuts the foundation for the self which the brotherhood of the sea provides, but more important for Conrad, it subverts as well an aesthetic which is an extension of the ethos of this brotherhood. If his novels are predicated on an act of openness between the writer and the men who move through the world of his novel, then the act of writing becomes no less a way into the darkness. Rather than assuring the novelist's identity, writing becomes much more than an act of bad faith. It is a form of suicide, for to identify himself with even so apparently strong a character as Lingard is to make him vulnerable to the darkness. This in turn suggests that perhaps *The Rescue* was such a threat to Conrad precisely because it required him to identify himself with Lingard and, therefore, undergo Lingard's experience of the darkness. Such a relationship is implicit in Conrad's sense that the irony of the novel's title applies as much to his own position as to that of Lingard. "The scales are falling off my eyes," he writes to Garnett concerning *The Rescue* manuscript, ". . . I am alone . . . in a chasm with perpendicular sides of black basalt. . . . Above, your anxious head against a bit of sky peers down—in vain—in vain. There's no rope long enough for that rescue."[21]

In one context, then, *The Rescue* marks not only the destruction of Conrad's belief in the integrity of man and his world, but the dissolution of his commitment to an art which is the expression of this belief. The visible world which seemed to provide a stable subject for the work now appears as a sham and a façade. The world of men which seemed infused with the solidarity of

[21] *Ibid.*, p. 153.

human brotherhood has become a collection of "fourbes, lâches, menteurs,"[22] even the best of whom, like Lingard, is vulnerable and suspect. Robbed of these two positive foundations, the act of writing is at best a lie, at worst a form of suicide.

Out of this destruction emerges in Conrad a sense of ironic detachment from both life and art. He becomes at times like Jörgenson, who regards all human activity in the context of the void beneath and thereby reduces it to "phenomena unrelated to his own apparitional existence" (XII, 382). With his full understanding of the darkness, it is no longer possible for Conrad to tell "the simplest fact in a simple way."[23] His view of the surface and the men who inhabit it is inevitably compromised, and although he will continue throughout his life to affirm a commitment to realism, it is always, appropriately, a qualified one. He praises Galsworthy for his "fidelity to the surface of life, to the surface of events,—to the surface of things and ideas"[24] and commends Daudet for the same quality, but Conrad's comments make it clear that he himself can see beneath this surface. "And Daudet," he remarks, "was honest; perhaps because he knew no better—but he was very honest. If he saw only the surface of things it was for the reason that most things have nothing but a surface. He did not pretend—perhaps because he did not know how—he did not pretend to see any depths in a life that is only a film of unsteady appearances stretched over regions deep indeed, but which have nothing to do with the half-truths, half-thoughts, and whole illusions of existence" (III, 22).

One result of *The Rescue* was to effect that polarization of Conrad's thought between commitment and detachment which determines the primary dialectic of his work. The essential characteristic of his consciousness at this time is the acuteness of the unresolved tension between these two points of view. During the years that he struggled with *The Rescue* he engaged in his most intense and ambivalent exchanges with Robert Cunninghame-Graham, exchanges which reveal, as we have seen, how Conrad was torn between a desire to involve himself in the world of men and things and a detachment forced on him by a sense of its

[22] C. T. Watts, *Letters*, p. 84.
[23] Garnett, *Letters*, p. 180.
[24] Jean-Aubry, *Life and Letters*, I, 224.

meaninglessness and unreality. Thus he can, characteristically, praise one of Cunninghame-Graham's travel books for revealing "acuteness of vision,—of sympathy . . . and through vision . . . expression as noble, unselfish and human as is only the gift of the best"[25] and close by saying that the book "pulled at my very heart strings."[26] Yet at almost the same time he can write Cunninghame-Graham concerning this same book and call the value of such a sympathetic involvement into question by remarking that mankind is only, after all, "a speck in the eternal night"[27] or elsewhere refer to earth as "l'ignoble boule [qui] rouleva toujours portant des êtres infimes et méchants dans un univers qui ne se comprend pas lui-même."[28]

In this context, the novels which develop out of Conrad's difficulties with *The Rescue* are no longer simply the restatement of the theme of Lingard's failure but appear in a slightly different light. The rhythm of their composition, in which Conrad would turn from *The Rescue* to another work only to return to it, suggests that the completed novels are attempts to explore the effects on his own art of the full vision of the darkness to which *The Rescue* inevitably led him. On this level their common subject is an effort to resolve the tension between an aesthetics which is the expression of the artist's commitment to the visible surface of life and a new perception which denies the validity of this surface. Although the last of these novels, *Lord Jim,* is the fullest exploration of this tension and the novel in which it is finally resolved, it is perhaps well to sketch at least briefly the place of *The Nigger of the "Narcissus"* and "Heart of Darkness" in this exploration.

Both these novellas reveal clearly the quality of Conrad's mind during this period, for both the narrator of *The Nigger* and Marlow stand, as Conrad did, at the intersection of the darkness and the light. Both begin their stories having undergone, at least implicitly, some experience which, like Conrad's experience with *The Rescue,* gives them a prior knowledge of the darkness. The opening description of the crew of the *Narcissus* in the doorway

25 *Ibid.,* I, 259.
26 *Ibid.*
27 C. T. Watts, *Letters,* p. 101.
28 *Ibid.,* p. 87.

appearing "very black, without relief, like figures cut out of sheet tin" (XXIII, 3) points to the narrator's dual knowledge of the surface and the depths. It is on the basis of this knowledge that he stands apart from their community and, in referring to them as "big children" (XXIII, 6), suggests that he has a maturity of vision which they lack. In the same way, when Marlow returns to the "sepulchral city" (XVI, 152) from the Congo he separates himself from his former existence on the basis of a similar vision and treats those he meets as "intruders whose knowledge of life was to me an irritating pretence" (XVI, 152).

Both Marlow and the narrator of *The Nigger* are alike, moreover, in the way in which they attempt to come to terms with this vision. Both work to reject it and the detachment which it brings, and attempt to return to their former state of innocence in order to live and, more particularly, to write from a commitment to the world. Their narratives are at once the record of this commitment and the agency by which it is obtained. The effect of the telling in each case is to draw them back to the life of men and this, perhaps, provides one way of understanding the inconsistencies of point of view in *The Nigger*. In this light they appear to be less the result of carelessness or technical immaturity than the record of a narrating consciousness which is gradually abandoning its initial detachment to participate in the world of the *Narcissus*, a participation which flows inevitably from the openness which is, in the terms of the novel's Preface, the source of the act of writing. In a slightly different way, Marlow's narration on the deck of the *Nellie* has a similar purpose; his story is a continuation of his lie to the Intended. Like his original journey, it serves to vindicate Kurtz's idealism and, in this way, to vindicate Marlow's belief in Kurtz and his goals.

Finally, in each case, this attempt to return to the life and art of an earlier innocent state of mind is compromised in a way which suggests precisely one source of Conrad's trouble with *The Rescue*. In both stories the movement toward an involvement with others on which the narrative is based results in the narrator's participation in another's experience of the darkness. On one level, then, *The Nigger* records not only the way in which the crew becomes "highly humanised, tender, complex, excessively decadent" (xxɪɪɪ, 139) through their sympathy with Wait, but the way in which the narrator, himself, is drawn into this "sentimental lie" (xxɪɪɪ, 155) and suffers a similar fate.[29] Again, it is not only Marlow's initial discovery of the darkness which comes from his attachment to Kurtz, from the fact that, in Marlow's words, it was "not my own extremity I remember best. . . . No! It it his extremity that I seem to have lived through" (xvɪ, 151). Marlow's attempt in his narrative to re-create and justify his "unforeseen partnership" (xvɪ, 147) leads him inevitably to live through this extremity once again and, once again, to lie to the Intended.

It is because these efforts to return to live inside the dream lead both narrators into the darkness that both their narratives have a circular quality. The narrator of *The Nigger*, for example, ends as he begins, contemplating from a distance the "dark knot" (xxɪɪɪ, 172) of sailors against the light. Marlow, in turn, finds that his story has left him where his journey did, at the mouth of a river which leads into the "immense darkness" (xvɪ, 162) that fills the estuary. This circular movement, a movement which suggests the pattern of Conrad's frustration with *The Rescue*, implies that such an attempt to bury the darkness is futile. The discovery of the darkness cannot be treated as if it were itself a nightmare from which man could awake and return to his everyday existence.

Balancing the apparent failure of this return to commitment, there appears in these stories another level of awareness, and another aesthetic, which embraces detachment for the protection which it may provide. It is this stance which is taken by the anonymous narrator whose consciousness records, and frames,

---

[29] On another level this same movement is suggested by the relation between the Preface to *The Nigger of the "Narcissus"* and the work itself. The Preface is Conrad's most explicit statement of an aesthetics directed toward the visible surface of life and the fellowship of men. Yet the term Preface is misleading. Conrad composed it after *The Nigger* was complete and, therefore, after such an aesthetics had been, at the very least, called into question. The Preface is not, in this sense, a pure expression of the blessed unsophistication in which Conrad wrote *Almayer's Folly*. Instead, it too takes on the character of a deliberate attempt to retreat from the experience of the darkness into the comforting haven of the illusion.

Marlow's story. Like his companion storytellers, this narrator has early ties both with the civilizing activity of modern man and with the community of the world of the sea. He, like all the passengers on the *Nellie* except Marlow, has left his life under sail for the shore, but all retain their ground in the brotherhood that unites this world. Between all on board the *Nellie*, the narrator remarks, "there was, as I have already said somewhere, the bond of the sea" (xvi, 45).

Yet for him, as for the narrator of *The Nigger* in the opening pages, this is a commitment which is qualified by another knowledge. The transition from sea to shore which these listeners have undergone suggests not only the passing of Singleton's generation, but the passing of the innocence of vision which was their greatest virtue. The narrator is characterized by an awareness which marks such a fall from innocence. He sees both the darkness which hovers over London and the way in which this darkness undermines the concept of solidarity. "The Director of Companies," he comments, "was our captain and our host. We four affectionately watched his back as he stood in the bows looking to seaward. . . . He resembled a pilot, which to a seaman is trustworthiness personified" (xvi, 45). Yet the narrator can see that this personification of trustworthiness has not escaped the darkness. "It was difficult to realize," he continues, "his work was not out there in the luminous estuary, but behind him, within the brooding gloom" (xvi, 45).

Unlike the narrator of *The Nigger*, however, this anonymous consciousness is never drawn out of his detachment. It is Marlow who makes, and narrates, the journey to Kurtz, and this double level of narration results in the existence of a double level of awareness throughout the story itself. We are introduced to Marlow in the story through the eyes of one whose comments on the Director of Companies and whose description of the "mournful gloom, brooding motionless over the biggest, and the greatest, town on earth" (xvi, 45) suggests that he knows already the lesson of Marlow's tale. This wider vision conditions our entire response to Marlow and to his attitude toward Kurtz. But more than this, because we hear Marlow's narrative through the consciousness of his anonymous listener, we never lose the sense of seeing Marlow, and reacting to Marlow's story, from this narrator's point of view.

"Heart of Darkness" is not, then, Marlow's story exclusively. And if we examine it for a moment as the creation of the nameless member of Marlow's audience, it takes on a different coloration. The narrator's inclusion of Marlow's story within his point of view appears as a deliberate attempt on his part to frame the concrete world and man's involvement with this world in a vision which negates the reality of both. "Heart of Darkness" creates for us the visible surface of life, but does so in such a way that we never forget that this surface is a lie. It leads us to Kurtz, but does so in such a way that we never accept his idealism at face value. And this destruction of both possible grounds for the self, grounds toward which all versions of the adventure for Conrad are directed, results in the radical transformation in the intent of writing. It is no longer one form of the adventure, an act by which man could assure his positive existence. For the anonymous narrator, writing performs precisely the opposite function. It becomes a way of destroying any idea of an act which can confer such an identity by destroying all belief in a reality toward which this act can be directed.

Thus for the narrator to place Marlow's positive, creative journey within the context of a negating darkness is for him to accept the insubstantiality of the self. It is to accept the fact that man can never transcend the conditional existence of his original, orphaned state, and it is this acceptance of his own insubstantiality which is the source of the narrator's strength. Because he exercises his knowledge not only against the world around him but against himself, because he seems to realize that "one's personality is only a ridiculous and aimless masquerade of something hopelessly unknown,"[30] he is able to confront the darkness with the proper attitude of cold unconcern. Like Kurtz and Marlow, the anonymous narrator makes his voyage into the darkness, a voyage defined by the *Nellie*'s swing during the course of the narrative from its position facing the "luminous estuary" (xvi, 45) to its final heading "into the heart of an immense darkness" (xvi, 162). Yet it is clear from the narrator's calm accept-

[30] Garnett, *Letters*, p. 46.

ance of this final vision, an acceptance which contrasts so strongly with Marlow's lie to the Intended, that he does not feel threatened. Because he has accepted the darkness to the point where even the final commitment to a positive self vanishes, he is not susceptible to the sense of vulnerability which overwhelms Marlow. He can say, in the words Conrad used to Cunninghame-Graham, "je ne regrette rien,—je n'espère rien, car je m'aperçois que ni le regret ni l'espérance signifient rien à ma personnalité."[31]

For this narrator, then, the act of writing "Heart of Darkness" is an act of self-denial, a self-denial which is apparent in the very tone of the narrator's voice. In contrast to Kurtz and Marlow, his voice has a curiously passive quality, so that, although he occasionally uses the first person, his statements do not really appear as acts of assertion by an "I." Significantly, he presents himself as a listener, not as an actor or speaker, and contents himself with weaving an abstract, symbolic frame in his descriptions of the setting of Marlow's story. If in giving us Marlow's narrative he creates a world, he does so only to deny its reality. Like the dark force at the center of creation, he brings forth an existence at the same time that he denies this existence. And like this force, he is characterized not by a positive identity but by his ephemerality. His anonymity defines him.

If Conrad's remark that the novelist lives in his work and that in writing he "is only writing about himself" (VI, xv) applies to Conrad's own situation, then we can say that he exists in "Heart of Darkness" in two radically distinct ways. He is at once Marlow and the anonymous narrator. He is at once engaged in the active creation of a world and at the same time cursed by the awareness that this world is a lie. The emergence of the anonymous narrator images the emergence of Conrad's destructive awareness of the ephemerality of creation, and the tension between Marlow and this narrator is precisely the tension between that level of consciousness which is able to create "whole paragraphs, whole pages, whole chapters" of *The Rescue* and that which robs him of "the belief, the conviction"[32] in their reality.

[31] C. T. Watts, *Letters*, p. 117.
[32] Blackburn, *Letters*, p. 26.

While *The Nigger* and "Heart of Darkness" clarify this tension they do not themselves offer a solution. For this, we must turn to *Lord Jim*, the last of the novels which Conrad began while he was still involved with *The Rescue*. This novel is, in many ways, a summary of Conrad's experience of the previous three years. It offers a systematic statement of the destruction of the visible surface of life by the darkness, but it does so in order to provide a context for the formulation of a new aesthetics, and it is here that Conrad makes his choice between Marlow and the anonymous narrator, between the dream and the darkness.

CHAPTER IV

Lord Jim: *The Search for a New Aesthetic*

I liked his appearance; I knew his appearance; he came from the right place; he was one of us. He stood there for all the parentage of his kind, for men and women by no means clever or amusing, but whose very existence is based upon honest faith, and upon the instinct of courage . . . he was outwardly so typical of that good, stupid kind we like to feel marching to the right and left of us in life. . .

(XXI, 43–44)

It is this symbolic quality of Jim's appearance, his ability to stand for "the parentage of his kind," which makes his case of such importance. This quality draws the crowd to his trial in "expectation of some essential disclosure as to the strength, the power, the horror of human emotions" (XXI, 56). It leads the French Lieutenant instinctively to make a distinction between Jim and the rest of the crew, and it reveals to Brierly the secret of human nature which results in his suicide.

This quality lies as well behind Marlow's fascination with Jim. It is, he tells us, Jim's vague appeal "like a symbolic figure in a picture" (XXI, 133) which is "the real cause of my interest in his fate" (XXI, 265). As was the case with Kurtz, Marlow's interest in Jim is an expression of his own concerns. Just as Kurtz symbolized to Marlow his own commitment to the ideal and to the enlightening mission of civilization, Jim is most obviously a test case for Marlow's allegiance to the group and the ethos defined by the phrase "one of us." In this, *Lord Jim* repeats once again the theme of *The Rescue* and in Jim's experience on the deck of the *Patna* we can see reflected the downfall of Lingard.

Yet, as this comparison with Lingard indicates, there are other issues involved. In the pattern that dominates Conrad's fiction of this period, a pattern in which the voyage of the adventurer becomes a metaphor for the act of writing, Jim's symbolic quality will inevitably have an aesthetic reference as well. He is, as we shall see, both sailor and artist, and in the *Patna* incident Conrad has given us an analysis not only of the destruction of Jim's dreams of heroism, but of the dissolution of a certain kind of art which is implicit in his dreams.

The key to this analysis lies in a series of associations in the early chapters which link Jim's dreams to both a particular kind of literature and a particular view of reality. His visions, we recall, have a literary origin. They are the product of a "course of light holiday literature" (xxi, 5), and the tone of the phrase implies that his reading is concerned with an impossible world of fanciful adventure. Although this implication is certainly there for the ironic narrator of the first four chapters, it is also impor tant to see that Jim himself obviously assumes that these books describe the actual world, "its secret truth, its hidden reality" (xxi, 20). Thus, when he climbs to the foretop in order to live in his mind "the sea-life of light literature" (xxi, 6) he does not think of himself as rejecting the reality around him. His dreams, like those of all Conrad's early adventurers, turn out into the world; they are visions of the successful attainment of that self-completing action which is the object of the adventure.

Consequently, Jim dreams not of some fantastic universe but accepts as his starting point the apparent stability of the surface of creation, a stability which implicitly images the simplistic world of his reading. It is for this reason that the act of dreaming for Jim always involves an impression of the security and serenity of nature. On the training ship, at his station in the foretop, Jim abandons himself to his imaginary life, but this activity is inextricably involved with his impression of a secure and stable world which frames it.

His station was in the fore-top, and often from there he looked down ... at the peaceful multitude of roofs cut in two by the brown tide of the stream.... He could see the big ships departing, the broad-beamed ferries constantly on the move ... with the hazy splendour of the sea in the distance, and the hope of a stirring life in the world of adventure. (XXI, 6)

The content and implications of this description are echoed again during Jim's sojourn in the hospital of the nameless Eastern port. Like his station on the foretop, the hospital is located on the heights, and Jim once again finds himself presented with a view which seems to provide the fulfillment of his dreams in a secure universe:

The hospital stood on a hill, and a gentle breeze entering through the windows, always flung wide open, brought into the bare room the softness of the sky, the languor of the earth, the bewitching breath of the Eastern waters. There were perfumes in it, suggestions of infinite repose, the gift of endless dreams. Jim looked every day over the thickets of gardens ... at that roadstead which is a thoroughfare of the East ... dotted by garlanded islets, lighted by festal sunshine, its ships like toys ... with the eternal serenity of the Eastern sky overhead and the smiling peace of the Eastern seas possessing the space as far as the horizon. (XXI, 12)

Here again, Jim's dreaming involves a view of an ordered world—the eternal serenity of the Eastern sky which offers Jim a life which fulfills the promise of his early reading. In this sense we can say that the early figure of Jim "stands for" not only that naïveté of vision which leads men like Lingard to accept the surface as reality and to make it the setting of their projected visions. Because Jim's vision flows from his taste in literature, he is implicitly representative of a kind of writing which shares the same quality. One can say, in fact, that the way in which he embodies his dreams, or projects them into the peaceful world around him, suggests the way in which the artist, for Conrad, incarnates his temperament in the realistic re-creation of this same visible surface. In this sense, Jim is symbolic not only of the assumptions which govern Lingard's action in *The Rescue* but, implicitly, of the assumptions which govern Conrad's writing of it.

These early descriptions of Jim's dreamlike world provide a context for understanding the implications of the *Patna* episode. Like those moments on the foretop and in the hospital, Jim observes the world from a height, from the bridge of the *Patna* whose "slim high hull" (XXI, 19) rises above the ocean. Again, it is a view in which the illusion of a stable natural order and the promise of the fulfillment of endless dreams are intermixed. Under the "inaccessible serenity of the sky" (XXI, 19), the *Patna* sails through a sea whose stillness "pervaded the world" and "seemed to shed upon the earth the assurance of everlasting security" (XXI, 17). Its propeller turns without check "as though its beat had been part of the scheme of a safe universe" (XXI, 17). Moreover, in the same way that he has accepted this security on the basis of its reflection in "the sea-life of light literature," here he makes an equivalent error and accepts this image of peace as it is mirrored in the stable level surface of the ship's chart. "From time to time," the narrator tells us, "he glanced idly at a chart pegged out with four drawing pins on a low three-legged table abaft the steering-gear case. The sheet of paper portraying the depths of the sea presented a shiny surface under the light of the bulls-eye lamp . . . a surface as level and smooth as the glimmering surface of the waters" (XXI, 20).

The effect of this serenity on Jim is once again to induce the "dreams of success" (XXI, 20) which seem to him the reality of his life, and the dependence of these dreams on the assumption of eternal peace is emphasized by the equation of Jim's immersion in his imaginary visions and his slow descent into a real sleep induced by the calm of his surroundings. It is this calm which turns Jim's body to "warm milk" (XXI, 21) and makes him feel that "life was easy and he was too sure of himself—too sure of himself . . . the line dividing his meditation from a surreptitious doze on his feet was thinner than the thread of a spider's web" (XXI, 25).

From this point of view, Jim's most fundamental error was less in his imaginative flight than in his more basic miscalculation that the shiny surface of the chart does in fact portray the depths of the ocean. In this incident, we can see precisely how the discovery of the darkness has reduced, for Conrad, an art of the visible surface to a dangerous lie. It is Jim's assumption that the surface does define the hidden truth of reality which fosters "the adventurous freedom of his thoughts" (XXI, 21), and it is because his eyes are fixed on the "unattainable horizon" (XXI, 19) which is associated at once with the peace of nature and his imaginative heroism that he cannot see the "shadow of the coming event" (XXI, 19).

If Jim, like Lingard, lives on the "visible surface of life" (XII, 210), a surface which seems to provide him with a safe and open field of action, then the collision with the derelict floating just beneath this apparently innocuous surface results not only in the destruction of Jim's dreams but of his more fundamental belief in the reality of this surface. It is precisely at the moment of the collision that the hitherto stable world of the senses takes on an appalling fragility. "What had happened?" he thinks, ". . . they could not understand; and suddenly the calm sea, the sky without a cloud, appeared formidably insecure in their immobility, as if poised on the brow of yawning destruction" (XXI, 26). Jim's terror before the worn bulkhead, or standing on the deck waiting for the sudden slant of the skyline which had seemed so firm, reflects that central experience of vulnerability which comes to those of Conrad's characters who discover that the darkness qualifies the apparent order of existence. Like the sailors of the *Narcissus* who discover that behind the peace of God there exists a force which attacks them "like a madman with an axe" (XXIII, 57), Jim has come face to face with the hostile force at the center of creation.

The storm which destroys the last of Jim's hope is an image of this force, and is characterized by the qualities of stillness and formlessness that Conrad attributes to the "ombre sinistre et fuyante."[1] Its arrival is marked by the apparent annihilation of all form. When Jim first notices it the "silent black squall" seems to have "eaten up" one third of the sky. "Opaque like a wall," it swallows the stars in whole constellations and "confounds sea and sky into one abyss of obscurity" (XXI, 101–2). And like Mrs. Travers's voyage into a similar night "without limit in space and time" (XII, 241), Jim's jump into the "great stillness" (XXI, 105) of this "tenebrous immensity" (XXI, 102) carries him to the center of a limitless darkness whose infinity and eternality are the negation of the ordered world of time and space. During the night he passes in the lifeboat, the "silence of the sea, of the sky merged

---

[1] C. T. Watts, ed., *Joseph Conrad's Letters to R. B. Cunninghame-Graham* (Cambridge: Cambridge University Press, 1969), p. 117.

into one indefinite immensity still as death" in which you "couldn't distinguish the sea from the sky" (xxi, 114). The coming of day, moreover, brings only a repetition of the experience. "I couldn't," Jim tells Marlow "see the water for the glitter of the sunshine.... All was light, light, and the boat seemed to be falling through it" (xxi, 125).

To experience this timeless and indefinite immensity which lies behind the ordered world of days and nights is to discover the formlessness behind all form, the meaninglessness behind all meaning. As the experience of Lingard, or Conrad himself with *The Rescue*, reveals, this discovery casts the surface of existence in the shadow, and gives it a hidden and terrible meaning. Like Marlow after his voyage up the Congo, Jim finds that facts cannot be simply accepted as facts, that the world of "surface-truth" (xvi, 97) is inevitably qualified by the new knowledge of what lies behind it. It is this sense of the ambivalence of facts which makes Jim so uncomfortable at the inquest. His feeling that "speech was of no use to him any longer" (xxi, 33) like Conrad's own feeling that he could no longer "tell the simplest fact in a simple way"[2] comes from a recognition that a language of the surface does not convey the dark truth of existence. "The facts those men were so eager to know," he thinks, "had been visible, tangible, open to the senses, occupying their place in space and time ... they made a whole that had features, shades of expression, a complicated aspect that could be remembered by the eye" (xxi, 30–31). This visible fact, however, is not the truth of Jim's experience. There was "something else besides, something invisible, a directing spirit of perdition that dwelt within, like a malevolent soul in a detestable body" (xxi, 31).

If Jim is symbolic of that aspect of the fellowship which for the world of the sea unites man and nature, he is perhaps even more obviously a representative of the brotherhood which in this world should bind each man to his fellow men. "We trust for our salvation," the narrator reminds us, not only in the stability of the physical world, "in the sights that fill our eyes, in the sound that fills our ears, and in the air that fills our lungs" but also "in

[2] Edward Garnett, *Letters from Joseph Conrad* (New York: Bobbs-Merrill, 1962), p. 180.

the men that surround us" (xxi, 21). Jim in this sense stands for man's ability to give his effective allegiance to a code. And as Marlow suggests when he remarks that "as with belief, thought, love, hate, conviction, or even the visual aspect of material things, there are as many shipwrecks as there are men" (xxi, 121), the *Patna* incident undercuts Jim's belief in this moral reality as well. It is precisely this idea of a moral identity, "this precious notion of a convention ... [with] its assumption of unlimited power over natural instincts" (xxi, 81) which, as we have seen, is so completely destroyed by the fear which robs Jim of his ability to will his action and leaves him helplessly frozen to the deck. His jump into the darkness, moreover, carries him into a realm which transcends, and negates, the structure of "belief" as effectively as it does "the visual aspect of material things." "Trust a boat on the high seas," Marlow remarks, "to bring out the Irrational that lurks at the bottom of every thought, sentiment, sensation, emotion" (xxi, 121), and in this lifeboat under "the shadow of madness" (xxi, 121) Jim finds himself in a world where ethics have no more reality than facts. "Nothing mattered," he thinks, "... no fear, no law, no sounds, no eyes" (xxi, 120). The freedom which he experiences is the terrifying freedom which comes with the nihilistic realization that man's moral codes have no foundation in reality. "When your ship fails you," Marlow explains, "your whole world seems to fail you; the world that made you, restrained you, taken care of you. It is as if the souls of men floating on an abyss and in touch with immensity had been set free for any excess of heroism, absurdity, or abomination" (xxi, 121).

In part Jim appears as a danger to those around him because he has shown he is not to be trusted, but this is not the whole issue. Conrad has made him an example of the unauthenticity of the fellowship of the sea, at least as it exists after the generation of Singleton. More than this, though, he has used Jim to illustrate, in ways which suggest again the aesthetic problems which concern him, how this fellowship has been transmuted into something destructive. Jim's real threat to those around him lies not only in his violation of their trust, as is the case with Marlow's friend or Jewel, but also in the particular quality of his life which leads others to be drawn into his experience. Precisely because there is "something indefinite and attractive in the man" (XXI, 58) which seems to suggest to others the best part of their own character, those who come in contact with Jim run the risk of seeing his experience as their own and of feeling the effects of the *Patna* incident as if they had undergone it themselves. Like the narrator of *The Nigger* or Marlow in "Heart of Darkness," they find themselves driven out of their sheltered conception of existence not by a direct encounter with the darkness but through a sympathetic involvement with another's confrontation.

Perhaps the most striking example of this destructive sympathy is the case of Brierly, one of the three judges at Jim's trial. "One of those lucky fellows who know nothing of indecision, much less self-mistrust" (XXI, 57), he presents to the world "a surface as hard as granite" (XXI, 58). Yet clearly in the same way that James Wait awakens in the crew of the *Narcissus* a knowledge of their own mortality and makes them egotistical, self-aware and corrupted, so Jim leads Brierly to look beneath this granite surface. "Such an affair destroys one's confidence" (XXI, 68), Brierly remarks, and it is clear to Marlow that "at bottom poor Brierly must have been thinking of himself" (XXI, 66). It is this self-concern, moreover, which determines his attitude at Jim's trial. "No wonder Jim's case bored him," Marlow observes, ". . . he was probably holding silent inquiry into his own case. The verdict must have been unmitigated guilt, and he took the secret of the evidence with him in that leap into the sea" (XXI, 58).

Both aspects of Jim's experience are particularly apparent in his relationship to Marlow, apparent in ways which point to the way *Lord Jim* grew out of Conrad's difficulty with *The Rescue*. On the one hand, Jim appears to Marlow throughout the latter's narrative as a problem in the reality of appearances, a problem which suggests Conrad's inability to "see images."[3] In the same way that Conrad discovers that "the progressive episodes of the story will not emerge from the chaos of my sensations"[4] or finds that "every image floats vaguely in a sea of doubt,"[5] Marlow remarks, "I cannot say I had ever seen Jim distinctly" (XXI, 221)

[3] Gérard Jean-Aubry, *Joseph Conrad: Life and Letters* (Garden City, N.Y.: Doubleday, 1927), I, 237.
[4] Garnett, *Letters*, p. 59.
[5] *Ibid.*, p. 155.

but only had an occasional "glimpse through a rent in the mists in which he moved and had his being" (xxi, 125).

For both Marlow and Conrad, the surface of facts, Jim's appearance as "one of us," for example, can no longer be accepted. Instead, they find that this surface continually dissolves into the darkness which lies behind it. The implications of Marlow's inability to see Jim, moreover, are made clear by his encounter with the chief engineer of the *Patna* in the hospital. The engineer's bizarre dreams make us forget that, in this scene at least, Marlow describes him in a way that associates him with the same world of youth and the sea to which Jim himself belongs. He has a "lean bronzed head, with white moustaches" which "looked fine and calm on the pillow, like the head of a war-worn soldier with a child-like soul" (xxi, 50).

This apparent calm, however, is qualified by "a hint of spectral alarm that lurked in the blank glitter of his glance, resembling a nondescript form of terror crouching silently behind a pane of glass" (xxi, 50). The movement of the engineer from composure to a state of hysteria is described by Marlow in terms of this fear, the "phantom of terror behind his glassy eyes" (xxi, 51), breaking through and destroying the calm surface. "His body trembled tensely," Marlow tells us, "like a released harp-string; and while I looked down, the spectral horror in him broke through his glassy gaze. Instantly his face of an old soldier, with its noble and calm outlines, became decomposed before my eyes by the corruption . . . of desperate fear" (xxi, 53).

This passage is, in many ways, a microcosm of the description of the storm striking the *Patna*. There, the wind and the rain appear "as if they had burst through something solid" (xxi, 102) and, in a similar manner, seem to dissolve the surface. More directly, however, and despite Marlow's comment that the engineer's case is irrelevant, it seems to echo a parallel scene between Marlow and Jim, a scene which suggests how the validity of Jim's appearance is destroyed in the same way as that of the engineer's. Together in his room after the court's final judgment, Marlow catches one of his many glimpses of Jim in a flash of lightning.

An abrupt heavy rumble made me lift my head. The noise seemed to roll away, and suddenly a searching and violent glare fell on the blind face of the night . . . I looked at him . . . planted solidly on the shores of a sea of light. At the moment of greatest brilliance the darkness leaped back with a culminating crash, and he vanished before my dazzled eyes as utterly as though he had been blown to atoms. (xxi, 177–78)

Here the destruction of Marlow's view of the lighted figure of Jim by the darkness is an image of the effect of Marlow's knowledge of the *Patna* incident on his belief in Jim's appearance and all it stands for. "I ought to know the right kind of looks," he says, "I would have trusted the deck to that youngster on the strength of a single glance ... and ... it wouldn't have been safe" (xxi, 45). As a result, Marlow's view of Jim is a view of a surface dissolved into a welter of atoms, of unrelated images, which form no coherent picture. "The views he let me have of himself," remarks Marlow, "were like those glimpses through the shifting rents in a thick fog—bits of vivid and vanishing detail, giving no connected idea of the general aspect of a country. . . . they were no good for purposes of orientation" (xxi, 76).

"We exist," remarks Marlow at one point, "only in so far as we hang together" (xxi, 223), and his comment about Jim's being no good for orientation implies—his relation to Jim suggests, too— the way in which the experience of the darkness destroys this brotherhood. But because Marlow is at once a fellow seaman and at the same time the author through whose narrative we have our principle access to Jim, this relationship involves as well the corruption of the bond between writer and subject. It is in this light that we should understand Marlow's constant references to his fear of Jim. Like Brierly, the fellowship invoked at least initially by Jim's appearance leads Marlow always to see Jim's experience as potentially his own, and to see the hidden truth of the *Patna* incident underlying his own life. "He was," Marlow tells his listeners, "too much like one of us not to be dangerous" (xxi, 106), and in his contact with Jim, he explains, "it seemed to me I was being made to comprehend the Inconceivable—and I know of nothing to compare with the discomfort of such a sensation. I was made to look at the convention that lurks in all truth and on the essential sincerity of falsehood" (xxi, 93). Under this influence, Marlow discovers that he is becoming self-aware in the same destructive way as the crew of the *Narcissus* discovers their latent egoism awakened by Wait. "If he had not enlisted my sympathies," he says of Jim, "he had done better for himself—he had gone to the very fount and origin of that sentiment, he had reached the secret sensibility of my egoism" (XXI, 152).

In a larger sense, then, Jim's symbolic status involves more than a moral question, more even than the destructive effect of the darkness on man's conception of a stable moral and physical reality. For Conrad, his initial attitude toward the validity of his art is rooted in this concept of a moral and physical reality, and thus Jim becomes, in one of his many sides, a symbol for the destruction of this attitude, his experience on the *Patna* an allegory of Conrad's own experience with *The Rescue*. In his role as symbol, however, Jim is only the center, not the real subject of the novel. Like James Wait, he is the pivot, the point of reference around which Jim's official and unofficial judges range themselves, and by the same token, their evaluations of Jim's case are more than ethical. Since each judgment implies a way of coming to terms with Jim's experience and of redefining the reality which this experience invalidates, each implies a way of writing which is in accord with this definition. The principle of these judges—Stein, Marlow, and the narrator of the early chapters—constitutes in this sense a systematic investigation of the range of aesthetic possibilities open to Conrad after the failure of *The Rescue*. Taken together, they define a spectrum of alternatives ranging from a possible return to live inside the dream to the studied detachment of the anonymous narrator of "Heart of Darkness."

The key to the first of these alternatives lies in Marlow's remark that "words also belong to the sheltering conception of light and order which is our refuge" (XXI, 313). For Marlow, his comment is a recognition of the unauthenticity of language, of the fact that it describes a world as safe but no more real than Jim's chart. Implicitly, there is another side to his remark which suggests that, even if language does not have the power to capture some reality external to itself, perhaps it is possible for words to create their own reality, a world of light and order in which the dream could exist. If language cannot be the agency through which the writer embodies his vision in the firm ground of "things as they are,"[6] then perhaps it can become itself the ground of this incarnation.

Such a course demands that the writer give up any nostalgia for realism and devote himself to the creation of a world of illusion, but this world would be an illusion of a different order from the apparent stability of the surface of creation. This surface had been generated by the darkness and, as the *Patna* incident proves, its order and stability will always be subject to the negating action of the force which produced it. To live in this illusion is to live in intimate contact with the darkness, and it is for this reason that Jim's attempt to bury the *Patna* incident and establish himself again in a new life does not work. He finds that he must continually confront the dark fact in his past and finds himself destined endlessly to repeat his jump from the *Patna*. He learns, as did the narrator of *The Nigger* and Marlow in "Heart of Darkness," that even if his state of former innocence can be regained such success is only momentary, and his life after the trial is governed by the same circularity which characterizes their narrative.

By embodying the dream not in an image of the surface of life but in a consciously created fiction, however, man could avoid this inevitable disillusionment. The source of this literary world would not be the darkness but consciousness itself. If mind cannot control the darkness, then perhaps language can create a world independent of the destructive force at the center of creation. In this way, the dream becomes no longer, as the image of the chart implies, a plan for action in the world but rather an object of aesthetic contemplation, a contemplation which allows us to achieve imaginatively a sense of fulfillment which the realities of existence deny us.

In adopting such an alternative man abandons any hope for establishing a substantial self grounded in some concrete reality, but perhaps this is the best alternative. Jim's father has passed his whole life safely in the "inviolable shelter of his book-lined, faded, and comfortable study" (XXI, 341), in the same manner that the accountant in "Heart of Darkness" protects himself from the chaos around him by withdrawing into the artificial order of

---

[6] Jean-Aubry, *Life and Letters*, I, 280.

his books. Similarly, when Jim lives in those moments when "all his inner being [is] carried on, projected head-long into the fanciful realm of recklessly heroic aspirations" (XXI, 83) he is able to penetrate to the heart of "the impossible world of romantic achievements" (XXI, 83) and he becomes transfigured by "a strange look of beatitude" (XXI, 83) which signifies his sense of a vision totally fulfilled. If Jim had contented himself with this experience, if he had settled for living "in his mind the sea-life of light literature" (XXI, 6) then his imagination would have been his friend and he too could have lived with this sense of fulfillment.

It is this deliberate retreat into the dreamlike world of fiction which determines the logic of Stein's life and is the center of his analysis of Jim's case. A man with a "student's face" (XXI, 202), Stein, like Jim's father, lives a "sedentary life" (XXI, 202) in the comfortable, circumscribed world of his study. This parallel is made even more meaningful by Marlow's history of the butterfly collection which is now the single object of Stein's interest. Originally, Stein's attraction to butterflies is associated with his early life of adventure in the world. He comes to the East with a Dutch naturalist in search of specimens, and throughout the romantic events which follow Marlow is careful to tell us that "Stein never failed to annex on his own account every butterfly . . . he could lay hands on" (XXI, 206). The prize of his collection, moreover, comes to him on that day when all his dreams seem to have been fulfilled. Recounting its capture, Stein tells Marlow that "on that day I had nothing to desire; I had greatly annoyed my principal enemy; I was young, strong; I had friendship; I had the love . . . of woman, a child I had, to make my heart very full —and even what I had once dreamed in my sleep had come into my hand, too!" (XXI, 211).

Neither Marlow nor Stein gives us an explicit reason for the latter's movement from an active search for butterflies to a contemplation of them; from an attempt to live the dream in the world to a passive life studying it. There are, however, suggestions in the various references to Stein's career which imply that he is not the God-like figure some critics have seen, but that this sudden alteration in his life had its roots in an experience similar to Jim's. There is, for example, Stein's reply when Marlow comments that, unlike Jim, Stein never let any occasions to realize the dream escape him. "And do you know how many opportunities I let escape," he replies, "how many dreams I had lost that had come in my way?" (xxi, 217).

The specific nature of these lost opportunities, moreover, is implied in the ambiguity of Stein's relationship to the world of Patusan and, specifically, to Jewel and Cornelius. Stein has been to Patusan himself in his youth and it is clear that the place holds less than pleasant memories for him. Stein's ambiguous comment, "The woman is dead now" (xxi, 219), combined with Marlow's remark, "I can only guess that once before Patusan had been used as a grave for some sin, transgression, or misfortune" (xxi, 219), tends to qualify his further comment that it is impossible to suspect Stein of any wrongdoing. Although Marlow himself ignores its implication, the most prominent grave in Patusan is that of Jewel's mother, and this pattern seems to support Cornelius's claim that he has been mistreated. Cornelius, in his conversations with Marlow, makes it clear that Jewel is not his daughter but that he has been paid by Stein to marry her mother. This, together with the description of Stein "grey-haired" and "paternal" (xxi, 350) bending over Jewel, gives some substance to the suspicion that it is Stein who has fathered Jewel and deserted her mother. There is, then, at least the implication of a biographical basis for the shadows which fill Stein's house, a suggestion that somewhere in Stein's past there is an act of desertion as shattering in its implications as Jim's desertion of the *Patna*, and that his knowledge of "the heart pain—the world pain" which comes when "you cannot make your dream come true, for the reason that you not strong enough are, or not clever enough" (xxi, 213) has its roots in personal experience.

This disillusionment with his ability to "make your dream come true" determines his present attitude toward his collection. The butterfly still remains a symbol of the dream, but it is a dream which, like Jim's literary visions of heroism, reflects an idealized imaginary nature. "The white tracings" and "gorgeous markings" of the butterflies' wings embody "a splendour unmarred by death" (xxi, 207) and image for Stein "the balance of colossal forces ... the mighty Kosmos in perfect equilibrium" (xxi, 208). This image, "this masterpiece of Nature—the great artist" (XXI, 208), however, is clearly recognized as only an aesthetic ideal, not a description of the actual conditions of man's life. The artist who made man, Stein reminds Marlow, was perhaps "a little mad" (XXI, 208) and rather than living in a perfectly balanced universe he "is come where he is not wanted, where there is no place for him" (XXI, 208).

The pattern of Stein's life thus seems to suggest that for him the only way to have the dream is to recognize it for what it is. It is to realize that it is a product of imagination opposed to the nature of man's life and capable of only the kind of imaginative expression which art affords. This movement from life into aesthetics of the dream is underlined both by Marlow's comment that "what followed [the adventurous part of Stein's life] was so different that . . . this strange part must have resembled a dream" (XXI, 207) and, even more so, by his description of Stein returning his prize specimen to its case:

He lowered the glass lid . . . and taking up the case in both hands he bore it religiously away to its place, passing out of the bright circle of the lamp into the ring of fainter light—into shapeless dusk at last. It had an odd effect—as if these few steps had carried him out of this concrete and perplexed world. (XXI, 213)

Here among his collection Stein is bathed in the "impalpable poesy" of a "crepuscular light" (XXI, 215) and his "tall form, as though robbed of its substance" concerns itself with the "immaterial cares" (XXI, 213) of butterfly collecting. Coming soon after Marlow's summary of Stein's career, this movement from a concrete to an immaterial world seems an obvious metaphor for the course of Stein's life, also a movement from the active world of commerce and adventure to the insubstantial twilight of his collection. As such, it reveals clearly the way in which Stein has attempted to substitute an imaginary reality for man's "concrete and perplexed world," and to withdraw entirely within the confines of the dream.

It is this description of Stein among his butterflies, moreover, which frames Stein's definitive analysis of Jim's case.

A man that is born falls into a dream like a man who falls into the sea. If he tries to climb out into the air as inexperienced people endeavour to do, he drowns—*nicht wahr?* . . . . No! I tell you! The way is to the destructive element submit yourself, and with the exertions of your hands and feet in the water make the deep, deep sea keep you up. (XXI, 214)

Stein gives his speech from the shadows where his voice seems "to roll voluminous and grave" (XXI, 213). When he later returns to the light, Marlow tells us, this light "destroyed the assurance which had inspired him in the distant shadows" (XXI, 214), and, in this context, his analysis seems to be an explicit statement of the rationale of his twilight existence, and this in turn provides a key to Stein's equation of the dream with the destructive element. In terms of Stein's metaphor, the sea only becomes destructive when you try to climb out of it; when, like Jim or the young Stein, you actually try to make your dream come true. It is this attempt, rather than the dream itself, which leads Jim, and by implication Stein, to their encounter with the darkness. Stein, however, suggests that the dream can be preserved by giving oneself over to it entirely, submitting oneself to it, and withdrawing completely from an involvement with the world. The phrase "with the exertions of your hands and feet in the water make the deep, deep sea keep you up" suggests not an attempt to realize the dream through action but rather the essentially passive life of the late Stein.

Lord Jim is concerned not only with the statement of alternatives, but also with an evaluation of their viability, and there are indications that Stein's attempt to create an independent, ethereal realm of the imagination is not, in Conrad's world, a truly adequate answer. Stein's butterflies, ironically, provide an insight into the logic of this failure. Marlow's initial description of them as "beautiful and hovering" (XXI, 203) seems to set them off from Stein's parallel collection of beetles—"horrible miniature monsters" in their "death and immobility" (XXI, 203). A closer reading suggests, however, that the similarities between the two are more essential, for the wings of the butterflies are as "lifeless" (XXI, 203) as the beetles and both are fixed in their glass cases. Stein's attempt to preserve the grandeur and beauty of the butterfly, and all this represents, succeeds only in reducing it to that immobility of death which is the final triumph of darkness over the spirit, and the implications of their lifelessness are made even more definite by the references at the end of the novel to Stein's own imminent death.

Perhaps the best argument for Stein's failure, however, is Jim's career in Patusan, for Stein's withdrawal from the world provides an insight into the rationale for Jim's final voyage to the East. It is on Stein's advice, of course, that Jim undertakes his last adventure, and, as Marlow describes it, it is an adventure which carries him in a new direction. This time he travels not toward the world but away from it. Patusan, as Marlow describes it, is associated not only with the heights which are the setting of Jim's early dreams, but also with a kind of art which, Stein suggests, allows the perfect embodiment of these dreams. Patusan is, for Marlow, a "distant heavenly body" (XXI, 218) where Jim can leave all his failings behind, but it is also for him a world created by imagination and described in terms which suggest the color and tracings on the wings of Stein's butterflies. In this sense, the distance between Patusan and man's concrete existence is precisely that between life and art. "But next morning," Marlow writes of his departure, "at the first bend of the river shutting off the houses of Patusan, all this dropped out of my sight bodily, with its colour, its design, and its meaning, like a picture created by fancy on a canvas, upon which, after long contemplation, you turn your back for the last time. . . . I had turned away from the picture and was going back to the world where events move, men change, light flickers, . . . But as to what I was leaving behind, I cannot imagine any alteration. . . . They exist as if under an enchanter's wand" (XXI, 330).

The constant emphasis on Patusan's isolation reinforces the parallel between Stein's withdrawal to his secluded house and Jim's withdrawal to Patusan. As he did with Stein, Marlow associates Jim in his native kingdom with the "impalpable poesy" of a light which seems to free objects from material involvement. The moon which Marlow and Jim watch rising above the ravine "as if escaping from a yawning grave in gentle triumph" (XXI, 221) is most obviously a symbol of Jim's apparent victory, of his ascent out of the abyss into which he jumped from the *Patna*. It also sheds a light which "robs all forms of matter . . . of their substance" (XXI, 246) in the same way that the twilight surrounding

Stein's collection seemed to rob his tall form of its substance. It is in this light that Jim recounts to Marlow the heroic adventures of his first years in Patusan among people who, he remarks, "are like people in a book" (xxi, 260).

These parallels tend to minimize the apparent difference between Stein's sedentary life and Jim's active one, and to associate them in the same project. All of these suggestions that Jim, too, is engaged in a withdrawal from the world of men into a world of the imagination are drawn together in the descriptions of Jim's second jump, the one which carries him from the Raja's compound into the creekbed. As in the case of his jump from the *Patna*, this leap carries Jim into the formless materiality which underlies existence. The "horrible cold shiny heap of slime" (xxi, 254) of the creekbed threatens to destroy in Jim "all semblance to a human being" (xxi, 254) in the same way that the dusk Marlow sees descending "like a steady fall of an impalpable black dust" threatens to dissolve "all the visible forms, effacing the outlines, burying the shapes deeper and deeper" (xxi, 306). Jim's movement from the moment when he finds himself immobilized in the mud until he attains the height of the firm bank is an attempt in the darkness "to crack the earth asunder, to throw it off his limbs" (xxi, 254).

In this context, Jim's jump becomes an image of his attempt to escape a world in which, as he discovers in the *Patna* incident, he is inextricably involved in the darkness, and to attain an immaterial world of his own making. The success of this second jump, a success on which his life in Patusan is founded, would seem implicitly to justify this attempt. But just as our last view of Stein qualifies the apparent validity of his life, so our last view of Jim through the eyes of Gentleman Brown points to Jim's ultimate failure. As he is described by Marlow, Brown becomes an embodiment of the same powers of the darkness which conspired against Jim in the *Patna* incident. His arrival in Patusan is arranged by that same seemingly "malevolent providence" (xxi, 159) which ordained the *Patna*'s collision. "Running his appointed course," Marlow remarks, "he sails into Jim's history, a blind accomplice of the Dark Powers" (xxi, 354), and we recall that Marlow had described the *Patna* incident in the same terms as "a sham from beginning to end, planned by the tremendous disdain of the Dark Powers" (xxi, 121).

In many ways, then, Jim's meeting with Gentleman Brown, a meeting which results in the destruction of his ordered world in Patusan and, eventually, in his death, is a repetition of the collision of the *Patna*.[7] The fact that the key encounter between Jim and Brown takes place at the same spot where Jim made his second leap into the creekbed emphasizes the impossibility of his attempt to free himself from the life of men, and in this there is a lesson not only for Jim as an adventurer but also for him in his role as artist. The Patusan episode seems in this light to be a statement of the inevitable failure of any artist who tries to create a hermetically sealed world. It is possible, as Jim has at least metaphorically done, for the artist to write himself into another, imaginative existence, to create and live in a world which is like a fanciful picture. Yet it is impossible, Conrad seems to say, for the artist to write himself out of his real life. Insofar as he exists, he does so as part of the surface of life which he is trying to escape, and, because of this, he remains subject to the darkness. This is the real meaning of the death which hangs over Stein and the shadows which haunt Jim, and it is a meaning which Marlow himself seems to read. When he describes Jim's world in Patusan as "a picture created by fancy on a can-

[7] Both Robert Heilman, "Introduction," *Lord Jim* (New York: Holt, Rinehart and Winston, 1957), and Morton Dauwen Zabel, "Introduction," *Lord Jim* (Boston: Houghton Mifflin, 1958) see Jim's decision to allow Gentleman Brown's escape and his death at the hands of Doramin as positive acts, the "final expiation" (i, xxvi) of his jump and the culmination of his "progression toward self-knowledge" (Heilman, p. xix). Both Zabel and Heilman ignore the implications of the "impalpable poesy" of the moonlight associated with Patusan, implications which suggest that Jim's flight there and his subsequent actions are not, as Heilman states, an effort to give his dreams "some substance in life" (p. xx), but a continuation of his retreat into illusion. Again the emphasis in the closing pages is not on Jim's redemption through a kind of ritual suicide or even on his breach of faith with Dain Waris. Instead, it is on his betrayal of Jewel, his violation "in a last flicker of superb egoism" (xxi, 413) of the promise he had made never to leave her. The description in the final scene in the novel of Jewel "leading a sort of soundless, inert life" (xxi, 416) suggests the way Conrad sees Jim's suicide as a breach of faith equivalent to his jump from the *Patna*. His own death makes him as responsible for Jewel's metaphoric death as he is for Dain Waris's actual one.

vas" he is careful to make clear that Jim himself has not attained such a purely imaginative existence. The people of this world, he remarks, "exist as if under an enchanter's wand. But the figure around which all these are grouped—that one lives, and I am not certain of him. No magician's wand can immobilise him under my eyes. He is one of us" (xxi, 330–31).

The conception of the work of art as a self-contained, imaginative and harmonious world which is the foundation of the later careers of Stein and Jim obviously looks two ways. On the one hand it is a nostalgic echo of a time when art could address itself to the ideal harmony which men thought existed beneath the phenomenal surface of events. In this way, for example, a metaphysical conceit points to a unity which reconciles apparent opposites or a poem by Pope rationalizes particulars by showing that they, like Stein's butterflies, are microcosms of an ordered cosmos. On the other hand, and perhaps more important, Stein and Jim look toward tradition of art which develops from the loss of belief in this transcendent order. In this tradition, the structure of the work, instead of reflecting some pre-existent harmony, becomes itself the harmonizing principle, and the creation of an independent world of language becomes a way of achieving unity in a fundamentally disordered world.

As innumerable critics have noted, a large part of post-Renaissance literature falls into this latter tradition, and although Stein occupies only a small part of *Lord Jim* the rejection of his alternative is no small matter. He represents, historically, an important development, and beneath Conrad's rejection of an art which creates and defines its own reality we can detect perhaps one of the constant elements in Conrad's temperament, an element which manifests itself in many aspects of his life. Conrad seems to have shared with Gentleman Brown and with many of his characters a horror of being imprisoned, of being confined in a closed space and, with this horror, a longing for a world and an art which opens on limitless horizons. Without venturing into the wilds of psychological criticism, it is perhaps not too much to suggest that such a horror and longing drove Conrad from a landlocked part of Poland to his life on the sea. This tendency is reflected, as we shall see, in Razumov's crucial rejection, in *Under Western Eyes*, of the closed, dead world of Geneva for the infinite plains of Russia. It would seem to afford, moreover, some insight into Conrad's choice of the image of the darkness. Part of the terror which the darkness holds for Conrad is the paradoxical sense it gives one of being lost in a void and at the same time buried in a closed space without perspective or power of movement. Thus, although the darkness is an infinite night, Conrad will write to Garnett that when he encounters it he feels as if he "is alone ... in a chasm with perpendicular sides of black basalt"[8] or again remark that "all the doors behind me are shut and I must remain where I have come blundering in the dark."[9] In the same way, when Jim finds himself in the "indefinite immensity still as death" (xxi, 114) into which he jumps from the *Patna*, he is struck by the inexplicable feeling that he and his companions are "like men walled up quick in a roomy grave" (xxi, 120).

It is perhaps this association of confinement with the darkness which allows us to understand best Conrad's rejection of the static, closed worlds of Stein and Jim. In Patusan, Jim achieves a marvelous control of his storybook world. "He had regulated," Marlow remarks, "so many things in Patusan! Things that would have appeared as much beyond his control as the motions of the moon and stars" (xxi, 221). Patusan is a world where Jim's "word was the one truth of every passing day" (xxi, 272), and associated as it is with his voice, Jim's control suggests the absolute power the consciousness of the artist exercises over the world he has brought into existence. Yet because this power results from the fact that this world defined by the work is self-contained, a world apart from the life of men, the creation of such a work inevitably involves the limitation of the consciousness of the artist. His power is only good in this fixed area. For this reason Stein's butterflies fixed on a pin in a glass case are an appropriate image of his life, and this imprisonment is reflected as well in the conditions which govern Jim's existence in Patusan. Marlow, we recall, can never shake the feeling that Jim, for all his success, is

8 Garnett, *Letters*, p. 142.
9 *Ibid.*, p. 153.

a prisoner of his world. "I can't with mere words convey to you," he remarks, "the impression of his total and utter isolation." He continues, ". . . This isolation seemed only the effect of his power" (XXI, 272). Jim, like the artist who creates such an enclosed work, finds that he has become the prisoner of his own creation. He finds, in the words of Marlow, that he is "imprisoned within the very freedom of his power" (XXI, 283).

It is not surprising, then, that in its search *Lord Jim* looks beyond Stein, for his is not the only possible alternative and it is not inevitable that the artist's language constitute a circumscribed world of illusion. Language, as we have seen, is for Conrad tied to the surface of life. It names and defines the discrete objects of this surface, and in the sense that the darkness negates the fundamental qualities of this surface—weight, dimension, etc.—which allow discrete objects to exist, it negates the structure of language as well. The darkness cannot be named in a positive, substantial sense for the same reason that the night "without limit in space and time" (XII, 241) cannot be measured. It can only be recognized as beyond measurement. We might say that it is precisely because it is "impossible de fixer l'image"[10] of the darkness that the darkness is for him unnameable.

Yet as this discussion indicates, it is possible to use language in such a way that it points beyond itself to a realm which transcends the word. Such an approach, in which the artist attempts to address himself to the ultimate reality of things, even if this reality is a negative one, is much more congenial to Conrad's temperament. The same basic commitment to an art grounded in the objective truth of things which lies behind his early realism would seem to demand that he come to terms directly with the darkness, and much of Conrad's language does have the quality of words straining to transcend themselves. As one critic has recently noted,[11] it is this attempt to reach an "ineffable" reality which lies behind what F. R. Leavis refers to as Conrad's "emotional insistence on the presence of what he can't produce."[12] It

10 C. T. Watts, *Letters*, p. 117.

11 James Guetti, *The Limits of Metaphor* (Ithaca: Cornell University Press, 1967), p. 5.

12 F. R. Leavis, *The Great Tradition* (Garden City, N.Y.: Doubleday, 1954), p. 219.

is also the rationale for Conrad's description of the darkness in terms of contradictions, such as calling it a matter of infinite tenuousity, in which the two terms, by cancelling one another out, indicate the presence of a world in which such distinctions are meaningless.

An approach in which the artist attempts to escape the bounds of language would seem to demand that he accept an unimpeded view of the darkness and recognize the way in which it negates the surface. If this were true there would only be two choices. One could either live in an illusion like Stein and Jim, or one could adopt a position of utter detachment like the anonymous narrator of "Heart of Darkness." Perhaps, however, there is another way. Language, it seems, has a definite ambivalence. It can both describe the surface and yet point to the depths beneath this surface, and perhaps this ambivalence can be turned to the artist's advantage. If language can be used in such a way that it has this dual reference then it is possible that it could provide a neutral ground in which the surface and the darkness could exist together. Such an art would combine two truths: the illusory, conditional truth of the surface and the reality of the darkness. If art could succeed in reconciling these two, then man could live with a twofold knowledge. He would be aware of the darkness, and thus would avoid the dangers which threaten those who, like Stein and Jim, want to withdraw completely into the illusion, but he would still maintain a hold on the surface of existence and therefore maintain a conditional, but effective, commitment to this surface. Such an art, in other words, provides a way of balancing two opposing levels of awareness in such a way that one does not destroy the other, so that the knowledge of the darkness does not render the visible surface of life so illusory that, like Lingard, men are reduced to passivity. If this were possible, then perhaps the only choice would be not between some version of Stein and the narrator of "Heart of Darkness," but between commitment to an illusion and detachment. There would exist a life, and an art, which at once recognized the truth of things and yet allowed man a positive existence.

Marlow's constant practice of playing the light side of Jim off against the dark, of invoking his success and his failure at the same time, suggests that his narrative is governed by such a prin-

ciple of ambivalence. He describes Jim's reserves, for example, as
the outcome of "manly self-control, of impudence, of callousness,
of a colossal unconsciousness, of a gigantic deception" (xxi, 78)
and the bewildering contradictions of this series of phrases are
echoed throughout the novel in the many contradictory judg-
ments Marlow seems to take pleasure in passing. What he refers
to at one point as Jim's deceptive illusion of passivity becomes
at a later one his "passive heroism" (xxi, 114). In another instance Marlow comments that Jim seems to have buried the
memory of his jump, only to remark several pages later that "he
did not try to minimize its importance" (xxi, 81), and it is precisely this shifting point of view which makes it so hard for the
reader to determine the ultimate success of Jim's wedding with
his shadowy Eastern bride.

It is possible, of course, to explain Marlow's contradictions by
seeing him as a larger version of Stein, as a man who would like
to retreat into the illusion but who is always defeated by a
knowledge of the darkness which will not be denied. Marlow's
attitude toward Jim, however, is much more contradictory than
this. While he will engage with Stein in a conspiracy to bury Jim
in Patusan, he does not abandon him and will, unlike Stein,
undertake a reasonably lengthy voyage to visit him. In addition,
Marlow's remark to his listeners that Jim "existed for me, and
after all it is only through me that he exists for you" (xxi, 224)
seems to imply that he is more aware of his narrative as a systematic presentation of Jim's case than it might first appear.
This, in turn, implies that his contradictions are the result of a
deliberate method.

Although Marlow is Stein's most forceful character witness,
moreover, there are indications that he sees the error of Stein's
approach and that he recognizes that the twilight world of Stein
and Jim is a form of death. In his first visit to Stein, Marlow had
equivocated the value of this immaterial twilight. Was it "a
crepuscular horizon on a plain at dawn," he asked, "or was it,
perchance, at the coming of the night? One had not the courage
to decide" (xxi, 215). But Marlow's further remark that it throws
its "deceptive light" over "pitfalls" and "graves" (xxi, 215) is
echoed by his much more straightforward evaluation of the
similar moonlight of Patusan. Shining on the grave of Jewel's

mother, it becomes a symbol to Marlow of death rather than regeneration. It is now a mournful, eclipse-like light which gives the flowers around the grave "shapes foreign to one's memory and colours indefinable to the eye, as though they had been ... destined for the use of the dead alone" (xxi, 322). This moonlight, he remarks elsewhere, is "to our sunshine, which ... is all we have to live by, what the echo is to the sound; misleading and confusing" (xxi, 246).

Marlow's affirmation of the sunshine reveals his hesitancy to abandon the surface for a consciously created world of illusion. Yet as his insistence on Jim's dark side shows, too, he realizes that to accept this surface completely is to live in a dream of a different order from, but just as ephemeral as, Stein's. Marlow's approach suggests that he is attempting to blend both sides of Jim, the light and the dark, by drawing the shadowy line between his success and failure so thin that the two are confused. If Jim's case could be made totally ambiguous, if Jim could be wrapped completely in the enigma, then perhaps a no man's land could in fact be established in which the darkness and the light could coexist. Marlow remarks about Jim's attitude toward his home that he knew "he felt ... the demand of some such truth or some such illusion—I don't care how you call it, there is so little difference, and the difference means so little" (xxi, 222). Marlow's narrative with all its length and complexities seems to be only an extension of this statement, an attempt to make the difference between truth and illusion mean so little that Marlow can at once maintain an awareness of the dark in Jim and a commitment to all the illusions which claim fellowship with Jim's appearance.

This attempt to show the darkness through the surface, "the truth," as Marlow puts it, "disclosed in a moment of illusion" (xxi, 323), is most apparent in Marlow's efforts to describe Jim. If Stein in framing his butterflies and Jim in composing his dreams on the canvas of Patusan are in their way artists, then so is Marlow who is engaged in his own kind of portraiture. We only have to recall how many times Marlow does attempt to describe Jim as "a symbolic figure in a picture" (xxi, 133) to realize how literally this can be taken. Marlow's long investigation of Jim can be described in this context as an attempt to resolve Jim's floating outlines" (xxi, 224). His narrative intends to assemble his isolated glimpses of Jim into a coherent picture and thereby to return him to the realm of clearly perceived objects.

To accomplish this would be to vindicate the reality of Jim's appearance, a reality which, as we have seen, was fragmented for Marlow by the dark implications of the *Patna* affair. This symbolic act of reconstitution would allow Marlow once again to live on the visible surface of life and to believe in the moral reality of the bond which seems to unite him to the young seaman. Although Marlow is obviously interested in reviving his belief in these illusions, however, it is important to see that he seems to have an equal interest in maintaining a constant awareness of what lies beneath them. For this reason, Marlow's "symbolic" descriptions of Jim reveal a constant, paradoxical pattern in which Marlow, in various ways, consciously juxtaposes Jim's appearance and the *Patna* incident, the surface and the darkness. During his visit to Patusan, for example, Marlow describes Jim at the high-water mark of his success. Yet even at this moment which, more than any other, would seem to provide Marlow with the necessary evidence of Jim's reality, Marlow is careful to recall the shadow which hangs over him.

And there I was with him, high in the sunshine, on the top of that historic hill of his. . . like a figure set on a pedestal, to represent in his persistent youth the power, and perhaps the virtues, of races that never grow old. . . . I don't know whether it was exactly fair to him to remember the incident which had given a new direction to his life, but at that very moment I remembered very distinctly. It was like a shadow in the light. (xxi, 265)

This deliberate juxtaposition of Jim's greatest success with his worst failure is the clearest possible imagistic expression of Marlow's tendency to cloud the issue of Jim's actions, and this symbolic moment, a moment when the tension between the darkness and the light appears to have been harmoniously balanced, is echoed at several points throughout the narrative. In these moments, Marlow, as he can here, is able to see Jim clearly, not as a welter of chaotic details and glimpses through the mist. "I seem to see him, returned at last," he writes in the letter to his unnamed listener, "no longer a mere white speck at the heart of an immense mystery" (xxi, 342). At times like this, Marlow is able to accept Jim at face value and there exists between the two moments "of real and profound intimacy ... like a glimpse of some everlasting, of some saving truth" (xxi, 241). Nevertheless, even as Marlow pictures him here "full stature ... with a stern and romantic aspect" (xxi, 342) he notes also that Jim is nevertheless "always mute, dark—under a cloud" (xxi, 342).

At such times, Marlow's ambiguities seem to have the desired effect. The juxtaposition of light and dark seems to achieve the harmonious balance which is necessary if Marlow is to preserve his involvement with the surface in the face of the darkness. These are only moments, however, and Marlow's final vision of Jim at the end of his last narrative casts doubt on the stability of this balance. In this final glimpse, the tenuous balance which existed between Jim's two sides, and Marlow's two levels of awareness, seems to have broken down and in its place there appears an unstable fluctuation between his conviction in the reality of Jim and an all-encompassing scepticism. "Now he is no more," he writes, "there are days when the reality of his existence comes to me with an immense, with an overwhelming force; and yet upon my honour there are moments, too, when he passes from my eyes like a disembodied spirit astray among the passions of this earth, ready to surrender himself faithfully to the claim of his own world of shades" (xxi, 416).

This passage implies that the kind of balance which Marlow seeks can only be achieved and maintained for an instant. At the root of Marlow's failure is the failure of language to maintain effectively a double reference to the surface and to the darkness, and the reason for this is simple. Such an approach might be possible if language were itself independent of the darkness, but this, as we have seen, is not the case. Language, like all of man's creations, is a part of this surface, and to bring it into direct contact with the darkness is simply to confront it with its own negation.

It is for this reason that in the same way Jim experiences the darkness as a shipwreck of the visible world, Marlow experiences it as the destruction of language. Those moments when Marlow approaches closest to the darkness are precisely those moments when speech fails him and he is left without the net of words in which he hopes to capture surface and depths. The evening Marlow invites Jim to his room after the court has passed judgment is such a time. Watching Jim relive his experience of the *Patna*, Marlow finds himself overpowered by a sense of Jim's unreality which is beyond the power of language to counteract. At this moment, Marlow remarks, "I . . . who a moment ago had been so sure of the power of words . . . now was afraid to speak. . . . It is when we try to grapple with another man's intimate need that we perceive how incomprehensible, wavering, and misty are the beings that share with us the sight of the stars. . . . The envelope of flesh and blood on which our eyes are fixed melts before the outstretched hand, and there remains only the capricious, unconsolable and elusive spirit that no eye can follow, no hand can grasp" (xxi, 179–80).

Marlow's encounter with Jewel on his last night in Patusan is a repetition of this experience. Here again Marlow is drawn into the darkness through his contact with Jewel's "sudden dread, the dread of the unknown depths" (xxi, 312) of Jim's existence, and again, Marlow finds himself at a point where language and the world it describes fail him. At this moment, he remarks, he had allowed a "sense of utter solitude to get hold of me so completely that all I had lately seen, all I had heard, and the very human speech itself, seemed to have passed away out of existence" (xxi, 323). Because speech is human, Marlow discovers as Kurtz did, that rhetoric is no protection, and when he attempts to convince Jewel of Jim's reality he is helpless, seeming "to have lost all . . . words in the chaos of dark thoughts" (xxi, 313).

The failure of Stein and Marlow leaves the reader, where I believe it left Conrad, with the ironic narrator of the first four chapters. This narrator is the logical and dramatic extension of the disengagement from the dream which begins with the first chapter of *The Nigger of the "Narcissus."* He, like Jörgenson, views life with an "unearthly detachment" (xii, 248), a detachment which rests in his awareness of the darkness and which manifests itself in a similar "strange contempt for what his eyes could see" and an "unbelief in the importance of things and men" (XII, 431–32). It is this detachment which governs his attitude toward Jim in these chapters. His ironic location of the source of Jim's dreams in his "light holiday reading" (XXI, 6), his mock-heroic amplification of Jim's job as water clerk all point clearly to the way in which he sees that the soft spot renders all dreams, Lingard's as well as Jim's, ridiculous as well as dangerous. Unlike Stein and Marlow, he does not consider the illusion a shield against the darkness. Rather, he utilizes the detachment which comes with his knowledge of the darkness to protect himself against the destructive self-awareness which haunts Jim and, in their own ways, Marlow and Stein, Kurtz and Wait. To take this position, to accept that the darkness renders all life and all action meaningless is to reduce oneself to a life of almost total passivity, yet it is only by taking this position that the narrator seems to provide himself with the one viable and stable ground in the novel.

It is toward this detachment that Conrad turns in *Nostromo* and *The Secret Agent*. On one level, *Nostromo* investigates the failure of Charles Gould to achieve, on a grand scale, the realization of the ideals of justice and pity which motivated Lingard. In this sense, the novel is one more step in Conrad's investigation of man's ability to conquer and control the darkness. It considers this struggle, however, not from the partially sympathetic vantage point of a Marlow or the divided consciousness of the narrator of *The Nigger of the "Narcissus,"* but from the detached point of view of the anonymous narrator of *Lord Jim*. Although the narrator of *Nostromo* does not indulge in the same sarcastic touches, his vision is no less grounded in a dual awareness of the surface and the darkness which is the essence of Conradian detachment. In this sense, *Nostromo* is the culmination of Conrad's gradual movement toward detachment. In this novel the narrator's detachment is directed not against a lone representative of civilization, but against the structure of society itself.

CHAPTER V

Nostromo: *The Ironic Vision*

> *...the level of the Sulaco Valley... unrolled itself, with green young crops... from the blue vapour of the distant sierra to an immense quivering horizon of grass and sky.... Men ploughed with wooden ploughs and yoked oxen, small on a boundless expanse, as if attacking immensity itself. The mounted figures of vanqueros galloped in the distance, and the great herds fed with all their horned heads one way, in one single wavering line as far as the eye could reach across the broad potreros.* (IX, 87)

The landscape of *Nostromo* is a revelation of the darkness. For all its size, it does not give the impression of massive solidity, of a world of "matter ... as vulgarly understood."[1] Dominated by "boundless" (IX, 87) plains which pass into "the opal mystery of great distances" (IX, 8) and by the peaks of the Cordillera which appear "as if [they] had dissolved ... into great piles of grey and black vapours" (IX, 6), this landscape suggests instead the infinite substance of "inconceivable tenuity" from which creation has sprung. At the center of the geography of *Nostromo* lies the darkness of the Golfo Placido. Like the night "without limit in space and time" (XII, 241) which Edith Travers encounters, it negates the forms of creation and confounds the objects of everyday life into one homogeneous obscurity: "Sky, land, and sea disappear together out of the world when the Placido—as the saying is—goes to sleep under its black poncho" (IX, 6). In the "vastness" (IX, 7) of the gulf at night, "your ship floats unseen under your feet, her sails flutter invisible above

---

[1] Edward Garnett, *Letters from Joseph Conrad* (New York: Bobbs-Merrill, 1962), p. 143.

your head" (IX, 7). All things are "merged into the uniform texture of the night" (IX, 302).

The darkness of the Golfo Placido not only transcends the physical structures of creation. It transcends, and negates, all levels of consciousness—both rational and emotional—as well. It is the source and end of both the empty, formal eloquence of Don Juste and Avellanos and the more primitive irrationality and barbarism of the Monteros. When Decoud voyages into the Placido, he finds that "no intelligence could penetrate the darkness of the Placid Gulf" (IX, 275) and that he was robbed of his power of analysis. He finds that his one emotional hold on the world, his love for Antonia, evaporates too and that, like Edith Travers, he is reduced to a state of enervated languor in which his appearance is like "that of a somnambulist" (IX, 499).

In *Nostromo* the landscape does not exhibit toward men the active hostility of the jungle in "Heart of Darkness." As the name Placido suggests, its chief characteristic is its imperturbability. It has about it a sense of "universal repose" (IX, 494) which reflects the stability of being that the darkness possesses. Outside of time and space, the matter of the "eternal something"[2] cannot decay or die, and for Conrad, as we have seen, all material objects share in this stability insofar as they are in their essence material. The silver of the mine is, by virtue of this fact, incorruptible; although its form can be changed from ore to ingot it remains in some sense unaltered, and for this reason it can be trusted to "keep its value for ever" (IX, 300).

It is the intuition of matter's self-contained being which the characters of the novel find so destructive. Perhaps in no other work by Conrad does one find such a sense of the "immense indifference of things" (IX, 501) toward man; denied an equivalent stability by the fact that mind is not in essence material, consciousness sees this indifference as a constant reminder of its own insubstantiality. When Nostromo descends into the "shadowy immobility" (IX, 422) of the plain of Sulaco after his unsuccessful attempt to save the treasure, he finds that "its spaciousness, extended indefinitely by an effect of obscurity, rendered more sensible his profound isolation" (IX, 422). And Nostromo's

[2] *Ibid.*

sense of isolation here, flowing from the felt tension between the infinity and eternality of matter and the vulnerability of his own personality, marks the change which overtakes the Capataz after his failure. It measures precisely the distance between the permanence of things and the corruptibility of human identity.

We are introduced to Costaguana through the narrator's description of its geography in the opening chapter, and throughout the novel the landscape exists as a constant, detached presence of which the reader is always aware. Like the white dome of the Higuerota, "a colossal embodiment of silence" (IX, 27) whose "cool purity seemed to hold itself aloof from a hot earth" (IX, 26), the landscape envelops the human world, yet stands apart from it. In his Author's Note, Conrad describes his first, imaginative glimpse of this landscape as a "vision of a twilight country . . . with its high shadowy Sierra and its misty Campo for mute witnesses of events flowing from the passions of men" (IX, ix). While reading the novel, we are continually made conscious of such a perspective which measures the temporality of man's existence from the vantage point of the eternality of things.

In its symbolic role, the physical setting of the novel does more than provide an area of action; it defines a level of awareness which views men against the darkness, a view permeated by "the crushing, paralyzing sense of human littleness" (IX, 433). This level of awareness characterizes the narrator of *Nostromo*. The narrating consciousness of this novel is typified by its air of cool dispassionate analysis. The narrator rarely involves himself in the world of his story and then only parenthetically. He recalls, for example, that "those of us whom business or curiosity took to Sulaco . . . can remember the steadying effect of the San Tomé mine" (IX, 95), or again remarks that to Decoud "as to all of us, the compromises with his conscience appeared uglier . . . in the light of failure" (IX, 364). To compare the occasional quality of these instances of the narrator's assertiveness with the involvement of Marlow in his story of Jim is to measure in some degree the distance which exists between the narrator of *Nostromo* and his creation.

We should not allow this distance, however, to mislead us into thinking that *Nostromo* is written from some objective point of view by a consciousness which passively reflects the world before it. Conrad has given us, in his Author's Note, an insight into the conditions which governed his writing of the novel. Paradoxically, this was not for him a time of placid disengagement but rather of deep involvement with his characters and their world when Costaguana became as real for Conrad as England. He speaks of his two-year "sojourn" (IX, x) there and remarks that "on my return I found (speaking somewhat in the style of Captain Gulliver) my family all well, my wife heartily glad that the fuss was all over, and our small boy considerably grown during my absence" (IX, x). It is clear, moreover, that his sense of being involved in the reality of Costaguana extended to its inhabitants. As to their histories, he continues, "I have tried to set them down, Aristocracy and People, men and women, Latin and Anglo-Saxon, bandit and politician, with as cool a hand as was possible in the heat and clash of my own conflicting emotions. . . . I confess that, for me, that time is the time of firm friendships and unforgotten hospitalities" (IX, xi).

In this context the narrator's reserve seems the result less of an intrinsic impersonality than of a studied restraint, less of the absence of emotion than of the deliberate negation of it. If there is a distance between himself and his world, it is a distance which the narrator has imposed, and in this sense the writing of *Nostromo* involves again a twofold movement. It demands initially the creation of a realistic world, of the visible surface of life inhabited by men and women with whom one can establish "firm friendships." This positive act of creation, an act in which the consciousness of the artist journeys outward to involve itself with things and men in what is for Conrad one version of the adventure, is implicit in the existence of the novel. But as in "Heart of Darkness" and *Lord Jim*, although in a much more thoroughgoing way, this positive act is deliberately framed in a vision which negates it just as Marlow's voyage to Kurtz is framed in the vision of his nameless listener. The world of Costaguana is created only so that it may be imposed against the darkness of the Golfo Placido, the narrator's ties to this world are invoked only so that they can be dismissed as irrelevant.

112

The anonymity of the narrator is thus the deliberately chosen stance of a consciousness which has abandoned the adventure and, with it, any hope for a positive self. He sees that to attempt to win such an identity from the darkness is, in fact, like "attacking immensity itself" (IX, 87) and it is against the vision of this immensity, imaged in the Sierras and Campos of Costaguana, that he frames the stories of the two principal adventurers in the novel, Charles Gould and Nostromo.

The origins of both Charles Gould's and Nostromo's adventures lie in similar experiences of the vulnerability and transience of the self. For Gould, this experience comes when, as he learns of his father's death, the recognition that "by no effort of will, would he be able to think of his father in the same way" (IX, 66) fills him with a "vague and poignant discomfort of mind . . . closely affecting his own identity" (IX, 65–66). For Nostromo it comes much later in the narrative when he awakens, on the morning after his attempt to save the treasure, with the strange sense that he had somehow "gone out of existence" (IX, 419). In both cases, their discovery flows from the recognition by consciousness of its own nature and position in the world. Their sense of mortality reflects mind's ironic realization that it has no positive ground, that it lacks the same stable existence which the silver of the San Tomé possesses, and this realization by consciousness of the void at its center is emphasized by the quality of the expressions of Gould and Nostromo at this crucial moment. Nostromo's glance on awakening, a glance "fixed upon nothing from under a thoughtful frown" (IX, 412) echoes Charles Gould's expression when, on learning of his father's death, he had stared past Emma's head "at nothing" (IX, 63). And the parallel here suggests how, for Conrad, their new awareness of death is founded in a profound sense of the insubstantiality of consciousness itself.

The lives of Stein and Jim in *Lord Jim* are a statement of the impossibility of consciousness's escaping from the threat of this void by retreating to a self-enclosed world of its own creation. If man is to avoid abandoning himself to the anonymity and detachment of the narrators of "Heart of Darkness" and *Lord Jim* and win for himself a positive identity, then he must do so by facing the darkness directly. He must subjugate the tenuous materiality of the eternal something to the rule of consciousness, and, by doing so, assimilate to consciousness this matter's completeness of being.

For both Gould and Nostromo, the adventure has as its object just such a conquest. The silver which is the center of both their lives is an image of the lower levels of creation from which consciousness has sprung. In one aspect it suggests in its power to evoke the irrationality of men like Sotillio and Montero, the level of emotion which has given birth to rational consciousness, but beyond this, in its repose, it evidences the stability of being which is denied man. Both Gould and Nostromo in their dealings with the silver suggest that the ultimate end of their quest is to possess just this quality.[3] Both accept the fact that they cannot avoid what Conrad referred to, in a letter to Garnett, as "the contest of man interlocked with matter—the mortal in alliance with the immortal to make utility in the gross."[4] At that critical point for Conrad's characters where mind and world meet, where the imagination seizes on some aspect of the material world and attempts to give it form, to control matter and make it subservient to spirit, they do not turn away. In this same letter, Conrad had spoken of "material . . . gripped, moulded . . . by man,"[5] and the relations of Gould and Nostromo to the silver are described in terms which suggest just such a contest. Nostromo yearns "to clasp, embrace, absorb, subjugate in unquestioned possession this treasure" (IX, 529). In the same manner, Gould feels his father had not "grappled" (IX, 62) with the San Tomé mine in the

[3] In 1923 Conrad wrote to Ernest Bendz that "Nostromo has never been intended for the hero of the tale of the Seaboard. Silver is the pivot of the moral & material events" (Gérard Jean-Aubry, *Joseph Conrad: Life and Letters* [Garden City, N.Y.: Doubleday, 1927], II, 296), and in this sense, the real subject of the novel lies not in the story of any one character but in the relation of mind to matter. Both Eloise Knapp Hay, *The Political Novels of Joseph Conrad* (Chicago: University of Chicago Press, 1963), pp. 101–2, and Albert Guerard, *Conrad the Novelist* (Cambridge: Harvard University Press, 1958), pp. 177, 183, note that the central theme of the novel is the process of idealization itself.

[4] Garnett, *Letters*, pp. 84–85.

[5] *Ibid.*, p. 85.

proper way and tells his wife "I shall know how to grapple with this" (IX, 63).

At first this would seem an impossible task. The experience of Kurtz has already demonstrated the inability of reason alone to control the darkness. It has not the power. In the opening pages of *Nostromo*, the narrator describes the financier and the chief engineer of the railway surveying its route:

This was not the first undertaking in which their gifts . . . had worked in conjunction. From the contact of these two personalities, who had not the same vision of the world, there was generated a power for the world's service—a subtle force that could set in motion mighty machines, men's muscles, and awaken also in human breasts an unbounded devotion to the task. Of the young fellows at the table . . . more than one would be called to meet death before the work was done. But the work would be done; the force would be almost as strong as a faith. Not quite, however. (IX, 41)

The relationship of the two men is an image of all men's attempts to translate, through their own strength, vision into fact. It would seem, too, that it is a final pronouncement on the failure of this attempt, an assurance that the force of mind will never be equal to its faith.

Perhaps there is another way. Even if man's innate strength is not enough to triumph over the darkness there is still an alternative possibility. If he cannot defeat the darkness in a face to face confrontation then perhaps there is some way he can use the darkness against itself. It may be possible, in other words, that he can harness the darkness in the same way that men harness other natural forces.

It is this strategy which governs Gould's attitude toward the San Tomé mine. His father, he thinks, was wrong in "wasting his strength and making himself ill by his efforts to get rid of the Concession" (IX, 60). The inevitability of his involvement with the mine and the force it symbolizes is a fact which he accepts. The younger Gould, however, sees latent possibilities in this situation. Mines, he thinks, "might have been worthless, but also they might have been misunderstood" (IX, 59). Using a different approach, he implies, the mine might itself become the means of achieving a rational end, and Gould defends his interest in the silver as just such an employment of the darkness to realize a spiritual vision:

I pin my faith to material interests. Only let the material interests once get a firm footing, and they are bound to impose the conditions on which alone they can continue to exist. That's how your money-making is justified here in the face of lawlessness and disorder. It is justified because the security which it demands must be shared with an oppressed people. A better justice will come afterward. (IX, 84)

Gould is, in this sense, an idealist and, like Kurtz, he represents himself as an emissary of light in a land of darkness. As Decoud remarks, Charles Gould "cannot act or exist without idealizing every simple feeling, desire, or achievement" (IX, 214–15). He is, however, an idealist with a difference. As his aversion to Avellanos's "claptrap" (IX, 83) rhetoric shows, he sees the uselessness of opposing the darkness with the unaided power of idealism. In his argument with Antonia, Decoud clearly draws the distinction between Gould and the traditional liberalism of her father. "You write all the papers," he tells her, "all those State papers that are inspired here, in this room, in blind deference to a theory of political purity. Hadn't you Charles Gould before your eyes? . . . He and his mine are the practical demonstration of what could have been done. Do you think he succeeded by his fidelity to a theory of virtue?" (IX, 182–83). Unlike his father, then, Gould does not attempt to suppress the corruption of Costaguana. He faces it and attempts to use it so that he can employ the power of the silver to establish rational justice in his country. "Charles Gould," the narrator observes, "was competent because he had no illusions. The Gould concession had to fight for life with such weapons as could be found at once in the mire of a corruption that was so universal as almost to lose its significance. He was prepared to stoop for his weapons" (IX, 85).

Is it really possible to use the darkness in this way? Initially the answer seems to be yes. Through his directorship of the San Tomé mine, Gould becomes the controlling force in the province. His control is based on the advantage which the silver gives him in the game of bribery which is politics in Costaguana, but it is an advantage which he uses not to enrich himself but to bring about the rule of order. In this way, Gould transforms the silver, initially the center of the country's irrationality and corruption, into "a rallying point for everything . . . that needed order and stability to live" (IX, 110). Gould's success in mastering the political chaos of Costaguana is indicative of a more fundamental conquest of the alien materiality of the darkness. By using the silver to realize his dream of security in Costaguana, Gould seems in fact to have achieved the act of incarnation which marks the successful assimilation by consciousness of its source. The Concession no longer appears to him, as it did to his father, as something alien and hostile. Instead it has become imbued with a spiritual quality which allies it to the nature of consciousness itself. It is surrounded by "the marvellousness of an accomplished fact fulfilling an audacious desire" (IX, 105). Uniting vision and fact in this way, the mine would seem to be the realization of Emma's hopes when, laying her hands on the first bar of silver, she "by her imaginative estimate of its power . . . endowed that lump of metal with a justificative conception, as though it were not a mere fact, but something far-reaching and impalpable, like the true expression of an emotion or the emergence of a principle" (IX, 107).

Because Gould completes the act of incarnation he is allowed to exist for a time with the freedom which comes when the self achieves an independent being. Although he lives in Costaguana, Gould remains untouched by the darkness of the land. His mind, unlike Kurtz's, "preserved its steady poise as if sheltered in the passionless stability of private and public decencies at home in Europe" (IX, 49), and this independence of consciousness appears most clearly in the political stance which he initially takes in Costaguana. Although he uses the power of the mine to assure that the circle of order he has drawn around Sulaco remains unbroken, he maintains a certain distance from the political situation. He does not back one government over another, but accepts each as an inevitable manifestation of the "persistent barbarism" (IX, 231) of Costaguana and maintains an "offensively independent" (IX, 92) attitude toward those he must bribe. Gould uses the force of the silver rather than Avellanos's abstract appeal to rational political principle, but he uses it with the "cold, fearless scorn" (IX, 143) of a man who is sure of his control of it and of the stability of his own existence.

The complete history of the Gould Concession, however, reveals that Gould's power and his sense of stable existence is only transitory. Gould's initial sophistication protects him from Lord Jim's sudden and destructive discovery of the darkness beneath his dreams. But although Gould does win an early victory, he does not escape the fundamental process of Conrad's world in which the source of life continually negates and reabsorbs its own creation. In Gould's case, this process of reabsorption manifests itself not in a sudden onslaught of the darkness but rather in the slow transformation of his rational dream into more and more primitive levels of awareness.

The first step in his transformation is marked by the appearance of an undertone of irrationality in Gould's idealism, and Conrad is careful to emphasize that this irrationality does not emerge independently of Gould's initial vision but is a mutation of this vision. "Charles Gould's fits of abstraction," observes the narrator, "depicted the energetic concentration of a will haunted by a fixed idea. A man haunted by a fixed idea is insane. He is dangerous even if that idea is an idea of justice" (IX, 379). It is this same "picturesque extreme of wrong-headedness into which an honest, almost sacred, conviction may drive a man" (IX, 200) that also attracts Decoud's attention. "It is like madness," he thinks, "it must be—because it's self-destructive. . . . It seemed to [Decoud] that every conviction, as soon as it became effective, turned into that form of dementia the gods send upon those they wish to destroy" (IX, 200).

The practical effect of this emerging madness is to make Gould increasingly concerned with the physical safety of the Concession. From an ideal conception of political order which was to be implemented through the mine, Gould's vision gradually contracts to an obsession with the security of the mine itself. The ideal of rational justice ceases to exist "on its only real, on its immaterial side" (IX, 75) and becomes identified with the material agency through which it was to be realized. No longer the means to an end, the mine becomes the end itself, whose preservation and well-being are, in Gould's eyes, equivalent to the successful achievement of his dream.

118

The gradual transformation of reason into madness marks the destruction of the feeling of independence and freedom which had characterized the early period of Gould's success. Under increasing pressure to assure the safety of the Concession, Gould abandons his stance of a distanced manipulation of local politics and intervenes directly. "The extraordinary development of the mine," the narrator observes, "had put a great power into his hands. To feel that prosperity always at the mercy of unintelligent greed had grown irksome to him. . . . It was dangerous" (IX, 143). As a result, Gould comes to feel that "there must be an end now of this silent reserve. . . . The material interests required from him the sacrifice of his aloofness" (IX, 378). Yet with his surrender to material interests, Gould, instead of controlling the darkness, becomes controlled by it. The founding of the Occidental Republic which is the eventual result of Gould's decision to give his direct and open support to Ribera, represents consequently not the triumph of light but only another manifestation of the persistent tyranny which has always characterized Costaguana. This is the meaning of Dr. Monygham's prophecy: "the time approaches when all that the Gould Concession stands for shall weigh as heavily upon the people as the barbarism, cruelty, and misrule of a few years back" (IX, 511).

In *Nostromo*, the slow decay of idealism into irrationality is imaged as a process of petrification in which spirit is gradually materialized. Such a transformation is suggested not only by the allusions to the growing weight of the mine's autocracy or its increasing power to "crush innumerable lives in the expansion of its greatness" (IX, 521), but is also implied in the references to the history of the financier Holroyd. Like Gould, Holroyd begins as an imaginative materialist who attempts to use material interests to establish his vision of a "pure form of Christianity" (IX, 317). In a way which suggests the ultimate end of Gould's venture, however, fact has come to rule spirit in Holroyd's empire. His "religion of iron and silver" (IX, 71) has decayed into a "sort of idolatry" (IX, 71) and manifests itself in "the great Holroyd building (an enormous pile of iron, glass and blocks of stone . . .)" (IX, 80). In a similar manner, the only evidences of the Spanish attempt to civilize and Christianize the country are ruins

—"heavy stonework of bridges and churches" (IX, 89)—which "proclaimed the disregard of human labour" (IX, 89) in the same way Holroyd's business has destroyed his employees and "devoured their best years" (IX, 81).

The absorption of mind by matter appears most clearly, however, in the novel's description of the slow solidification of Gould's consciousness. As the material interests of the Concession increasingly come to dominate his attention, Gould sinks beneath the level of irrationality to a point at which all awareness seems to disappear in an almost total identification with the physical fact of the mine. Mrs. Gould herself is both witness to and unwilling participant in this process. "The fate of the San Tomé mine was lying heavy on her heart," we are told; ". . . It had been an idea. She had watched it with misgiving turning into a fetish, and now the fetish had grown into a crushing weight. It was as if the inspiration of their early years had left her heart to turn into a wall of silver bricks . . . between her and her husband. He seemed to dwell alone within a circumvallation of precious metal" (IX, 522). As a result of this movement from idea to matter, Gould becomes a figure of almost inhuman coldness, described by those who know him as "the embodied Gould Concession" whose "impenetrability" has its "surface shades" (IX, 203).

The destructive transformation of Charles Gould reveals that the whole idea of incarnation is a trap. Lord Jim had failed because he had been prevented from ever completing this act, but Gould's defeat is a direct result of his initial period of success. Paradoxically, his very ability to inform matter with consciousness and to make the mine an expression of a spiritual principle only leaves his consciousness more susceptible to the darkness. While Jim finds himself constantly rebuffed in his attempts to establish a substantial being and must remain the eternal youth, Gould's fate is precisely the opposite. The gradual emergence of "material interests" leaves him imprisoned in his own creation. Like a symbol in which the vehicle has destroyed the tenor, the San Tomé mine is no longer the "true expression" (IX, 107) of Gould's self but rather its tomb, a tomb in which he remains as fixed and immobile as one of Stein's butterflies. It is this same gradual process in which incarnation becomes imprisonment that is at the center of Nostromo's story.

The reader is introduced to Nostromo through a series of descriptions of what might be called his public figure. We see him first through the eyes of Captain Mitchell as a man "above reproach" (IX, 13), then as the rescuer of Viola where he is one whose "mere presence in the house would have made it perfectly safe" (IX, 19–20). Throughout the early narrative, he appears in his role as Capataz de Cargadores, the locus of power among the common people of Sulaco just as Gould is among the upper classes. Yet whereas the reader is given access to Gould's subjectivity immediately, during the long account of Gould's relation to the San Tomé mine, he encounters Nostromo through "the spell of that reputation the Capataz de Cargadores had made for himself by the waterside, along the railway line, with the English and with the populace" (IX, 20). Until late in the novel, the reader never penetrates the surface of this public image.

There is a reason for this. It is because Nostromo's consciousness is completely defined by its surface. Nostromo's life is one "whose very essence, value, reality, consisted in its reflection from the admiring eyes of men" (IX, 525). Like Willems's existence in Macassar, Nostromo is an example of a man whose entire identity lies in its relation to those outside himself. The key to Nostromo lies in his naïve and unconscious acknowledgment of this principle, his unquestioning acceptance of the fact that his being is defined entirely by his social context. His world is limited entirely to this one dimension, and things only have meaning for him if they manifest themselves on this level. As Decoud observes, "the only thing he seems to care for . . . is to be well spoken of . . . . He does not seem to make any difference between speaking and thinking" (IX, 246). His acceptance of this principle is symbolized by his acceptance of his name, "Nostromo," from the English. "This is our Nostromo!" remarks Signora Teresa, "What a name! What is that? Nostromo? He would take a name that is properly no word from them" (IX, 23).

Nostromo's acceptance of this principle governs the parallel between him and Charles Gould. Unlike the Englishman, Nostromo is not committed to the realization of an abstract ideal, a theory of rational liberty. But he is, in a similar way, committed to the perfect fulfillment of his public role. Although Captain Mitchell accepts Nostromo as the embodiment of virtue, the more perceptive Decoud realizes that Nostromo is, in reality, "made incorruptible by his enormous vanity, that finest form of egoism which can take on the aspect of every virtue" (IX, 300). In a way, Nostromo's allegiance to the Gould Concession is arbitrary. He could as well have thrown his lot with Montero. Nostromo does not think of himself, any more than he does of other people, as having an innate nature apart from his role in society. His egoism is without content. It manifests itself in his attitude to playing this role, for having accepted one he feels compelled to fulfill it completely. "Since it was the good pleasure of the Caballeros to send me off on such an errand," he says of his attempt to rescue the silver, "they shall learn I am just the man they take me for" (IX, 267). His gift of his last dollar to an old lady, performed without witnesses, has "still the characteristics of splendour and publicity" (IX, 414). Like his efforts to make himself indispensable to his employers and his talent for the picturesque, for the act which strikes the imagination, this gift is the expression of his attempt to give his reputation the widest possible currency and to maintain its total consistency. Nostromo understands clearly, if only intuitively, that, given his assumptions, the validity of his person lies in the consistency of this public image. For Nostromo, identity finds its strength and source not in its internal dedication to some principle but in the extent to which it gives itself a social reality. "It concerns me," he tells Viola's wife, "to keep on being what I am: every day alike" (IX, 253).

In this sense, then, Gould and Nostromo are parallel figures: both are attempting to achieve the incarnation of an ideal in society, although for Gould this ideal is a substantial theory of political liberty and for Nostromo it is a radically different conception of personal renown. In the opening chapters of the novel, we meet Nostromo at the high point of his success. His life to the moment when he undertakes the rescue of the silver has been "in complete harmony with his vanity" (IX, 414). The nature of this success, however, suggests not only the similarities between these two figures but also important differences. Like Gould's early achievements, Nostromo's are based on the power of silver. It is not only in the last episodes after he has stolen the treasure that Nostromo is associated with silver. This association is constant throughout the novel, although the terms of the association change in a significant way. Nostromo rides a "silver-grey mare" (ix, 22) and wears a sombrero "with a silver cord and tassels . . . enormous silver buttons . . . silver plates on headstall and saddle" (ix, 125). He seems "to disdain the use of any metal less precious than silver" (ix, 225). The scene in which he gives the silver buttons to Morenita is an illustration of the way in which his reputation is based, as firmly as Gould's political power, on the force of material interests. "But young or old," he tells Decoud, "they like money, and will speak well of the man who gives it to them" (ix, 247). Like Gould at the beginning of his career, Nostromo is interested in the silver only as a means. He uses it to establish his reputation in Sulaco in the same way that Gould uses it to establish his ideals of political stability and justice. Dr. Monygham makes the analogy explicit when he remarks to the chief engineer that Nostromo has "not grown rich by his fidelity to you good people of the railway and the harbour. I suppose he obtains some—how do you say that?—some spiritual value for his labours, or else I don't know why the devil he should be faithful to you, Gould, Mitchell, or anybody else" (ix, 321).

Although both employ the silver in this way, however, they approach their tasks in much different frames of mind. Gould's involvement with the San Tomé mine flows from his awareness of its destructive effects on his father. He understands clearly the nature of the forces he plans to use. Nostromo's relation to the silver, on the other hand, is characterized initially by that same quality of unconsciousness which appears also in his acceptance of the terms of his identity in Sulaco. His character, as Decoud notes, is at once naïve and "practical" (ix, 246), and Nostromo falls in that class of characters who are protected against the effects of the darkness, as Conrad himself once was, by a kind of blessed lack of sophistication.

It is in the context of this essential difference between these two "racially and socially contrasted men" (ix, xi) that we should consider the change which overtakes Nostromo when he awakens on the morning after his unsuccessful attempt to escape with the silver, for this change is explicitly a movement to another level of awareness:

Nostromo woke up from a fourteen hours' sleep.... Handsome, robust, and supple, he threw back his head, flung his arms open, and stretched himself with a slow twist of the waist and a leisurely growling yawn of white teeth, as natural and free from evil in the moment of waking as a magnificent and unconscious wild beast. Then, in the suddenly steadied glance fixed upon nothing from under a thoughtful frown, appeared the man. (IX, 411–12)

The key to the particular form this new awareness takes for Nostromo is in the way his partial failure to rescue the silver affects his public existence. To this point, Nostromo has lived on the surface of life, a surface which he has defined as the two dimensional world of overt actions and attitudes. Wherever he has turned in this world, he has seen the "perfect form of his egoism" (IX, 301) in the "reflection from the admiring eyes of men" (IX, 525), and in keeping with all of Conrad's characters who are protected by their unconscious naïveté he has never thought to question the solidity of this surface. He is like Jim who before the collision accepts the apparent peace of the ocean as a stable medium on which to project his dreams of adventure.

The real effect of Nostromo's failure is not so much in his inability to escape with the silver but in the way in which the attempt compromises him in Sulaco and thus separates him for the first time from this surface. His last act before leaving Sulaco, the gift of a dollar to an old lady, had still, we remember, "the characteristics of splendour and publicity" (IX, 414) and as such was in keeping with the tenor of his life. It is exactly these qualities which are denied him now. "But this awakening in solitude, except for the watchful vulture, amongst the ruins of the fort," the narrator remarks, "had no such characteristics. His first confused feeling was exactly this—that it was not in keeping. It was more like the end of things" (IX, 414).

The effect of his failure on Nostromo is, therefore, similar to the effect of the collision on Jim. It serves to drive a wedge between self and world, to effect that detachment which causes both to realize the instability of the surface of things. Just as at the moment of collision the visible surface of nature, hitherto stable, appears to Jim "formidably insecure" (XXI, 26) in its immobility, Nostromo is here made aware of the insubstantiality of the surface of society which is the foundation of his own existence. "The necessity of living concealed somehow, for God knows how long, which assailed him on his return to consciousness," we are told, "made everything that had gone before for years appear vain and foolish, like a flattering dream come suddenly to an end" (IX, 414).

The destruction of his unconscious acceptance of the surface world is experienced by Nostromo not simply in negative terms as the fragility of what he had thought real, but more positively as the discovery of an alien force behind this apparent solidity. Nostromo's awareness of this alien force appears as a sudden recognition of the antagonistic subjectivity of others. The flight of the Europeans and the maneuverings of Gould, acts which destroy the social fabric of Sulaco, appear to him acts of personal infidelity. His sense of betrayal expresses his feeling that he has been used without an understanding of his real nature. Nostromo's resentment at being chosen to rescue the silver has its source in the same realization. His entire reputation hangs on the success or failure of this mission. He is, Nostromo tells Decoud, "going to make it the most famous and desperate affair of my life" (IX, 265). Yet he understands clearly that he has been asked to risk what is, in effect, the foundation of his existence though those who have asked him have not understood what was involved. "Those gentlefolk," he tells Decoud, "do not seem to have sense enough to understand what they are giving one to do" (IX, 280). This same sense that he has not been understood, and that, because of this, his identity has been violated, lies behind his feeling of betrayal on this morning:

His imagination had seized upon the clear and simple notion of betrayal to account for the dazed feeling of enlightenment as to being done for, of having inadvertently gone out of his existence on an issue in which his personality had not been taken into account. A man betrayed is a man destroyed. (IX, 419–20)

Nostromo's realization of the worlds of subjectivity behind the social surface of life, worlds in which he himself exists only as a surface, an object to be used, is a revelation of the fragility of his former existence. It is this realization which governs his reaction to Dr. Monygham in the long exchange which takes place between them in the Custom House. The essence of this encounter lies in the tension between the reactions of these two characters to their unexpected meeting, in the way in which "the diversity of their natures made their thoughts born from their meeting swing afar from each other" (IX, 431). This tension, however, is more than a simple statement of individuality. It is a function of the way in which men, impelled by their particular fixed ideas, reduce others to the level of objects. Nostromo and Dr. Monygham meet at the precise point when each has been claimed by such a fixed idea. For Nostromo it is the silver, for Dr. Monygham, it is the "unlawful wealth" (IX, 481) of his devotion to Emma Gould. In his desire to save her, Dr. Monygham accepts the return of Nostromo without question, interested in him only as a necessary part of his plan:

Nostromo's return was providential. He did not think of him humanely, as of a fellow-creature just escaped from the jaws of death. The Capataz for him was the only possible messenger to Cayta. (IX, 431–32)

During the extended conversation which follows, Nostromo waits in vain for some expression of interest in the most desperate affair of his life, interest which will assure him that he has, in fact, been taken into account. The narrator moves continuously from one consciousness to another, contrasting Dr. Monygham's obsession with Mrs. Gould to the way in which Nostromo experiences this lack of interest in himself as a kind of death. Meeting Dr. Monygham, the narrator tells us, Nostromo felt "communicative. He expected the continuance of that interest which, whether accepted or rejected, would have restored to him his personality —the only thing lost in that desperate affair. But the doctor, engrossed by a desperate adventure of his own, was terrible in the pursuit of his idea" (IX, 434).

This scene confirms the validity of Nostromo's awakening to the insubstantiality of his former existence. If it is true that his real life lies in the place he occupies in the thoughts of others, then he is continually at the mercy not only of the darkness which lies at the center of his own being, but of the irrationality which is at the center of theirs as well. To become, for another, an object in the way Nostromo does for Dr. Monygham is to die.

For this reason, the narrator returns again and again to the figure of Hirsch which hangs with "the immobility of a disregarded man" (IX, 458) over this conversation. The "persistent immobility of the late Señor Hirsch" (IX, 454) is a symbol for the kind of death Nostromo experiences at the hands of Dr. Monygham:

And the Capataz, listening as if in a dream, felt himself of as little account as the indistinct, motionless shape of the dead man whom he saw upright under the beam, with his air of listening also, disregarded, forgotten, like a terrible example of neglect. (IX, 435)

By seeing Nostromo's new awareness as resulting from an experience of mortality different in form but essentially the same as Gould's we can understand Nostromo's destructive relation to the silver in the last third of the novel. In this final section, he attempts to create a new identity, that of Captain Fidanza, to replace the one he has lost:

Nostromo, the miscalled Capataz de Cargadores, had made for himself, under his rightful name, another public existence, but modified by the new conditions, less picturesque, more difficult to keep up in the increased size and varied population of Sulaco. (IX, 527)

In one sense, this new identity is, like the old, a "public existence." "Captain Fidanza was *seen*," the narrator remarks, and "the generation that would know nothing of the famous ride to Cayta was not born yet" (IX, 527). But its real source, the foundation of Fidanza's image, is the San Tomé treasure. Before, Nostromo had used the power of silver in much the same way to support his public existence, but he had done so unaware of the insubstantiality of this existence. Now, his attempt suggests the more conscious strategy of Gould. Flowing, too, from an experience of vulnerability, Nostromo's actions in the last chapters are best seen as an illustration of what can only be called the jealousy which man has for matter's completeness of being. Like Gould's desire to grapple with the mine, Nostromo's urge to "subjugate in unquestioned possession" (IX, 529) this treasure is ultimately a desire to share in this completeness, to found his identity as Captain Fidanza in an unshakable source.

As it did for Gould, however, the act of incarnation becomes a trap for Nostromo. Although he is successful in protecting the secret of the silver and in maintaining his new identity, Nostromo finds that his new life is one increasingly dominated by material interests. He, too, is afflicted with that fixed idea which is like madness, and suffers continually, the narrator tells us, "from the concentration of his thought upon the treasure" (IX, 523). Beyond his madness, Nostromo discovers that the moment in which he "welded that vein of silver into his life" (IX, 526) results in a bondage to the darkness which finds him "chained to the treasure" (IX, 495) and "imprisoned in silver fetters" (IX, 546). Despite his apparent success, Nostromo, like Gould and, in fact, the entire population of Sulaco, falls victim to the weight of the San Tomé mine. "The feeling of fearful and ardent subjection," the narrator remarks, ". . . weighed heavily upon the independent Captain Fidanza, owner and master of a coasting schooner whose smart appearance . . . [was] so well known along the western seabord of a vast continent" (IX, 526–27).

The lives of both Gould and Nostromo trace a pattern in which consciousness rises above and masters the darkness only to be reabsorbed into it. The inevitability of this pattern makes the adventurer's attempt to return to the source of life and ground his self in his control of this source futile. Even if momentarily successful, such an attempt leads at best to the imprisonment suffered by these two characters.

In *Nostromo*, however, the implications of this pattern are not confined to the lives of individuals. The novel suggests that a similar logic is operative in the whole range of human activity. The process by which Gould's idealistic visions of rational justice are born in reaction to the moral darkness of Costaguana and then are, in turn, transformed into only another manifestation of this darkness is symbolic not only of the law which ordains his personal fate but of the law which has determined the whole history of his country.

In the years immediately before Charles Gould, Costaguana had witnessed another such self-defeating attempt. Beginning in the general South American revolt against Spanish rule led by Bolivar in the 1820's, it resulted, in Costaguana, in the period of

Federation.[6] Like the Separatist movement of Charles, the Federation is led by a Gould, by his uncle Henry, who also takes up the banner of reason and liberty:

> Just as years ago, calmly, from the conviction of practical necessity, stronger than any abstract political doctrine, Henry Gould had drawn the sword, so now, the times being changed, Charles Gould had flung the silver of the San Tomé into the fray. The Inglez of Sulaco, the "Costaguana Englishman" of the third generation, was as far from being a political intriguer as his uncle from a revolutionary swashbuckler. Springing from the instinctive uprightness of their natures their action was reasoned. (IX, 142)

The period of Federation, however, results not in the establishment of political liberty but first in the tyranny of Guzman Bento and finally in the chaos of greed and corruption which destroy Gould's father. The references to the growing tyranny of the San Tomé mine, then, suggest that, in solidifying into autocracy, the movement supported by Gould is only mirroring the fate of many earlier revolts. And Father Corbelan's prophecy of a time when "the people, prevented from their aspirations, should rise and claim their share of the wealth and their share of the power" (IX, 510) points to yet another uprising of the spirit against its bondage to material interests.

For Marlow at the opening of "Heart of Darkness," the progress of all civilization has been marked by the steady conquest of the darkness by the idea, of matter by form, of emotion by reason. From this point of view, the history of man is a logically sequential progression beginning in the darkness and pointing toward the light. To Captain Mitchell, who is the spokesman in *Nostromo* for this "historical" (IX, 475) point of view, the career of the Gould Concession describes such an upward curve and he speaks confidently in the closing chapters of the "great future" (IX, 483) of the Separatist movement which has saved the San Tomé mine "intact for civilization" (IX, 483). It is this assumption of progress, and of the fulfillment of Gould's ambitions to turn the power of the mine to the service of the idea, which determines the form of Captain Mitchell's long narrative in the

---

[6] On the underlying consistency of the chronological structure of *Nostromo*, see Ben Kimpel and T. C. Duncan Eaves, "The Geography and History in *Nostromo*," *Modern Philology*, LVI (August, 1958), 45–54.

last chapters of the novel. Mitchell accepts the chronological order of history, speaks of the statue of Charles as an "anachronism" (IX, 482), and follows the natural order of events because this linear progression expresses to him the reality of the historical process. The structure of Mitchell's narrative reflects the assumptions of all those who accept the validity and success of the humanizing work of civilization and who see history as the record of this irreversible process.

The narrator, who frames the story of Gould against the darkness which is at once its source and end, sees that Mitchell's sense of historical progress is an illusion. The real movement of history for him is not linear but cyclical. It traces not a rise from the darkness but repeats the pattern of Costaguana politics in which revolution is inevitably transformed into an autocracy, which in turn gives rise to revolution. The narrator undermines belief in historical progress not only by making the senile Captain Mitchell its spokesman and placing his monologue at a time when the reader is able to see clearly the distance between Captain Mitchell's confident assertions of historical improvement and the real effect of the San Tomé mine on Costaguana. More than this, he presents the monologue itself as a prepared speech which is given to each important visitor. In this context, Mitchell's carefully rehearsed program, "relentless, like a law of Nature" (IX, 481), loses its linear quality and takes on a certain circularity. The Captain's constant repetition of this history of the revolution ironically images the constant repetition of the revolution in history, and the narrator emphasizes this by referring to "the cycle" (IX, 486) of Mitchell's monologue—remarking at its end, for example, that "the coxswain's voice at the door, announcing that the gig was ready, closed the cycle" (IX, 489).

The narrator's vision of the landscape thus frames not only the lives of Gould and Nostromo but the whole movement of human history. From this point of view, all civilization is destined to be reabsorbed into this landscape to become, like the efforts of the Spanish conquerors of Costaguana, "heavy stonework" (IX, 89) or "some ruinous pile" (IX, 89). This rejection of civilization and, by implication, of the adventure as it represents man's attempt to control the darkness, echoes and affirms the ironic stance of *Lord Jim*'s anonymous narrator. If it is true that the adventure is inevitably unsuccessful, then the detachment of these narrators would seem to be the only logical alternative. To commit oneself to realizing the dream is to invite the destruction which envelops Gould and Nostromo. It is to become, like the two gringo adventurers who go in search of the treasure of the Azuera, the prisoner of the darkness. In forsaking the adventure and taking his stance outside the dream, the narrator of Nostromo protects himself against this fate. *Nostromo*, it seems, presents man with two choices: one a way into the darkness, one a way to survival. Apparently the only strategy left to Conrad is a succession of novels in which the world of men is created only to be denied.

CHAPTER VI

From Nostromo *to* Under Western Eyes:
The Retreat from Irony

T he two novels which follow *Nostromo*, *The Secret Agent* and *Under Western Eyes*, repeat *Nostromo*'s disillusionment with the work of civilization. *The Secret Agent* presents a world in which the most conservative politicians and "the most ardent revolutionaries" (XIII, 81) are committed only to their own well-being. If they are seeking, like Gould, a kind of peace, it is not the peace which comes with the establishment of an ideal of rational justice but is instead "the peace of soothed vanity, of satisfied appetites, or perhaps of appeased conscience" (XIII, 81). The Russia of *Under Western Eyes* is, in turn, a place like Costaguana where "virtues themselves fester into crimes" (IX, 356) and both the tyrannical ruling party and the revolutionaries are characterized by the irrationality which *Nostromo* shows to be the beginning and end of all idealism. "The ferocity and imbecility of an autocratic rule rejecting all legality and in fact basing itself upon complete moral anarchism," Conrad writes in the Author's Note, "provokes the no less imbecile and atrocious answer of a purely Utopian revolutionism" (XXII, x).

For all its rhetoric of freedom, then, the Geneva movement in *Under Western Eyes* is only "senseless desperation provoked by senseless tyranny" (xxii, viii). It provides no more of a valid alternative than do the anarchists of *The Secret Agent* and in the fundamental identity of the establishment and the revolutionary in both novels we can see the end, for Conrad, of any possible commitment to political idealism. Marlow in "Heart of Darkness" suggests that the development of civilization is a movement toward more and more abstract and conceptual levels of awareness. The unspoken brotherhood of the crew of the *Narcissus* gives way to Kurtz's allegiance to a consciously articulated idea. *Nostromo* and *Under Western Eyes* show this movement as a circular one which leads back into the darkness. Since the force of idealism becomes a form of madness, or, as in *The Secret Agent*, decays into the passive self-interest of the anarchists, the idea provides neither the power to defeat the darkness nor the basis for a common world to be shared by all men. It does not provide the means by which men can establish an openness with one another but offers to each the lonely and inhuman prison of the fixed idea. Far from being man's salvation, the idea has become his curse. When Natalia Haldin tells Razumov that her brother "told me once to remember that men serve always something greater than themselves—the idea" (xxii, 352), his only thought is: "I wonder who is the greatest victim in that tale?" (xxii, 353).

Both *The Secret Agent* and *Under Western Eyes* agree that the attempts to reform all of human society and to sweep "all falsehood . . . out of the world" (xxii, 22) is an impossibility. But this agreement is misleading in some ways because it conceals a more radical dissimilarity between the two novels. "A sustained effort in ironical treatment of a melodramatic subject,"[1] *The Secret Agent* extends the narrative mode of *Nostromo*. It is also the product of a detached anonymous consciousness, and this consciousness realizes, perhaps more clearly than the narrator of *Nostromo*, the end of man's contest with the darkness. Although created, like the San Tomé mine, as an expression of man's vision and power, the London of *The Secret Agent* has become a

[1] C. T. Watts, ed., *Joseph Conrad's Letters to R. B. Cunninghame-Graham* (Cambridge: Cambridge University Press, 1969), p. 169.

chaotic ruin. It is an "enormity of cold, black, wet, muddy, inhospitable accumulation of bricks, slates and stones, things in themselves unlovely and unfriendly to man" (XIII, 56). Within the framing vision of this town, a town where "there was room enough ... to place any story ... darkness enough to bury five millions of lives" (XIII, xii), the narrator views the adventure as a hopeless attempt to transform existence into "a world planned out like an immense and nice hospital, with gardens and flowers" (XIII, 303). In this context, *The Secret Agent* represents the culmination of Conrad's movement toward ironic detachment which begins with the disruption in *The Nigger of the "Narcissus"* of the narrator's identification with the world of his novel, and it would seem to confirm the implication that after *Nostromo* Conrad has no choice but to embrace completely an aesthetics of irony.

Such, however, is not the case. In *Under Western Eyes*, Conrad abandons the radical irony of the narrator of *The Secret Agent* for the much more limited detachment of the English Teacher who narrates this novel. *Under Western Eyes*, moreover, calls into question even the limited detachment of its narrator. If there is any character in this novel who finds the answer to the "formula of peace" (XXII, 5), which the English Teacher assures us is the ideal all men search for, it is the servant Tekla, and she finds it not through detachment and irony but rather by devoting herself to the crippled and dying Razumov "with the pure joy of unselfish devotion" (XXII, 379). Nor do the novels which follow *Under Western Eyes* return to an ironic vision. *Chance, Victory, The Arrow of Gold,* and *The Rover* all assume the necessity of a commitment to the world of men. Rather than being studies in irony, these novels are concerned almost entirely with problems of human intersubjectivity and investigate, even in the face of Conrad's rejection of political idealism, ways in which men can commit themselves to others. How is this reversal to be explained?

The rationale of Conrad's surrender of his seemingly impregnable position of ironic detachment is suggested by the career of the last of the three principal characters of *Nostromo,* the

"Frenchified—but most un-French" (IX, 152) Martin Decoud. Decoud's personality suggests in many ways a portrait of the narrator.[2] In Decoud, too, there exists a latent involvement with the world around him, an involvement that echoes the "firm friendships" (IX, xi) which the narrator established during the time of composition. In the case of Martin Decoud, his positive relation to the world is concentrated in his love for Antonia Avellanos and his connections with the liberal movements in Costaguana are a reflection of his increasing involvement with her. Through this involvement, Decoud comes, at times, to be motivated by the same idealism which is at the center of Gould's life. His attempt to rescue the silver, the narrator tells us, reflects "the toils of an imaginative existence, and that strange work of pulling a lighter seemed to belong naturally to the inception of a new state, acquired an ideal meaning from his love for Antonia" (IX, 265–66).

For Decoud, as for the narrator, however, his involvement is for the most part latent, hidden behind his "barren indifferentism" (IX, 152) to life. Decoud, too, tries to stifle his ties to the world by adopting a detachment which is at once aesthetic and philosophic. He describes the events in Costaguana as a kind of play, *"une farce macabre"* (IX, 152), a "tragic comedy" (IX, 176), a "burlesque" (IX, 155), and can, moreover, "imagine himself to derive an artistic pleasure" (IX, 200) from watching Charles Gould's idealism petrify into madness. "Life is not for me a moral romance derived from the tradition of a pretty fairy tale" (IX, 218), he remarks, and thereby puts himself outside of the "fairy tale" (IX, 487) of Captain Mitchell's history and acknowledges that the work of civilization is an illusion. Decoud is, Father Corbelan tells us, "a sort of Frenchman—godless—a

---

[2] Many critics have noticed the resemblance between Decoud's attitude and that of the narrator, although almost all have identified the narrator with Conrad himself. See particularly Albert Guerard, *Conrad the Novelist* (Cambridge: Harvard University Press, 1958), p. 199; and F. R. Leavis, *The Great Tradition* (Garden City, N.Y.: Doubleday, 1954), p. 199, who remarks that although Decoud's scepticism seems to be rejected it still remains at the center of the work. "In fact, though Decoud is so decisively dealt with in the action, he remains the center of the book, in the sense that his consciousness seems to permeate it, even to dominate it. That consciousness is clearly very closely related to the author's own personal timber."

materialist" (IX, 198) who has "no faith in anything except the truth of his own sensations" (IX, 229).

The significance of Decoud, then, lies not simply in the way his "familiar habit of ironic thought" (IX, 191) suggests the irony of the narrator, but in the way his character reflects the tension between irony and involvement present in the narrator's stance. Decoud's story is a re-examination of this tension and of the conflicting alternatives of commitment and detachment, implicitly an investigation of the apparent success of the narrator's strategy in *Nostromo*, a success which Decoud's suicide calls into question.

In a similar manner *The Nigger of the "Narcissus"* had studied this tension. The narrator of this tale had been drawn into the darkness through his openness to others. Decoud meets his fate, however, as a result of embracing the opposite alternative. His death is a consequence not of his involvement with the world but of his movement to an extreme point of detachment. The major part of *Nostromo* concerned with Decoud is devoted to the attempt to rescue the silver from Sotillo. The narrative of his experiences during this attempt is an explanation of the way in which this detachment lies behind his suicide.

The detachment of the narrator of *Nostromo* is founded in an unrestricted view of the darkness. It requires that he move outside of the dream of civilization and recognize it for what it is. Decoud's voyage on the lighter into the Golfo Placido is the record of a parallel movement out of the dream. When he begins this voyage, Decoud is at his point of greatest involvement with Antonia and, through her, with the attempt to establish the Occidental Republic. "Part of a living world" (IX, 283), he is deeply enmeshed in the life of men. The journey in the lighter, however, carries him away from this life. He moves across the Waters of Oblivion and into contact with the "circumambient darkness in which land, sea, sky, the mountains, and the rocks were as if they had not been" (IX, 262). Contact with this formless night destroys his involvement with the affairs of the shore by destroying his belief in their reality. Surrounded by the "smooth darkness" (IX, 302) of the Gulf, the inhabitants of Sulaco appear to Decoud "unreal and terrible, like jibbering and obscene spectres" (IX, 498). He discovers that "even his passionate devotion to Antonia into which he had worked himself up out

136

of the depths of his scepticism had lost all appearance of reality" (IX, 267).

In this moment, Decoud stands where many of Conrad's characters have stood; he exists with a sense of distance from and independence of the world. Importantly, however, Decoud's journey carries him beyond a detachment from society to a point where he is forced to view not only the life of men, but his own life as "unreal and terrible" (IX, 498). In order to understand the logic of this process it is necessary to recall again that, for Conrad, even the most abstract forms of consciousness are grounded in the level of sensation and perception. Decoud, who professes to adopt a sceptical attitude toward all human illusions, still retains his belief in one. He still accepts the reality of the world of perception. Because mind does have its source in this world, to accept its validity is, implicitly, to accept that consciousness is founded in a positive source. Decoud's "intellectually self-confident" approach in which he "analyzed fearlessly all motives and all passions, including his own" (IX, 275), is founded on his implicit assumption of "the truth of his own sensations" (IX, 229). Since Decoud believes this "truth" does give mind a firm ground, he is able to detach himself from the unauthentic world of affairs, of loves, of revolutions and still exist independently of these things.

The relationship between Decoud's acceptance of the reality of the world of perception and his assumption of the independence of consciousness is the key to his suicide, for the detachment which results from his encounter with the darkness is not limited to this world of affairs and revolutions. It comes to extend to the perceptual world, to the "sights and sounds of the shore" (IX, 262), which is the source of awareness itself. The particular quality of Decoud's detachment on the Placido is in the way it isolates him from this fundamental level of experience, "Decoud," the narrator remarks, "lay on the silver boxes panting. All his active sensations and feelings from as far back as he could remember seemed to him the maddest of dreams" (IX, 267).

Decoud experiences the tension between the darkness and the surface of creation as one between the sensory flux of the shore and the stillness of the gulf. The tension between the shore world of "sights and sounds" (IX, 262) and the stillness of the gulf is one formulation of the basic paradox of Conrad's universe, the absurdity by which formlessness has given birth to and sustains order. The world of the shore is one of mutability, of shapes and colors. The world of the gulf is an image of the darkness, of the basic homogeneous materiality of existence. In this world outside of space and time, color, form and sound have no meaning. To see this "enormous stillness, without light or sound" (IX, 262) lying behind the world of "sights and sounds" (IX, 262) of the shore in Sulaco is to see this world resting on its own negation.

His recognition of dark stillness behind the world of sensation leads Decoud to confront directly the void at the center of consciousness. While he can preserve the illusion of a stable ground his detachment provides an answer. Decoud's ironic vision allows him to withdraw in good order to such a stable ground where, cut off from any destructive contact with the world, he is presumably protected from the darkness. But his voyage into the "solid stillness" (IX, 276) of the Placido destroys for him this stable ground by revealing to him that his identity is itself a product of the illusory world of the surface. His lonely vigil in the "absolute silence" (IX, 496) of the Grand Isabel forces him to confront directly the darkness which lies beneath the surface of the world of sensation. For the mind to do so is for it to recognize that it is itself an illusion, that it has no true foundation in reality. The narrator describes Decoud's awareness of the way in which the "solid stillness" behind the world of sense experience negates the reality of consciousness when he remarks that

solitude from mere outward condition of existence becomes very swiftly a state of soul . . . . It takes possession of the mind, and drives forth the thought into the exile of utter unbelief. After three days of waiting for the sight of some human face, Decoud caught himself entertaining a doubt of his own individuality. It had merged into the world of cloud and water, of natural forces and forms of nature. (IX, 497)

This doubt of his own individuality leads to the "want of faith in himself" (IX, 496) which the narrator tells us is the cause of Decoud's death. His suicide is the inevitable result of his movement to a point of detachment at which the mind is forced to recognize its own insubstantiality. At this point, Decoud discovers "the affectations of irony and scepticism have no place" (IX, 497). Rather than protect man from the darkness, they serve only to reveal more clearly how the darkness undercuts and invalidates his consciousness. The indifference which captures Decoud on the eve of his death when he pictures the "silence of the gulf like a tense, thin cord to which he hung suspended . . . without fear, without surprise, without any sort of emotion" (IX, 498) does not protect him from the darkness. It marks instead the moment before his consciousness is extinguished in the unbroken silence of the gulf.

To face the unreality of existence by framing it against the darkness leads one inevitably to confront the unreality of one's own self. Conrad had written to Cunninghame-Graham that "once the truth is grasped that one's own personality is only an aimless masquerade of something hopelessly unknown, the attainment of serenity is not very far off."[3] The suicide of Martin Decoud reveals that this serenity—a state "without fear, without surprise, without any sort of emotion" (IX, 498)—is in fact the peace that comes with death. There is, it seems, an inherent contradiction in the stance of Conrad's detached narrators. It is impossible to make a recognition of the self's ephemerality the rationale of its continued existence. Decoud's story lays bare this contradiction and, with this, the whole strategy of detachment is discredited.

If this is true, there would appear to be nowhere for Conrad to go after *Nostromo* and *The Secret Agent*. These two novels together mark not only the end of the attempt by consciousness to assure itself by assimilating and controlling the darkness. *Nostromo* also implicitly undercuts the detachment which has been the constant alternative to this attempt. Conrad's fiction after *Nostromo* and *The Secret Agent* accepts this fact. It accepts that "the contest of man interlocked with matter"[4] has been lost and that there is no possibility of the self establishing a founda-

3 Edward Garnett, *Letters from Joseph Conrad* (New York: Bobbs-Merrill, 1962), p. 46.
4 Garnett, *Letters*, p. 84.

tion either in the mastery of its ultimate source or in the circle of peace which detachment had seemed to promise.

Yet there is still one possible alternative, an alternative which is, paradoxically, suggested by the very rejection of a deep, ontological ground for the self. If man abandons the search for such a ground, then he admits that he is a creature of the surface whose existence can have no more solidity than this surface. But perhaps a superficial existence is man's proper essence. This possibility points to the truth of Nostromo's early acceptance of the reality of his public existence. Initially, before the attempt to rescue the silver, he had directed his actions not toward the darkness but had devoted himself entirely to the world of men and had endeavored to embody his ideal conception of his self in the eyes of those around him. By achieving this incarnation, he had given his identity a foundation. His conception of himself was no longer totally subjective, a dream, but had a social reality. This reality is, of course, a conditional one. It exists always in parentheses. But possibly it is the best man can hope for.

The novels which follow *The Secret Agent* investigate this alternative. In these novels, Conrad accepts the fact that identity can have at best only an intersubjective ground. The ultimate level of the darkness remains implicit in the fiction after *The Secret Agent*, imaged, for instance, in the seeming infinity of Russia in *Under Western Eyes* and in the snow which "covered the endless forests . . . the plains of [that] immense country, obliterating the landmarks, the accidents of the ground, levelling everything" (xxii, 33). These images of an infinite and formless materiality exist to remind us, if you will, of the brackets around the surface of existence. As we have seen, moreover, Conrad accepts the fact that even this limited intersubjective ground cannot be achieved through men's rational commitment to an ideal. If there is any salvation in this direction, it must come not through the idea but through the individual's discovery of some direct and immediate relation to another.

Under Western Eyes is the story of Razumov's discovery of this salvation. His discovery begins with his realization of what it means to exist in a society dominated, as the Russia of this novel is, by opposed but equally irrational political forces. Initially, Razumov lives free from the conflict of autocrat and revolutionary. On the one hand, he maintains no political allegiance to either party. Razumov, the narrator tells us, "shrank mentally from the fray as a good-natured man may shrink from taking definite sides in a violent family quarrel" (xxii, 11), and avoids facing the consequences of this "quarrel" by focusing instead on the apparent order of day to day life. "One of those men who, living in a period of mental and political unrest, keep an instinctive hold on normal, practical, everyday life" (xxii, 10), he counts for his "inward quietness" (xxii, 53) on the fact that "the exceptional could not prevail against the material contacts which make one day resemble another" (xxii, 54). On the other hand, he presents to his associates and fellow students a "frigid English manner" (xxii, 16) and thereby avoids any intimate contact with those around him.

In part, Razumov's lack of involvement with people and events is a result of his lack of family ties. The role of a "self-contained, thinking" (xxii, 19) man comes naturally to one whose lack of any "filial relation" (xxii, 344) has left him with " 'a breast unwarmed by any affection' " (xxii, 344). For the same reason, he has no natural political ties. "Did it ever occur to you," he asks Haldin, "how a man who had never heard a word of warm affection or praise in his life would think on matters on which you think first with or against your class, your domestic tradition?" (xxii, 61). "Officially and in fact without a family," the narrator observes, "he was as lonely in the world as a man swimming in the deep sea. The word Razumov was merely the label of a solitary individuality" (xxii, 10).

Insofar, however, as Razumov's solitary life is chosen by him and results from his conscious adoption of a reserved manner and a neutral political position, it has another implication. His self-imposed isolation is a reflection of Razumov's fundamental belief that he has the power and freedom to define his own life. Razumov is aware of his solitude and is aware, moreover, that because "a man's real life is that accorded to him in the thoughts of other men" (xxii, 14) it is necessary for him to "get acknowledged in some way" (xxii, 60). He believes that he will be able to dictate the form of this acknowledgment and will his identity by becoming a professor. At that time when he had won the silver medal and "conquered a name" (XXII, 71) he would no longer be a solitary but a celebrated professor and "a celebrated professor was a somebody. Distinction would convert the label Razumov into an honoured name" (XXII, 13–14). This belief in the efficacy of his will enables him to reject any life in the present for his projected life in the future. "The unrelated organism bearing that label [Razumov]," the narrator tells us, "was of no importance to any one. . . . The true Razumov had his being in the willed, in the determined future" (XXII, 77).

Haldin's abrupt entrance into Razumov's life destroys Razumov's belief in his ability to choose his identity and brings to him the dark and unhappy knowledge of the irrationality which lies at the center of the world of *Under Western Eyes*. On one level, the disruptive presence of Haldin forces Razumov to confront the political chaos beneath the surface of "practical, everyday life" (XXII, 10). Razumov's whole dream of becoming a professor is dependent upon the continuity of the government, a continuity which is threatened by Haldin and the movement he represents. A man who concentrates on the "material contacts which make one day resemble another" (XXII, 53), Razumov "forgot the dangers menacing the stability of the institutions which give awards and appointments" (XXII, 11).

Razumov's central experience of the way in which Haldin undermines "the safety of his lonely existence" (XXII, 21), however, lies on a more personal level. It lies in his realization of the way in which he exists for other people. Razumov discovers that the fanaticism not only of Haldin but of General T—— and Councillor Mikulin has blinded them to what he considers his real nature and has led them to take him for someone he is not. He finds that, like Nostromo, he has been used without being taken into account.

To be ignored in this way is a kind of death. Razumov experiences this death as a loss of the freedom to determine his self which was the basis of his dream of the future. Caught between the "lawlessness of autocracy . . . and the lawlessness of revolution" (XXII, 77), Razumov finds that "the feeling that his moral personality was at the mercy of these lawless forces was so strong that he asked himself seriously if it were worth while to go on accomplishing the mental functions of that existence which seemed no longer his own" (xxII, 77–78). Throughout the days following Haldin's visit, the sense of a lost freedom, and with it a lost identity, haunts Razumov. He feels that he has "lost all hope of saving his future, which depended on the free use of his intelligence" (xxII, 83), and experiences constantly the "sensation of his conduct being taken out of his hands" (xxII, 82).

Razumov's sense of not belonging to himself is a revelation of the way in which we are at the mercy of the irrationality which governs others. The twin curses of misunderstanding and mistrust which Haldin visits on Razumov bring with them more than an intellectual or emotional alienation from those around him. It would be wrong to interpret Razumov's experience on such a superficial level because it would imply that there was a distinct and independent entity, Razumov, who was cut off from others. The truth is more frightening. What is at the basis of Razumov's lost freedom is his discovery that his identity has been defined for him. It is not that he has been denied a role in society, but that he has been given one over which he has no control. This is the real meaning of his inability to escape the ghost of Haldin. The feeling that he "no longer belonged to himself" (xxII, 301) reflects his discovery that his whole life has been defined for him by Haldin's mistaken act of trust. Although he can avoid this ghost when he is locked alone in his rooms, "whenever he went abroad he felt himself at once closely involved in the moral consequences of his act. . . . The dark prestige of the Haldin mystery fell on him, clung to him like a poisoned robe it was impossible to fling off" (xxII, 229). For Conrad, the process through which an individual is given an identity and forced to act on it is unavoidable. It is Razumov's attempt to live apart from others, to take the "attitude of an inscrutable listener" (xxII, 5) and remain apart from the warring political forces which earns him a "reputation of profundity" (xxII, 6) and attracts Haldin to him. As Razumov complains to General T——, "even the silent contempt of a serious mind may be misinterpreted by headlong utopists" (xxII, 48).

Razumov's discovery that "he had been made a personage without knowing anything about it" (xxII, 82–83) is at the heart of the "new knowledge of his own nature" (xxII, 78) which this experience brings. The sense of vulnerability which attacks him is not, like Lord Jim's, an awareness of the irrationality at the center of his own self but rather a recognition of the way in which he is inextricably involved in the irrationality of others. His complaint, "I want to guide my conduct by reasonable convictions, but what security have I against something—some destructive horror—walking in upon me as I sit here?" (XXII, 78), embodies his knowledge that his self can be defined for him by those around him. To be subject to this is to be inevitably caught up in the "series of calamities overtaking private individuals and flowing logically from each other through hate, revenge, folly, and rapacity" (IX, 399) which is, to Father Roman in *Nostromo*, the workings of society. In such a world, there is no certainty, and no plans are valid. Reason is useless because the acts from which this chain flows are not rational and therefore not predictable.

He thought with a sort of dry, unemotional melancholy; three years of good work gone, the course of forty more perhaps jeopardized... because events started by human folly link themselves into a sequence which no sagacity can foresee and no courage can break through. Fatality enters your rooms while your landlady's back is turned; you come home and find it in possession bearing a man's name.... It asks you, "Is the outer door closed?"—and you don't know enough to take it by the throat and fling it downstairs.... "Sit down," you say. And it is all over. You cannot shake it off any more. It will cling to you for ever. Neither halter nor bullet can give you back the freedom of your life and the sanity of your thought. (XXII, 83)

With his awakening, Razumov has two choices. The first, and the one he initially adopts, is to attempt to live in this world on its terms. Conrad conceives of the irrationality which drives both the autocrats and the revolutionaries as manifesting itself in a world founded on the manipulation of others. In part, this tendency to use others is the inevitable result of the political fanaticism which drives most of the characters in the novel, but it also has another function. It is a way of living in this kind of society and still maintaining your freedom. If you can manipulate those around you, then you can control your world and preserve the freedom of action in which Decoud tells us "we find the sustaining illusion of an independent existence" (IX, 497). The leaders of both the government and the Geneva movement exhibit this compulsion to control. "Don't you understand," Tekla remarks, "that Peter Ivanovitch must direct, inspire, influence? It is the breath of his life. There can never be too many disciples. He can't bear thinking of any one escaping him" (XXII, 237). Consequently, Tekla, like Nostromo, finds herself reduced to the level of an implement. When Razumov asks her if she overhears the conversations at the chateau she replies, "So do the tables and chairs" (XXII, 235). In a similar way, Mikulin thinks of Razumov as "that tool so much finer than the common base instruments, so perfectly fitted, if only invested with sufficient credit, to penetrate into places inaccessible to common informers" (XXII, 307).

In *Under Western Eyes,* the struggle to manipulate others is a struggle to understand them without yourself being understood. To understand someone, to know his secret life, is to be able to control him. Councillor Mikulin owes his position to his ability to do this. "Things and men have always a certain sense, a certain side by which they must be got hold of if one wants to obtain a solid grasp and a perfect command. The power of Councillor Mikulin consisted in the ability to seize upon that sense, that side in the men he used" (XXII, 307). Peter Ivanovitch's desire to control appears, in a similar manner, in his dictum that "everybody had to be thoroughly understood before being accepted" (XXII, 270). In this world, safety comes only through concealment, through the power to keep your real life hidden. Razumov's face, the English Teacher remarks, "was really of the very mobile sort . . . the absolute stillness of it was the acquired habit of a revolutionist, of a conspirator everlastingly on his guard against self-betrayal in a world of secret spies" (XXII, 187). The necessity of protecting yourself in this way is behind the "bizarre" fact that "secrecy should play such a large part in the comfort and safety of lives" (XXII, 52). It is significant that Razumov's first interview with Madame de S—— brings to his mind "the epigrammatic saying that speech has been given to us for the purpose of concealing our thoughts" (XXII, 261).

Under these conditions, the effort to know someone becomes an act of aggression. It is characterized not by passive analysis

145

but by a positive effort to breach an essential reserve. The eyes of the characters in this novel have an ambivalent character. They reflect, on the one hand, the impassive and artificial masks behind which these characters hide themselves. Madame de S——'s eyes are "lifeless, as though they were as artificial as her teeth" (XXII, 225), Sophia Antonovna has a glance which is "black and impenetrable" (XXII, 261), Peter Ivanovitch hides from the world behind his dark glasses, and Councillor Mikulin appears to Razumov as "an idol with dim, unreadable eyes" (XXII, 95). At the same time, they reveal the active, aggressive character of the attempt to know others. Razumov is described as "plunging his glance into the black eyes" *(*XXII, 260) of Madame de S—— and receiving in turn her "black, penetrating gaze" (XXII, 241).

By betraying Haldin and choosing instead to confide in Prince K——, "the man who once had pressed his hand as no other man pressed it—a faint but lingering pressure like a secret sign" (XXII, 40), Razumov chooses to enter this struggle. The major part of the novel, and particularly the long second and third sections which critics usually dismiss as extraneous, are a dramatization of his attempt to penetrate the thoughts of others while concealing his own. This theme runs throughout his interview with General T—— and Councillor Mikulin in Russia and his conversations with the English Teacher and Sophia Antonovna in Geneva. In his relations with these characters, Razumov is caught continually in a tension between the necessity "not to be drawn into saying too much" (XXII, 87) and the need to understand their motives.

This tension is particularly apparent, however, in the long confrontation between Razumov, Peter Ivanovitch and Madame de S——. John Hagan has shown how the interview motif in *The Secret Agent* and *Under Western Eyes* works to dramatize the tension between appearance and reality, between the character's inner world and his actions,[5] but he misses the sense of contest which permeates such interviews in this novel. On the one hand, Razumov struggles to fathom the "impenetrable earnestness" (XXII, 213) of Peter Ivanovitch's blue glasses and

[5] John Hagan, "The Design of Conrad's *The Secret Agent*," *ELH*, XXII (June, 1955), 148–64.

answer the question, "What is the meaning of this performance?" (XXII, 217), while remaining himself "outwardly impassive" (XXII, 217). At the same time, these two search to discover the "something inflexible and secret" (XXII, 208) in Razumov which makes him, in Madame de S——'s words, "darkly self-sufficient" (XXII, 224). Razumov himself recognizes the character of this interview when he thinks, "I won't move from here till he either speaks or turns away. This is a duel" (XXII, 229).

It is a duel which Razumov wins. Aided by the "invincible nature of human error" (XXII, 282) appearing in the form of a letter placing the blame for Haldin's betrayal on Ziemianitch, Razumov finds that he has made himself "absolutely safe" (XXII, 317). Protected by the shield of his false identity and in a position through his friendship with Tekla to penetrate the movement's most secret conferences, he believes "nothing could touch him now" (XXII, 340). Yet this moment which would seem to mark success of this strategy of manipulation and deception brings to Razumov an awareness of its ultimate failure, of the impossibility of living in the "choking fumes of falsehood" with "the thought of being condemned to struggle on and on in that tainted atmosphere without the hope of ever renewing his strength with a breath of fresh air" (XXII, 269).

The explanation for Razumov's claustrophobia is simple: this strategy is self-defeating. It is possible to win the struggle to manipulate and to remain an enigma while solving the riddles of those around you. In this way, you avoid being reduced to an object as Tekla is. You escape as well being controlled in a direct way by the fanaticism of others. Instead of having an identity thrust on him, as was the case in his meeting with Haldin, Razumov in Geneva adopts a role and is able to impose it on the revolutionaries. It is, however, a hollow victory because this role is, by definition, false. The strategy of role-playing fails because it does not allow him to establish a positive identity. Because he must remain always hidden or risk being controlled, he is forced to live a series of lies. Yet to keep himself hidden in this way is, in fact, not to exist, for the only way in which he can give his true self reality is by embodying it in the "thoughts of other men" (XXII, 14).

Razumov learns that his life in Geneva is no more real than his dream of a life as a celebrated professor. Recording the findings of his secret mission, he is overcome by a sense of futility. "Even then he could not believe in the reality of his mission. He looked round despairingly, as if for some way to redeem his existence from that unconquerable feeling" (xxii, 316). The lesson behind this lack of faith in his own reality comes to Razumov near the close of the novel when he visits Haldin's mother. Here he encounters once again the ghost of Haldin, but a ghost which, paradoxically, has a stronger existence than his own self. "It was the other," he realizes, "who had attained to repose and yet continued to exist in the affection of that mourning old woman, in the thoughts of all these people posing for lovers of humanity" (xxii, 341). This dead, remarks the narrator, "can live only with the exact intensity and quality of the life imparted to them by the living" (xxii, 304). This, however, is a condition which holds as well for "the living" themselves. Razumov, by adopting the alternative of the secret life, has denied himself an equivalent place in the affections and thoughts of others. In betraying Haldin, "It's myself," he thinks, "whom I have given up to destruction" (xxii, 341).

There is an alternative to the slavery of lies into which Razumov has betrayed himself. This alternative is the way of confession. Throughout the novel, confession is present in opposition to Razumov's life of secrecy. When he first decides to betray Haldin, Razumov is stricken with an urge to return to him and "to pour out a full confession in passionate words that would stir the whole being of that man to its innermost depths; that would end in embraces and tears; in an incredible fellowship of souls—such as the world had never seen" (xxii, 40). Again, when he leaves his interview with Mikulin, having successfully concealed his visit to Ziemianitch, "the consciousness of his position presented itself to him as something so ugly . . . the difficulty of ever freeing himself from the toils of that complication so insoluble, that the idea of going back and, as he termed it to himself, *confessing* to Councillor Mikulin flashed through his mind" (xxii, 297). As the narrator suggests early in the novel, confession seems the solution to the "formula of peace" (xxii, 5) which, he assures us, is all men are really after. It is this way which Razumov takes when he admits to Natalia that he delivered Haldin to the police.

The way of confession suggests a return to the starting point of Conrad's fiction. In "The Return," Alvan Hervey, like Razumov, had waked to find that his life was a slavery to the lie. He, too, found that he was trapped in the prison of the self tormented by a "fiery sense of dangerous loneliness" (viii, 173). As Hervey learns, the only escape seems to lie in a return to the source of life, to the dark river of passion. To make this journey, which Hervey only glimpses but Nina Almayer and Willems actually take, is not only to give up your old way of life but also to abandon your will to your passion for the other and thereby be delivered over to the other. Yet only through this act of surrender can you hope to reach the "certitude of love and faith" (viii, 180) which gives access to a common world "serene and eternal, like the infinite peace of space above the short tempests of the earth" (viii, 178). "I have delivered my soul into your hands for ever," Dain tells Nina, "I breathe with your breath, I see with your eyes, I think with your mind" (xi, 178).

In *Under Western Eyes*, Razumov's confession to Natalia is seen as an equivalent act of sacrifice. By it, he destroys, at a moment when "the strength of falsehood seemed irresistible" (xxii, 360), the "absolute safety" (xxii, 317) which he had secured in his role as revolutionary. As in the case of other characters in Conrad's early fiction, the abandonment of Razumov's solitary existence, in which "his main concern was with his work, his studies, and with his own future" (xxii, 10), is marked by a surrender to his love for Natalia. Like Dain, he gives himself up to an "overmastering passion" (xi, 69) which delivers his will into the hands of Natalia. His written confession is a testament to his passion and therefore to "the sudden power Natalia Haldin had gained over him" (xxii, 362). In this confession, the narrator tells us, Razumov, overcome "by the novelty and the mysteriousness of that side of our emotional life to which his solitary existence had been a stranger" (xxii, 357–58), is "trying to express in broken sentences . . . the sovereign (he uses that very word) power of her person over his imagination" (XXII, 358).

In *Almayer's Folly*, Taminah was brought to "the full consciousness of life" (XI, 115) through her love for Dain. In a similar way, Razumov's surrender to the mystery of the emotional side of life paradoxically lifts him to a new level of awareness. In his crucial meeting with Natalia outside her mother's sitting-room, he gradually loses "that look in his eyes of dull, absent obstinacy" (XXII, 342). "It was as though he were coming to himself in the awakened consciousness of that marvellous harmony of feature, of lines, of glances, of voice, which made of the girl before him a being so rare, outside, and, as it were, above the common notion of beauty" (XXII, 342–43). In the context of Conrad's first novel, this new awareness would have seemed to offer the possibility of a positive answer. If Razumov and Natalia could in fact share the common world of Dain and Nina, if they could "see through each other's eyes" (XI, 179), then they would both achieve the solution to the formula for peace. In such a case, Razumov would no longer be haunted by a feeling of vulnerability. His life would be founded in the "certitude" (VIII, 181) of his knowledge of Natalia. "I wish," Razumov tells her, "I could know the innermost depths of your thoughts, of your feelings" (XXII, 352).

Yet, if Razumov's confession does mark a return to the starting point of the early works, Conrad returns with a full awareness of what has intervened. *An Outcast of the Islands* and *The Rescue* both pointed to the way in which the common world these lovers share is an illusion, and the surrender to passion a way into the darkness. None of the characters in these novels ever succeeds in transcending himself and escaping an existence which, in the words of Nina Almayer, is "like a captive thinking of liberty within the walls of his prison cell" (XI, 151–52) and listening "to the voice of my own self" (XI, 179). Natalia affirms her belief in a time when discord shall cease and men will be united in love, but the time is not yet. The new awareness which comes to Razumov and which is the result of his surrender to his love for her brings with it no common world based in a perfect understanding and trust. Instead, as in *An Outcast of the Islands*, the

150

surrender to passion is a kind of suicide. The moment when Razumov confesses his love is also, as he recognizes, the moment which marks not only his inevitable separation from Natalia but the beginning of a slow death as well. "I felt," he writes to her, "that I must tell you that I had ended by loving you. And to tell you that I must first confess. Confess, go out—and perish" (xxii, 361).

CHAPTER VII

Chance: *Marlow and the Double Perspective*

C onfession, then, is no answer. Both Razumov and Natalia achieve a kind of peace at the end of *Under Western Eyes*, but it is not the peace which comes to Dain and Nina through their participation in a common world. If Natalia and Razumov achieve a similar openness through their surrender to their love, it lasts for only a brief moment, a moment which brings with it a recognition of their inevitable isolation from one another. As in *An Outcast of the Islands*, this surrender is ultimately destructive. The act which promises to consummate this openness and gives to Razumov an identity free of falsehood results not only in his deafening but in his separation from Natalia.

The peace which they find is based on an acceptance of isolation and, consequently, on an acceptance of the impossibility of founding the self in that precious and immaterial certitude of another. This realization lies behind the independence and safety which Razumov celebrates at the moment of his confession to the revolutionaries. "To-day, of all days since I came amongst you," he tells them, "I was made safe, and to-day I made myself free from falsehood, from remorse—independent of every single human being on this earth" (xxii, 368). As he recognizes, however, this freedom comes with the inevitability of failure. "Have I then the soul of a slave?" he asks himself, "No! I am independent—and therefore perdition is my lot" (xxii, 362). Natalia's tranquility is based in a similar recognition. Her self-forgetfulness expresses her realization of the impossibility of giving the self any valid ground. Thus the English Teacher, at their last meeting, finds himself "lost in wonder at her force and her tranquillity. There was no longer any Natalia Haldin, because she had completely ceased to think of herself" (xxii, 375).

Yet Conrad is not willing to accept this conclusion. *Under Western Eyes* does point to one more possible way to establish such an essential understanding. It is the way which is suggested by the English Teacher who narrates Razumov's story. As Tony Tanner has shown, the English Teacher is the representative of the dead society of the West.[1] By choosing Geneva he has chosen a world which, like the London of the Herveys, has cut itself off from the source of life. While Russia is dominated by the overt irrationality of autocrats and revolutionaries dedicated to their utopian visions of the future, Geneva and the West have made their "bargain with fate" (xxii, 134). The people of the West have withdrawn to live, passionless and decorous on the surface of life. "You belong to a people which has made a bargain with fate," Natalia tells the narrator, ". . . You shrink from the idea of revolutionary action for those you think well of as if it were something—how shall I say it—not quite decent" (xxii, 134). The liberalism of the West, the narrator remarks, "is a matter of words, of ambitions, of votes (and if of feeling at all, then of the sort of feeling which leaves our deepest affections untouched)" (xxii, 318). This abhorrence of emotion is reflected in the character of the town itself, the "respectable and passionless abode of democratic liberty" (xxii, 357), which is "indifferent and hospitable in its cold, almost scornful, toleration—a respectable town of refuge to which all . . . sorrows and hopes were nothing" (xxii, 338). Even the surrounding landscape reflects the superficiality of this world. While the immensity of Russia embodies undisguised

[1] Tony Tanner, "Nightmare and Complacency: Razumov and the Western Eye," *Critical Quarterly*, IV (Autumn, 1962), 199–201.

the character of the darkness, the landscape of Geneva appears to Razumov like "a pretty, dull garden, where dull people sat ... under the trees. ... To his right, beyond the toy-like jetties, he saw the green slopes framing the Petit Lac in all the marvellous banality of the picturesque made of painted cardboard, with the more distant stretch of water inanimate and shining like a piece of tin" (XXII, 288).

Because the people of the West have made this bargain and have agreed, with Winnie Verloc, that life doesn't stand much looking into, they are able to free themselves from an immediate knowledge of the darkness. Like Stein, they have retreated into the illusion, but in doing so they have suffered his fate. If Geneva is an example of the safety which comes with such a withdrawal, it shows as well the death which accompanies it. Walking through the town which is "the very perfection of mediocrity attained at last after centuries of toil and culture" (XXII, 203), Razumov turns onto "the Boulevard des Philosophes, more wide, more empty, more dead—the very desolation of slumbering respectability" (XXII, 335). The inhabitants of Geneva exhibit the same passivity that characterizes Stein at the end of *Lord Jim*. The English Teacher, waiting with Natalia in the park, idly observes "a solitary Swiss couple, whose fate was made secure from the cradle to the grave by the perfected mechanism of democratic institutions in a republic that could almost be held in the palm of one's hand. The man, colourlessly uncouth, was drinking beer out of a glittering glass; the woman, rustic and placid, leaning back in the rough chair, gazed idly around" (XXII, 175). Like the owners of the stationery store where Razumov mails his reports, a "morose, shabby old man" and "a thin woman in black, with a sickly face, who are "safe to deal with because they no longer cared for anything in the world" (XXII, 316), these people illustrate the basic paradox of Conrad's world: the fact that the darkness is both hostile to and yet the source of life. To embrace the irrational in the way Russia does is to live always at the mercy of a lawless tyranny, yet to cut yourself off from it and live on the surface is to die.

The narrator is a part of the surface world. He, too, exhibits an abhorrence of emotion and a compulsion to keep his deepest affections untouched. This quality is particularly apparent in his relations to Natalia. It is clear from the English Teacher's occasional comments that his interest in her is more than that of a chance acquaintance. He introduces her as "Miss Haldin— Nathalie, caressingly Natalka" (xxii, 100). During the time he tutors her, the English Teacher tells us he "became aware ... how attractive physically her personality could be to a man capable of appreciating in a woman something else than the mere grace of femininity" (xxii, 102). Yet despite this obvious interest, he remains only a distant friend fated always, he remarks, "to be a spectator" (xxii, 339) in her life. At times, the narrator attributes to his age his failure to pursue his attraction. The real reason, however, seems to lie elsewhere. At one point, discussing his relation to Natalia, he remarks, "I had the sense of being out of it—not because of my age, which at any rate could draw inferences—but altogether out of it, on another plane whence I could only watch her from afar" (xxii, 170). In this context, his reticence reflects his spiritual alliance with Geneva and his consequent attempt to avoid any deep emotional contacts. This attitude is marked at crucial points by the English Teacher's deliberate refusal to involve himself in Natalia's affairs even when he believes such an involvement is called for. When he finds her alone with Peter Ivanovitch, for example, he accepts without protest the gap between their two worlds despite the fact that he sees Ivanovitch as a threat to Natalia. "I made no claim to a special standing for my silent friendship" he explains. "Removed by the difference of age and nationality as if into the sphere of another existence, I produced, even upon myself, the effect of a dumb helpless ghost, of an anxious immaterial thing that could only hover about without the power to protect or guide by as much as a whisper" (xxii, 126). Again, he admits that he avoids Mrs. Haldin because the intensity of her grief for her son unsettles him. "I had shirked calling of late," he tells us, because "I confess she frightened me a little" (xxii, 318).

She was one of those natures, rare enough, luckily, in which one cannot help being interested, because they provoke both terror and pity. One dreads their contact for oneself, and still more for those one cares for, so clear it is that they are born to suffer and to make others suffer, too. ... A faintly ironic resignation is no armour for a vulnerable heart.

Mrs. Haldin, struck at through her children, was bound to suffer afresh from the past. . . . She was of those who do not know how to heal themselves, of those who are too much aware of their heart. (xxii, 318)

The narrator's attitude toward the Haldins is representative less of the discreet reticence of an old man than a deliberate attempt to use the mask of an aging language teacher to protect himself from becoming involved in any way that would leave the narrator "too much aware" of his heart. The same strategy appears to govern his attitude toward Razumov in particular and Russia in general. The narrator constantly shelters himself behind his Westernism when faced with any contact with the forces which drive Razumov. This is the rationale both of his elaborate and often repeated statements that he is simply editing a manuscript and that he lacks the imagination to create such a character as Razumov, and of his constant reminders of the impossibility that the West will ever understand the East. Both are denials of any involvement in the irrational, affirmations that the people of the West have, in fact, succeeded in cutting themselves off from this level of experience. "To begin with," he opens, "I wish to disclaim the possession of those high gifts of imagination and expression which would have enabled my pen to create for the reader the personality of the man who called himself . . . Kirylo Sidorovitch-Razumov. . . . I could not have observed Mr. Razumov or guessed at his reality by the force of insight, much less have imagined him as he was. Even to invent the mere bald facts of his life would have been utterly beyond my powers" (xxii, 3). In a similar manner, he assures his readers that "it is a vain enterprise for sophisticated Europe to try and understand these doings" (xxii, 126). Like the inhabitants of Geneva, he hides the darkness behind an artificial surface, a surface of words. If he has been blessed with any gifts of the imagination, he tells us, "they have been smothered out of existence a long time ago under a wilderness of words. Words, as is well known, are the great foes of reality. I have been for many years a teacher of languages. It is an occupation which at length becomes fatal to whatever share of imagination, observation, and insight an ordinary person may be heir to" (xxii, 3).

From one point of view, the role-playing of the English Teacher suggests the detachment of the ironic narrators of *Nostromo* and *The Secret Agent*. If, as Decoud's death illustrates, a total detachment is impossible, then perhaps the studied restraint, the "faintly ironic resignation" (xxII, 318) of the narrator is the best that can be hoped for. There are several elements in the novel which suggest that the English Teacher has consciously adopted his role. His comments on the deadness of Geneva and on "the corrupt frivolity of a Western mind, like my own" (xxII, 126), point to his awareness of the limitations of the Western bargain. His comment, in passing, that he was "born from parents settled in St. Petersburg" (xxII, 187) reveals that he is not as unaware of the forces which characterize his native country as he would have the reader believe. It is this element of conscious choice behind his role as an unimaginative English teacher, the way in which it seems to have been adopted with a full knowledge of the darkness as a protection against this knowledge, which allies him in spirit with these ironic narrators rather than with the unconscious acceptance of illusion of a character like Alvan Hervey.

Yet it is impossible to accept even this role-playing at face value. Despite the fact that the narrator does strive to avoid intimate contact with others, the very fact that he does undertake the task of "editing" Razumov's diary suggests that he is concerned with putting himself in some kind of limited relation with the emotional, irrational, but life-giving world of Razumov and Natalia. In this sense, the role of English Teacher serves as more than a protective shield; it serves as a base from which he can enter into a kind of controlled contact with others. He adopts this role with Natalia but uses it to establish a limited intimacy with her. Whenever this intimacy threatens to become too close, he becomes again a "silent friend." His relation to her is not that of a consistent detachment but rather a fluctuation toward and away from intimacy. "I was," he remarks, "only too ready to stay near Nathalie Haldin, and I am not ashamed to say that it was no smiling matter to me" (xxII, 180). But, he continues, in a remark which defines the two poles of this fluctuation, "I stayed, not as a youth would have stayed, uplifted, as it

157

were poised in the air, but soberly, with my feet on the ground and my mind trying to penetrate her intention" (xxii, 180).

This fluctuation informs the entire narrative structure of *Under Western Eyes*. From this point of view, the transitions from Razumov's story to the narrator's comments are more than simply his annotations on a manuscript. Instead, they reflect the narrator's fluctuation between involvement and detachment. This alternation suggests that the English Teacher has made use of Razumov's diary to "penetrate" his intention and to enter his world, but that he does so with his feet on the ground. He never abandons the detachment which is his ultimate protection. Consequently he is never drawn into Razumov's world in the destructive way Marlow is into Kurtz's, just as with Natalia he is never brought to the point of Razumov's equally destructive surrender to love. By exploiting this ambivalence, the narrator makes an attempt to live in both worlds while avoiding the dangers of either.

Although *Under Western Eyes* makes no explicit comment on the success of the narrator's strategy, the fact that he loses Natalia at the end implies that Geneva and Russia cannot be so easily reconciled. His strategy, however, does suggest another way of knowing others. The phrase "with my feet on the ground and my mind trying to penetrate her intention" (xxii, 180) implies a blending not only of two emotional attitudes but also of two modes of vision. The early narrators of *Almayer's Folly* and *The Nigger of the "Narcissus"* enter the world of their characters primarily through an act of emotional identification. The narrators of *Nostromo* and *The Secret Agent* adopt instead a stance of cool, uninvolved analysis. In adopting this stance, they suggest the way by which Decoud had come to know and understand Nostromo. Decoud, we are told, "had tried to understand this man thoroughly. He had discovered a complete singleness of motive behind the varied manifestations of a consistent character" (ix, 278). This passage implies an analytical process in which understanding moves from the overt actions of a character to the "singleness of motive" which these actions reveal. Perhaps by using both these approaches to complement one another, by combining an analytical process with the limited measure of sympathetic identification which the narrator's approach allows him, man can achieve the understanding which is his last hope. *Chance* is an investigation of this possibility.

Chance accepts the logic which governs the world of *Under Western Eyes*. It assumes that men, in some fundamental way, will always be isolated from one another. At one point in his narrative, Marlow is discussing Powell's surprise at his first meeting with Captain Anthony and Flora:

> The surprise, it is easy to understand, would arise from the inability to interpret aright the signs which experience (a thing mysterious in itself) makes to our understanding and emotions. For it is never more than that. Our experience never gets into our blood and bones. It always remains outside of us. That's why we look with wonder at the past. And this persists even when from practice . . . we come to the point when nothing that we meet in that rapid blinking stumble across a flick of sunshine—which our life is— . . . surprises us any more. Not at the time, I mean. If, later on, we recover the faculty . . . it is probably because this very thing that there should be a past to look back upon, other people's, is very astounding in itself when one has the time, a fleeting and immense instant to think of it. . . . (II, 282–83)

On one level, what Marlow is discussing is the surprise that accompanies our discovery of the unique, subjective world of others. Earlier, he has described this same sensation when he remarked on the people passing him and Flora in the street outside Anthony's London hotel. They were, he said, "mere unconsidered existences whose joys, struggles, thoughts, sorrows and their very hopes were miserable, glamourless, and of no account in the world" (II, 208). "And," he adds, "when one thought of their reality to themselves one's heart became oppressed" (II, 208). It is this realization that "there should be a past to look back upon, other people's," which constitutes their "reality to themselves" which is the source of Powell's astonishment.

There is, however, more to Marlow's comments. They imply that the recognition of the subjective reality of others brings with it, as *Under Western Eyes* also suggests, a perception of our exclusion from this reality. The experience to which Marlow refers here is not our experience of the natural world but our experience of others—the way Natalia understands Razumov and

Flora, Anthony. The sentences, "Our experience never gets into our blood and bones. It always remains outside of us," are a statement of the impossibility of completely entering a common world with another. They imply that no matter how completely Razumov or Natalia surrender themselves to their love, to the influence each has over the other, they can never really lose themselves in this passion. There will always remain at the center of consciousness a detached awareness which stands apart from experience. For this reason, we can never escape the prison of our own ego, and although a man can realize the existence of the private worlds of others, he can never enter them totally. When de Barral first strikes up a conversation with Powell, the latter finds himself not only "surprised" (II, 292) by his perception of de Barral's world, but made profoundly aware of his own isolation. At this moment, the horizon, effaced by the clouded night, "traced no reassuring limit to the eye . . . it was the immensity of space made visible—almost palpable. Young Powell felt it. He felt in it the sudden sense of his isolation . . . before that unexpected old man becoming so suddenly articulate in a darkening universe" (II, 292–93).

Because our awareness of others brings with it an awareness of the distance separating us from them, confession is a failure. Marlow sees clearly that the emotions which a confession gives rise to result not in a common vision but only in an increased perception of isolation. At one point, he explains that our laughter at others is based in a recognition of our separation from them. We laugh, he comments, not out of sympathy. It is not an expression of fellowship but rather it arises "from a sense of superiority. Therefore, observe, simplicity, honesty, warmth of feeling, delicacy of heart . . . are laughed at, because the presence of these traits in a man's character often puts him into difficult, cruel or absurd situations and makes us . . . feel pleasantly superior" (II, 283–84). In the same way, confession only gives rise to a sense of superiority which also testifies to an equivalent awareness of separation:

What a sell these confessions are! What a horrible sell! You seek sympathy, and all you get is the most evanescent sense of relief—if you get that much. For a confession, whatever it may be, stirs the secret depths of the hearer's character. Often depths that he himself is but dimly aware of. And so the righteous triumph secretly, the lucky are amused, the strong are disgusted, the weak are either upset or irritated.... And all of them in their heart brand you for either mad or impudent.... (II, 212)

At the same time, *Chance* accepts the need for some kind of human communion. In the Author's Note, Conrad reaffirms "the soundness of my belief in the solidarity of all mankind in simple ideas and in sincere emotions" (II, xi) and this communion, in the novel, is related to our ability to understand others. From our "provision of understanding," explains Marlow, "there springs in us compassion, charity, indignation, the sense of solidarity; and in minds of any largeness an inclination to that indulgence which is next to affection" (II, 117–18). Marlow's insistence on the necessity that Flora and Anthony should consummate "the embrace, in the noblest meaning of the word" (II, 427), and his proposal of the fact that they "fail in understanding" (II, 426) as the source of all their trouble, reveals clearly that he sees this understanding as the only hope for man.

As the short introductory interlude between Marlow and Powell shows, the world of the sea provides a common ground which allows such an understanding to exist. "A temperamental difference," Marlow observes about his relationship to Fyne, "is the parent of hate" (II, 54). Yet despite such a temperamental difference, Marlow and Powell are able to maintain a common ground which transcends this difference. "That an excellent understanding should have established itself between my old friend and our new acquaintance was remarkable enough. For they were exactly dissimilar—one individuality projecting itself in length and the other in breadth, which is already a sufficient ground for irreconcilable difference.... Between two such organisms one would not have expected to find the slightest temperament accord" (II, 32). But, the narrator continues, "the men of the sea understand each other very well in their view of earthly things, for simplicity is a good counsellor and isolation not a bad educator" (II, 33).

This common understanding forged by life at sea is not, in *Chance*, a real alternative. For Conrad, the particular communion of this world once lost, can never be regained. As Anthony's fruitless attempt to take Flora to sea with him emphasizes, the understanding which Marlow and Powell share is not the result of a place but of the sharing of a kind of vision. Their concord exists not to point the way to an answer but to emphasize the temperamental discord which pervades the world of the land.

The relationship between Flora and Anthony is representative of the temperamental differences which block understanding and dictate that our experience of others shall always be an experience of our separation from them. In one aspect, of course, they exemplify the temperamental variations between man and woman which, as Marlow never ceases to remind the reader, is one of the obstacles which stand between them. More importantly, however, Flora and Anthony both are dominated by the irrational in ways which, although different, effectively imprison them in their own worlds. In the case of Flora, this domination manifests itself in a sense of vulnerability which leads her, as it does those who live in the world of *Under Western Eyes*, to seek protection in secrecy. This vulnerability results from her loss of "that ignorance, or better still, of that unconsciousness of the world's ways, the unconsciousness of danger, of pain, of humiliation, of bitterness, of falsehood" (II, 99). This loss coming not "by a gradual process of experience and information" (II, 99) but "with desecrating circumstances like a temple violated by a mad, vengeful impiety" (II, 99) has left her "a passive victim, quivering in every nerve, as if she were flayed" (II, 164). Consequently, Flora is cursed with the same sense of insecurity which is brought to Razumov by his encounter with Haldin. You may imagine, Marlow tells the narrator, the force of the shock when the woman who had been "the wisdom, the authority, the protection of life, security embodied and visible and undisputed" (II, 117), had turned on her, a shock which has its source "in the intuitive perception not merely of danger . . . but in the sense of the security being gone" (II, 117). Because her experience with the governess had resulted in this hypersensitivity and "had implanted in her unlucky breast a lasting doubt, an ineradicable suspicion of herself and others" (II, 232), she becomes one of those women "to whom perfect frankness is impossible, because so much of their safety depends on judicious reticences" (II, 261).

On the other hand, Anthony becomes the prisoner of a fixed idea. Like Gould, Anthony is possessed by his "need for embodying in his conduct the dreams, the passion, the impulses" (II, 328) which are the source of his heroic vision of himself as Flora's savior. Anthony's love for Flora, too, has its source in an idealistic vision, but throughout the novel Marlow describes his love in a manner which suggests, first, the way in which idealism becomes a madness and, second, the way madness blinds a man to others. Anthony becomes "intoxicated with the pity and tenderness of his part" (II, 261) to the point where he "discovered that he was not the proud master but the chafing captive of his generosity" (II, 395). His passion for Flora reveals again the tendency which idealism has, on reaching the point of madness, to turn in on itself and cut itself off from the world. When Marlow describes Anthony, lost in the strange elation which comes to him with his renunciation of Flora, so that "he saw no one or anything, though he went about restlessly, here and there, amongst men and things," and attributes it to a "special state . . . peculiar to common lovers" (II, 339), he is being ironic. The description, however, does foreshadow the way in which Anthony's involvement in his own role blinds him to the few tentative attempts Flora does make to reveal her true feelings. In the same way that Mrs. Gould finds herself cut off from her husband behind a wall of silver, Flora finds herself relegated by Anthony's "blind generosity" (II, 343) to a role in which "she existed, unapproachable, behind the blank wall of his renunciation" (II, 396).

For Conrad, both the vulnerability which inhibits Flora and the idealism which possesses Anthony, and which walls them in "that solitude, that moral loneliness, which had made . . . life intolerable" (II, 428), are a result of man's involvement in a world governed by the laws of chance and accident, a universe "without thought, without conscience, without foresight, without eyes, without heart."[2] "By accident," explains Marlow, "I mean that which happens blindly and without intelligent design" (II, 36), and the whole history of Flora and Anthony has its source in a series of such accidents. The Fynes's marriage is the result of "pure accident" (II, 37). Marlow's own involvement in Flora's

[2] C. T. Watts, ed., *Joseph Conrad's Letters to R. B. Cunninghame-Graham* (Cambridge: Cambridge University Press, 1969), p. 56.

life is the work of "an accident called Fyne" (II, 36). More significantly, Flora's "mystic wound" (II, 118) results from de Barral's chance selection of a governess who was not simply "a perfectly harmless, naïve, usual, inefficient specimen" (II, 100). Discussing her loss of innocence, Marlow remarks that she was only a young girl, "almost no more than a child—this was what was going to happen to her. And if you ask me how, wherefore, for what reason? . . . Why, by chance! By the merest chance, as things do happen, lucky and unlucky, terrible or tender . . . even things which are neither, things so completely neutral in character that you would wonder why they do happen at all if you didn't know that they, too, carry in their insignificance the seeds of further incalculable chances" (II, 99–100).

Chance is thus the expression of the chaotic principle which determines human life. It is important to see that, for Conrad, this is not simply a question of man's being an essentially free agent acting in a limited situation. It is rather that the very structure of an individual's awareness, the source of his supposedly free action, is being determined by forces over which he has no control. In *The Secret Agent*, Michaelis had found "the secret of fate discovered in the material side of life; the economic condition of the world responsible for the past and shaping the future; the source of all history, of all ideas, guiding the mental development of mankind and the very impulses of their passion" (XIII, 45). In a similar way, Marlow sees the force of chance determining not only the largest configuration of human culture, all history and all ideas, but also the most intimate and individual, the "mental development" of men and "the very impulse of their passion." The way in which Marlow stresses that the poetic temperament which the inarticulate Captain Anthony has inherited from his father lies behind his overwhelming passion for Flora emphasizes how Anthony's action is determined by circumstances outside his control. "Genius," remarks Marlow, "is not hereditary but temperament may be. And he was the son of a poet with an admirable gift of individualizing, of etherealizing the commonplace" (II, 193). Man is a prisoner of his past not only in the way his external situation is imposed on him but in the way his temperamental reaction to this external situation is also a product of the past.

For Conrad, the way in which mind is bound by determining forces appears most fundamentally in the manner in which it is under the influence of sensation and emotion. On this level, Flora's sense of vulnerability is explained by the fact that "we live at the mercy of a malevolent word. A sound, a mere disturbance of the air, sinks into our very soul sometimes" (II, 264). Anthony's love, too, has its ultimate references in the mind's susceptibility to such a level of experience. The act by which "chance had thrown that girl in his way" (II, 328) appears fundamentally in the mysterious power of physical appearance to give rise to overpowering emotions. "But it is a fact," Marlow comments, "that in every man ... there lives a lover; a lover who is called out in all his potentialities often by the most insignificant little things—as long as they come at the psychological moment: the glimpse of a face at an unusual angle, an evanescent attitude, the curve of a cheek often looked at before, perhaps, but then, at the moment, charged with astonishing significance. These are great mysteries, of course. Magic signs" (II, 217). To Marlow, all human action has its origin in this relationship between mind and sensation: "all these revolts and indignations, all these protests, revulsions of feeling, pangs of suffering and of rage, expressed but the uneasiness of sensual beings trying for their share in the joys of form, colour, sensations—the only riches of our world of senses" (II, 62).

The bondage of mind to the forces which determine it is seen clearly in its involvement in time. The fact that man is determined by his past is the expression of his imprisonment in the present moment. The scene in which Flora meets her father on his release from prison is a dramatization of his bondage to the past. On the one hand, the prison itself is a symbol of the spirit's incarnation in matter. "There is," Marlow says, "something infernal about the aspect of every individual stone and brick of them, something malicious as if matter were enjoying its revenge of the contemptuous spirit of man" (II, 352). On this level it images the inexorable movement which carries man toward death. It embodies the force of time that, "blind and insensible ... seems inert and yet uses one's life up by its imperceptible action, dropping minute after minute on one's living heart like drops of water wearing down a stone" (II, 396). For Marlow, "the very lines and angles" of the walls image this inevitable movement toward death; the "fall of time, drop by drop, hour by hour, leaf by leaf, with a gentle and implacable slowness" (II, 354), and the "unholy claustration of a jail" (II, 354) express man's imprisonment in the fall towards death.

De Barral's imprisonment, however, is symbolic not only of the entrapment of all men in this movement, but of the way in which each is walled in the prison of his own subjectivity. To each individual, the experience of time is not one of a process which he shares with others. Rather, he experiences it as the sum of all the particular influences which have determined his temperament and life. The real meaning of the scene between Flora and her father lies in the way de Barral's experience in prison cuts him off from Flora. To de Barral, isolated for seven years, his former life retains an immediacy which it has lost for his daughter. In jail, says Marlow, "old pains keep on gnawing at your heart, old desires, old deceptions, old dreams, assailing you in the dead stillness of your present where nothing moves except the irrecoverable minutes of your life" (II, 354–55). Consequently, de Barral's trial was "to him like yesterday, a long yesterday, a yesterday gone over innumerable times, analyzed, meditated upon for years. It had a vividness and force for that old man of which his daughter who had not been shut out of the world could have no idea" (II, 357). The feeling Flora has that there was "something between them, something hard and impalpable, the ghost of these high walls" (II, 355), and that, in embracing her father, she was "pressing [her face] against a stone" (II, 355), images the way de Barral is caught up and isolated from her in his own past. Because in de Barral's time the past seven years constitute only a "long yesterday" and, therefore, he has no sense of the passage of time in Flora's world, Flora feels he is "strangely, unnaturally incurious" to know "what she had gone through" (II, 358). In the same way, de Barral's perception of his isolation from Flora rests in his intuition that she, too, lives in her own time, and he is "resentful that the child had turned into a young woman without waiting for him to come out" (II, 356). In both cases, the character's sense of alienation is a function of his inability to penetrate the other's individual sense of the past, and in this we can see the logic of Marlow's association of an individual's subjective world with his unique history, with the fact that "there should be a past to look back upon, other people's, is very astounding in itself" (II, 283). This past expresses for Conrad the particular set of influences, accidents and chances which have determined an individual's consciousness and, in doing so, have isolated it from others.

She laid her hand on his arm soothingly. "Is it worth while talking about that awful time? It is so far away now." She shuddered slightly at the thought of all the horrible years which had passed over her young head; never guessing that for him the time was but yesterday. (II, 356)

If the wall which exists between Flora and Anthony is symbolic of their bondage to time, their history also suggests a possible way to escape this isolation. If it is true that a man is the product of his past, then one way to understand him is to understand this past. By explaining the origins of Flora's "mystic wound" (II, 118) and Anthony's misguided idealism, perhaps the groundwork for their mutual understanding can be established. If this is done, moreover, they can be freed from their subjugation to chance and time. Once they understand the forces which determine them, they will no longer be the passive pawns of these forces. Although life will still be in large measure the product of accident, men will have a measure of control because of this understanding. Conrad's epigram for the novel points to the way *Chance* is concerned with the possibility of this kind of limited, but real, freedom.

This possibility underlies the role of Marlow in the novel. It is too much to expect individuals to reach understanding for themselves because they are too close to the problem. As the narrator reminds us, "people, whether mature or not mature . . . are for the most part quite incapable of understanding what is happening to them" (II, 117). Yet perhaps someone who stands apart from these influences can understand them. *Chance* is founded on this possibility. It assumes that "we . . . have the inestimable advantage of understanding what is happening to others" (II, 117), a "provision of understanding" (II, 117) from which springs in us "compassion, charity, indignation, the sense of solidarity"

(II, 117). It is Marlow's function in *Chance* to investigate the effectiveness of this provision.[3]

To reach this level of insight, Marlow employs more than one source of information concerning Flora and Anthony. His approach is based first on the accumulation of a large amount of factual material which he draws not only from personal experience but from the reports of the Fynes, of Powell, from a chance meeting with a newspaper reporter. One purpose of this accumulation of material is to allow Marlow to build a coherent, chronological account of the major events in the characters' lives. The first part of the novel which concerns for the most part the early life of Flora gives such an account and is the product of Marlow's ordering of data from several sources. "You understand," remarks Marlow, "that in order to be consecutive in my relation of this affair I am telling you at once the details which I heard from Mrs. Fyne later in the day, as well as what little Fyne imparted to me with his usual solemnity during that morning call" (II, 107).

A more important function of this factual material is suggested by Marlow when he jokingly identifies himself to Mrs. Fyne as "a physiognomist" (II, 151). In an earlier passage Marlow had spoken of the surprise which arises "from the inability to interpret aright the signs which experience . . . makes to our understanding and emotions" (II, 282). While this passage is, as we have seen, a statement of man's ultimate imprisonment in his own subjectivity, it points to one limited way in which men reveal themselves to one another. While individuals cannot know each other directly through an act of confession, they give an insight into their motives, conscious and unconscious, through these signs. For Marlow, what is important is not the larger outlines of a character's actions and expressions but the nuances which are the

---

[3] For another view of the role of Marlow in *Chance*, see William York Tindall, "Apology for Marlow," in R. C. Rathburn and M. Steinmann, Jr., eds., *From Jane Austen to Joseph Conrad* (Minneapolis: University of Minnesota Press, 1959), pp. 284–85. Tindall, at a loss to explain Marlow's reappearance in the novel, tries to make him a portrait of the artist giving body to otherwise trivial material. From my point of view, a more reasonable explanation lies in the parallel between the ambivalence of Marlow's view of Jim and of his view of the Flora-Anthony affair. In both cases his stance is defined by a shifting point of view.

key to response mechanisms of which the character himself may not be aware. Discussing Powell's encounter with the bizarre marriage of Flora and Anthony, Marlow remarks that "in the majority of ships a second officer has not many points of contact with the captain's wife. He sits at the same table with her at meals . . . he may now and then be addressed more or less kindly on insignificant matters, and have the opportunity to show her some small attentions on deck. And that is all. Under such conditions, signs can be seen only with a sharp and practised eye. I am alluding now to troubles which are subtle often to the extent of not being understood by the very hearts they devastate or uplift" (II, 272). For this reason, Powell only begins to understand the situation after events "had sharpened the perceptions of the unsophisticated officer of the *Ferndale*" and made him "alive to the slightest shade of tone" (II, 293). It is these shades of tone which, like the "play of physiognomy" (II, 214) that gives Marlow an insight into the reasons Flora accepts Anthony's proposal, are the key to our understanding others. These "insignificant little things . . . charged with astonishing significance" (II, 217) are the source not only of Anthony's love for Flora but of our understanding of the rationale of this love.

Such subtleties of action and expression are "the signs which experience . . . makes to our understanding and emotion" (II, 282), but they are never more than signs. Their meaning lies not open on the surface but rather in their enigmatic reference to the inner world of the character. To be understood, they must be interpreted by a "sharp and practised eye" (II, 272). It is Marlow's ability to read these signs which makes him an "expert in the psychological wilderness" (II, 311). As the narrator tells him, he is like "the honest backwoodsman" who "with his incomparable knowledge follows the track and reads the signs of [Flora's] fate in a footprint here, a broken twig there, a trinket dropped by the way" (II, 311).

In following this track and interpreting these "magic signs" (II, 217) Marlow employs several methods. His approach involves a systematic application of the English Teacher's ambivalence between sympathetic identification and detachment. On the one hand, Marlow often makes a conscious attempt to "enter into the feelings" (II, 87) of characters like Flora and Anthony and to re-

create through his "imaginative sympathy" (II, 143) the psychological mood of an action or a moment. In this attempt, he uses
such signs to "give my imagination its line" (II, 210–11). Discussing de Barral's final outburst at his trial, Marlow remarks, "I
seemed to understand that, with the shock of the agonies and
perplexities of his trial, the imagination of that man . . . had been
roused into activity. And this was awful. Just try to enter the
feelings of a man whose imagination wakes up at the very
moment he is about to enter the tomb" (II, 87). Such an "inner
knowledge" (II, 261) of an individual's emotional state at a crucial point is necessary because his distinctive world is not simply
the product of the objective events which have occurred since his
birth. Rather, it is the result of a complicated interaction between these events and his particular temperament. Anthony's
world on the *Ferndale* describes the vector resulting from the
meeting of his poetic temperament with Flora. To penetrate this
world, it is not enough to reconstruct the factual framework, the
meeting itself, but also the temperaments which cause the meeting to result in their marriage.

Without this intuition, the mere knowledge of facts is worthless. Without Marlow's imaginative sympathy, his vision would
be limited, like the Fynes's, to the surface of events. On the
morning of Flora's loss of innocence, the Fynes sit at their win-
dow "watching like a pair of private detectives" (II, 111) the
events of the morning as if they were "some action on a stage"
(II, 114). Because they are "strangely consistent in their lack of
imaginative sympathy" (II, 143), however, they fail to understand
the effect of these events on Flora. Their vision stops with the
"face of the house cruelly impenetrable," with its "unchanged
daily aspect of inanimate things" (II, 123). In contrast, Marlow's
brief analysis of the rationale of the governess's attack on Flora
illustrates how Marlow uses this sympathetic power to reveal, to
use his term, the "inwardness" (II, 426) of events. His profile of
the governess begins with a reconstruction of her situation, using
facts gained from both Fynes. His discussion of this woman, he
tells the narrator, is not "a matter of conjecture but of actual
fact" (II, 102). He uses these facts as a starting point for his
imagination and re-creates the temperament of a woman who has
been forced to repress herself for forty years and has just been

denied her last chance for release. "I have no difficulty," Marlow remarks, "in imagining that . . . woman" (II, 101) and proceeds to re-create the emotions of the governess and her "nephew" on the evening of the day they learn of de Barral's failure:

disappointment had most likely made them touchy with each other . . . the secret of his careless, railing behaviour, was in the thought, springing up within him with an emphatic oath of relief, "Now there's nothing to prevent me from breaking away from that old woman." And that the secret of her envenomed rage, not against this miserable and attractive wretch, but against fate, accident and the whole course of human life, concentrating its venom on de Barral and including the innocent girl herself, was in the thought, in the fear crying within her, "Now I have nothing to hold him with." (II, 102–3)

In this way, Marlow is able to see that "mere disappointed cupidity" (II, 102) cannot, as the facts themselves suggest to the Fynes, account for the force of the governess's anger. Because he can see the real motive, he, unlike the Fynes, can understand the unique and terrible effect this anger has on Flora.

In contrast to such sympathetic involvement, however, Marlow frequently adopts a detachment like that of the narrators of *The Secret Agent* and *Nostromo* and at such times views the affairs of men as a comedy to be laughed at from a distance. His detachment has two sources: it is a reflection of his early life at sea, and the perspective which this life has given him on the affairs of the land. Marlow, the narrator remarks, has a kinship with "a turn of mind composed of innocence and scepticism . . . with the addition of an unexpected insight into motives, as of disinterested lookers-on at a game" (II, 34). The real source of Marlow's view of life as a game, however, lies somewhere else. Like Jörgenson's similar vision, it is rooted in a knowledge of the darkness which sets Marlow apart from the innocence of the world of the sea. Marlow has left the life of the sea, the narrator reminds us, and has become "an object of incredulous commiseration like a bird, which, secretly, should have lost its faith in the high virtue of flying" (II, 34). This secret knowledge destroys Marlow's innocence and gives his scepticism a sharper edge. When, early in the novel, he leaves with Fyne to search for the missing Flora he is met by "one of those dewy, clear, starry nights, oppressing our spirit, crushing our pride, by the brilliant evidence of the awful loneliness, of the hopeless obscure insignificance of our globe lost in the splendid revelation of a glittering, soulless universe" (II, 50). At this moment "Fyne fussing in a knickerbocker suit before the hosts of heaven, on a shadowy earth, about a transient, phantom-like girl, seemed too ridiculous to associate with" (II, 50). Marlow's detachment, like Decoud's, is grounded in a perception of the darkness which reveals the irredeemable littleness of the affairs of men. This vision, however, is implicitly the source of his attempt to understand Flora and Anthony, for it is a perception as well of the "awful loneliness" of men in a dark world and, therefore, of the necessity of their achieving a "sense of solidarity" (II, 117) with one another.

In reaching his understanding, the detachment which comes with such a perception of the darkness has a positive function. His detachment is necessary, because a concern with signs and with the imaginative empathy with momentary emotional states is misleading for two important reasons. The first is a result of the mind's openness to the influence of sensation. Speaking of Mrs. Fyne, Marlow remarks that she was "crudely amazing. . . . Why crudely? . . . Perhaps because I saw her then in a crude light. I mean this materially—in the light of an unshaded lamp. Our mental conclusions depend so much on momentary physical sensations—don't they?" (II, 56). In the same way Marlow lets his interpretation be determined by the immediate impression of the lamplight when Flora, in the course of telling Marlow of her second attempt at suicide, lowers "her glance unexpectedly till her dark eyelashes seemed to rest against her white cheeks" so that "she presented a perfectly demure aspect" (II, 214). Faced with the contrast between the subject of their conversation and Flora's appearance, Marlow discovers that he "could not help a faint smile" (II, 214). Both of these incidents are examples of the misleading effect of "a mere play of physiognomy" (II, 214) on our understanding.

Despite the fact that these momentary impressions are the key to our understanding of others, there is an obvious danger in accepting them in their immediacy. Although "it may be that a glimpse and no more is the proper way of seeing an individuality" (II, 85), for this glimpse to be understood properly the mind must achieve a proper detachment from and perspective on

it. Such a perspective is behind Marlow's distinction between his
mode of vision and that of the newspaper reporter covering the
de Barral trial. Commenting on their different reactions to de
Barral's final outburst, Marlow remarks that "the pressman dis-
approved of that manifestation. It was not his business to understand it. . . . It would lead him too far away from the actualities
which are the daily bread of the public mind. . . . His business
was to write a readable account. But I, who had nothing to write,
permitted myself to use my mind as we sat before our still untouched glasses. And the disclosure which so often rewards a
moment of detachment from mere visual impressions gave me a
thrill very much approaching a shudder" (II, 87). In this passage,
we can see how sympathetic identification and detachment are
not, for Marlow, opposing principles. In order for his "imaginative sympathy" (II, 143) to operate free from the influence of
"mere visual impressions" it must take advantage of the freedom
offered it by detachment. Marlow's ability to detach himself in
this way and to permit himself to use his mind allows him "to
enter into the feelings of a man . . . whose imagination wakes up
at the very moment he is about to enter the tomb" (II, 87). In
Chance, Marlow's sympathy always has this quality of intellectual
control. It is always based in a detachment which frees the mind
from the immediacy of the appeal which signs make to "our
understanding and emotions" (II, 282).

The second danger in a program of imaginative empathy lies
in the self-defeating nature of a too-close identification with one
point of view. In the early novels, the emphasis lay on the way
sympathetic identification with a character in the grip of the
irrational was itself a way into irrationality. In *Chance*, the
emphasis rests implicitly on the way such an identification would
blind Marlow to the very signs which his sympathetic approach
is designed to interpret. Anthony, under the control of his own
"blind generosity" (II, 343), ignores the signs of Flora's love. Mrs.
Fyne could, Marlow comments, "before the task of evolving the
philosophy of rebellious action had affected her intuitive sharp-
ness, perceive things which were, I suspect, moderately plain" (II,
91). At the time of Flora and Anthony's elopement, however, she
is as unconscious of Flora's real motives as Anthony will become.

For Marlow to involve himself too closely with either of these characters would be for him to become a prisoner of their blindness. He avoids this by retreating to a position of detachment whenever such a danger presents itself. The long conversation between Marlow and Mrs. Fyne in the chapters entitled "The Tea Party" and "Flora" is a dramatization of Marlow's fluctuation between sympathy and detachment. In this conversation, he moves from an initial reluctance to become involved in the Fynes's affairs to the moment when her "little cry of distress, quite genuine in its inexpressiveness, altered my feeling toward Mrs. Fyne" (II, 138). Throughout the conversation, Marlow exhibits the same ambivalence. He alternates constantly between a sympathy with Mrs. Fyne's compassion for Flora and with Fyne's own disagreement with his wife on the one hand and an assertion that "neither my affections nor my vanity was engaged" (II, 145) on the other. Thus the moment when Marlow's imaginative sympathy allows him to understand the depth of Mrs. Fyne's feelings, and allows him to see that "by Jove she's desperate too," is followed "by a movement of shrinking from this unreasonable and unmasculine affair" (II, 152–53).

The ebb and flow of Marlow's sympathy in this scene is not haphazard. His retreat to a detached point of view here gives him the same freedom of mind that "a moment of detachment from mere visual impressions" (II, 87) affords him in his conversation with the reporter. In this case, his freedom allows him to participate in all points of view, to enter the worlds of Anthony, Flora, and Mrs. Fyne, without being limited by any of them. By constantly alternating between imaginative sympathy and detachment, he avoids any danger of being drawn completely into one of these worlds in the way that the narrator of *The Nigger of the "Narcissus"* is drawn into the world of James Wait. Because of this, he is able to understand the relationships of all these points of view. "Marlow," remarks the narrator, "had the habit of pursuing general ideas in a peculiar manner, between jest and earnest" (II, 23). It is this peculiar manner, this blend of involvement and detachment, which characterizes Marlow's narrative throughout.

The way in which Marlow blends sympathy and detachment in this scene with Mrs. Fyne is again a reminder of how his imaginative sympathy always operates within a larger context of rational analysis and control. It is always used as one step in a deductive procedure which is founded in the perspective and freedom of mind which his detachment gives him. Although these excursions into sympathetic involvement are necessary to reveal the inwardness of events, such glimpses are meaningful only if they are correlated with other, objective material and formed into some kind of coherent theory. While "the purely human reality is capable of lyrism but not abstraction" (II, 310), such a systematizing process is necessary to reach a full understanding of this reality. "Nothing will serve for its understanding," Marlow continues, "but the rational linking up of characters and facts" (II, 310).

This rational linking up is the purpose of Marlow's narrative. The first part of *Chance* is an illustration of Marlow's use of this method to provide an insight into the worlds of Flora and Anthony through an investigation of their pasts. In his "old-maiden-lady-like occupation of putting two and two together . . . to produce a coherent theory" (II, 326) he sketches profiles of Flora and Anthony which have the composite quality of "a coherent theory" formulated by someone acting "as an investigator—a man of deductions" (II, 326). These profiles are not the result of a single, sudden insight or of a moment, like Razumov's moment of confession, which promises to reveal the whole truth of another in a flash. Rather they have the quality which is characteristic also of the thought of a detective who blends theory, fact, and experience to form the total picture of a person's actions.

This method is the subject of the novel. What dramatic quality *Chance* possesses results from the contrast between its use by Marlow and by Powell. The contrast is introduced in the opening incident concerning Powell's first job as second mate. Here, the naïveté of Powell concerning the motives of the shipping master is set off against Marlow's insight. Powell accepts his namesake in a straightforward manner as a spiritual father. Marlow, however, reveals his credentials as an expert in the psychological wilderness by suggesting a deeper level of motivation. "I cannot help thinking," he remarks, "that there was some malice in the way he seized the opportunity to serve you. . . . I am inclined to think your cheek alarmed him. And this was an excellent occasion for him to suppress you altogether. For if you accepted he was relieved of you with every appearance of humanity, and if you made objections . . . it was open to him to drop you as a sort of imposter" (II, 23–24). In the same way, the two parts of *Chance* contrast Marlow's subtlety with Powell's unsophisticated attempts to fit the facts of the situation on the *Ferndale* into some reasonable theory, to " 'get hold of that thing' by some side which would fit with his simple notions of psychology" (II, 308).

It is, of course, no real contest. Powell's failure to discover the "inwardness of what was passing before his eyes" (II, 426) serves only to emphasize the greater depth of Marlow's experienced vision, and to let us see the apparent confirmation of Marlow's strategy. Marlow does, in fact, seem to achieve a level of understanding which bridges not only the gap that exists between Flora and Anthony but those which separate all the characters in the novel. His comments on the way our ability to understand others is the foundation of our "sense of solidarity" (II, 117) with them come at the end of his psychological profile of the governess, and this profile is obviously an illustration of how such understanding brings "in minds of any largeness an inclination to that indulgence which is next to affection" (II, 117–18).

This profile also points, however, to the way Marlow, because he has access to the private worlds of these characters, can see how the situation between Flora and Anthony flows from the interaction of these worlds. Marlow's understanding provides the instrument by which Flora and Anthony can be freed from their pasts. Because only Marlow has the key to their "psychological cabin-mystery of discomfort" (II, 325), only he, it would seem, could bring about such a liberation, only he could provide the necessary perspective.

Flora and Anthony do achieve such a liberation. At the moment when Powell saves Anthony from de Barral, a moment when "the tension of the false situation was at its highest" (II, 426), both manage to break out of this false life. Their liberation, however, is the result not of an informed and considered intervention by Marlow but rather of an act of Powell, an act in which the role of *Chance* is deliberately emphasized. Powell's view of de Barral's attempted murder is the result, as Powell observes, of "the wonderful linking up of small facts," of the "precise workmanship of chance, fate, providence, call it what you will!" (II, 411). The fact that Flora and Anthony are saved by the very person whose lack of understanding is contrasted to Marlow's raises an important point. In the flow of Marlow's rhetoric the reader tends to forget that Marlow himself took an active part in Flora's history when he urged Fyne to accommodate his wife and visit Anthony in London. This is the visit, moreover, which results in Anthony's act of renunciation. Thus, while on one level the two parts of *Chance* contrast Powell's naïveté with the greater penetration of Marlow, they also present Powell solving a situation which the supposedly acute Marlow has created.

It is in the tension between action and understanding that the novel's judgment of Marlow's strategy lies. In order to free man from his bondage to time it is not sufficient for Marlow to achieve his understanding of Flora and Anthony. He must do so at a point and in a way that allows him to act on this understanding. In order for man to be assured of the certainty of Razumov's willed and determined future, it is not enough that he be given a way of understanding what is past. To free him from the "blind and insensible" (II, 396) force of time this understanding must give him a measure of foresight. Marlow's strategy, scientific in its marriage of facts and theory, ultimately must be judged on the scientific criterion of predictability. It is on this criterion that he fails. At the moment when, as he remarks, "I myself had played my part" (II, 309), he believes both that Anthony would not be impressed by Fyne and that Flora was in fact the aggressor in their marriage.

Marlow's failure of understanding is important because it emphasizes the way in which Marlow's vision is itself tied to the force of chance. His method is based on the accumulation and interpretation of facts, but it is chance itself which provides these facts. As Marlow himself remarks, he had been allowed a glimpse into Flora's world "simply by chance" (II, 311). At the time of his intervention, he simply does not yet have enough of the key facts which "give my imagination its line" (II, 210) to allow him to understand the probable effects of Fyne's action. No matter how sharp and practised Marlow's eye becomes it would seem that, because vision is tied to chance in this way, the future will always be the product of accident rather than design. Marlow's rational piecing-together is always one step behind events. He is a detective, but not a prophet.

Marlow himself seems to realize this. His narrative is studded with references to man's inability to penetrate the future. His analysis of the shipping master's attitude toward Powell is based on the fact that "it's certainly unwise to admit any sort of responsibility for our actions, whose consequences we are never able to forsee" (II, 23). The narrative itself is a proof of this inability, a testament to the fact that, "chance being incalculable" (II, 100), we live in a world determined by "forces which, for us, work in the dark because of our imperfect comprehension" (II, 327). Marlow's failure to provide such a basis for predictability, a basis which would allow men to will and determine their futures, throws a shadow over the seemingly happy ending of *Chance*. It is true that Flora and Anthony do finally consummate their embrace and that this embrace does bring the certainty which Alvan Hervey glimpsed and for which so many of Conrad's characters searched. "I loved and was loved," Flora tells Marlow, "untroubled, at peace, without remorse, without fear. All the world, all life were transformed for me" (II, 444). In the final scene Marlow, moreover, is able to protect Flora against a return of "the old mistrust, the old doubt of herself, the old scar of the blow received in childhood" (II, 445–46), and to urge Powell into declaring his love for her. In doing so, he seems in fact, through his insight into her, to have freed her from her past and allowed her to choose her own future.

Yet seen in the context of the tension between Marlow's understanding and the effects of his earlier action in Flora's life, Marlow's confident assertion "that the science of life consists in seizing each chance that presents itself" (II, 446) loses much of its force. By reminding us that it was not Marlow but chance which had provided, and taken away, Flora's earlier happiness with Anthony, this context undermines the optimism suggested by the marriage between Powell and Flora. Although Marlow seems certain that it will end happily, he was equally certain that

178

Fyne's visit would have no effect on Anthony. "The subterfuges of . . . passion," Marlow earlier remarked, "are not to be fathomed. You think it is going on the way it looks, whereas it is capable, for its own ends, of walking backwards into a precipice" (II, 103.) His comment describes exactly the involution of Anthony's love for Flora, but it also illustrates why Marlow's optimism at the end is unfounded. In a world in which the forces, external and psychological, which determine life are incalculable it is impossible to seize any chance with a full knowledge of the consequences. From this point of view, the brief and accidental happiness of Flora and Anthony serves more to underline the poignancy of man's inability to achieve such happiness by his own will than to put a seal of approval on Marlow's strategy.

Conclusion

The failure of Marlow's shifting point of view in *Chance* marked the end of Conrad's search for a way for man to establish the limited but positive identity potential in his relations with others. After this failure, Conrad returned to his position at the conclusion of *Under Western Eyes*. The novels which follow *Chance*, for all their varied settings, embody the common pattern already imaged in the logic of Razumov's career. *Victory*, *The Arrow of Gold*, and *The Rover* are all novels in which the protagonist passes, as Razumov did, from a state of limited awareness to one of "awakened consciousness" (xxii, 342). In *Victory*, this initial state is defined by Heyst's isolation, an isolation which reflects his decision to "have no connection with earthly affairs and passions" (xv, 60). In *The Arrow of Gold* it is defined by the naïveté of George on the eve of his first love and his first adventure. In *The Rover* it appears in the unconsciousness of old Peyrol, who, like Lingard and Singleton, begins the novel characterized by the innocence of the world of the sea.

Each of these characters is drawn from this initial state to a fuller sense of life by the force of passion. Peyrol, who had always acted "unemotionally, for such was his character formed under the sun of the *Indian Seas*" (xxiv, 1), finds that the first sight of Arlette "aroused a kind of intimate emotion which he had not known before to exist by itself in a man" (xxiv, 88). Heyst finds his similar experience with Lena reveals that his former isolated existence was a lie and that "the awakening of a tenderness, indistinct and confused" (xv, 82) which he first feels under her influence brings to him eventually "a greater sense of his own reality than he had ever known in all his life" (xv, 200).

Yet for these characters, as for Razumov, immersion in what Conrad, in "The Return," calls "the stream of life" (viii, 123) leads to death. The face of Arlette, which brings Peyrol his new consciousness is also, as Catherine tells him, the sign which death has made to him.[1] Their inability to achieve a positive self by their involvement in this force is apparent not only in the deaths of Peyrol and Lena and the near death of Monsieur George, but in the failure, before their deaths, to achieve a true openness with their lovers. Although her final minutes convince Lena of "the reality of her victory over death" (xv, 406) and bring to her a vision of Heyst taking her "into the sanctuary of his innermost heart—for ever" (xv, 407), her love in actuality fails to overcome "his fastidious soul, which even at that moment kept the true cry of love from his lips in its infernal mistrust of all life. He dared not touch her" (xv, 406). The impossibility of reaching the other is implicit, too, in Rita's desertion of George and in Peyrol's decision to leave Arlette and undertake Real's suicidal mission. They love, as Razumov loves, only to "go out—and perish" (xxii, 361).

The lives of Heyst, Lena, George, and Peyrol are, then, a restatement of the truth at the center of Conrad's world: the paradox that the source of life is also the force of death. The force of the darkness gives birth to awareness only to reabsorb it; Peyrol moves from "a simple, venturesome, precarious life, full

---

[1] Paul L. Wiley, *Conrad's Measure of Men* (Madison: University of Wisconsin Press, 1954), p. 190, remarks that *The Rover's* affirmation is reflected in the marriage of Real and Arlette. But *The Rover* is Peyrol's story and the emphasis falls on Arlette's destruction of his protective unconsciousness. Thus in the final moments of his life he is described as an "old man on whom age had stolen, unnoticed, till the veil of peace was torn down by the touch of a sentiment unexpected like an intruder and cruel like an enemy" (xxiv, 268).

THE METAPHYSICS OF DARKNESS

of risks and leaving no time for introspection" (xxiv, 173) to an "intimate inward sense" (xxiv, 173) of himself only to reach "that depth of despondency [where] there was nothing more before him but a black gulf into which his consciousness sank like a stone" (xxiv, 174). The meaning of the repetition of these characters' voyages into the darkness in Conrad's last novels is, however, equally clear. It implies not only a final recognition of this paradox but also a final acceptance of it, and it is an acceptance which does not abandon the voyage in the face of death but embraces this death as the inevitable price of a true self. The same necessity which Conrad has felt throughout his fiction to journey outward, to involve himself in some reality which transcends the limits of human awareness, would seem to lead him toward this adventure even in the light of a full understanding of its consequences. In Conrad's world, man must accept the fact that the darkness is, finally, the source of life, and if he wishes ever to transcend the ephemerality and abstractness of his initial, orphaned state, then he can do so only by returning to this source. Although this will result in the extinction of consciousness, it is only by such a final voyage that man can make the necessary and saving contact with the reality which has brought him into existence.

This is the true meaning implicit in the conclusion of *Under Western Eyes*. The force which drives Haldin in his destructive violation of Razumov's lonely existence in Russia is only another manifestation of the passion which eventually leads Razumov himself to destroy the isolation imposed on him by his role in Geneva. By confessing to Natalia and refusing to betray that woman with "the most trustful eyes of any human being that ever walked this earth" (xxii, 22), Razumov is only acknowledging Haldin's view of him as "an altogether trustworthy man" (xxii, 6). In accepting his self from Haldin in this way, he receives that "real life" which is founded "in the thoughts of other men by reason of respect or natural love" (xxii, 14), and at this moment, Razumov actually achieves the "solidity of character" (xxii, 15) which Haldin attributes to him. But if Razumov by this confession attains the solidity and reality which is the goal of the orphan's journey, he does so because in confessing he accepts his brotherhood not only with Haldin but with the forces of darkness which Haldin represents. For this reason, his decision to act on his love for Natalia leads inevitably not only to his confession but to his return to the plains of Russia, plains which in their immensity and emptiness image the fundamental level of the darkness. Because for Conrad the darkness is now the only source of a true life, Razumov's victory and his death on these plains are inextricably involved with one another.

From this point of view it is apparent that *Under Western Eyes* is, on a symbolic level at least, anything but an affirmation of the West. Both the English Teacher and Razumov are men who, like Conrad himself, were born in Russia but adopt a Western personality.[2] In their denial of their "illogical" (xxii, 4) Slavic origins and their cultivation of the "frigid English manner" (xxii, 16) of "self-contained, thinking men" (xxii, 19), they suggest the hostility which exists between consciousness and the darkness which has given it birth. But if *Under Western Eyes* affirms Razumov's abandonment of his pose as "a regular Englishman" (xxii, 22) and his acceptance of his Russian birthright, then it implies as well the rejection of the narrator who, despite his attraction to Natalia, insists upon maintaining his self-contained, Western pose. The deadness which characterizes both the English Teacher and the city in which he makes his home reveals Conrad's final disillusionment with the attempt by consciousness to achieve, through its own resources, the stable ground of its existence. The superficiality of the landscape of Geneva, which appears to be "made of painted cardboard" (xxii, 288), suggests that all man's efforts in this direction have resulted only in the creation of a world which mirrors his own lack of solidity.

The hollowness of the English Teacher, however, implies not only the failure of consciousness to achieve a "self-contained" existence. His opening statements on the nature of language emphasize that he presents himself not only as one who sees the world through Western eyes but as one who writes of it from this perspective as well. The Western attempt to hide the darkness behind a painted surface appears, in microcosm, in the

[2] Jocelyn Baines, *Joseph Conrad: A Critical Biography* (London: McGraw-Hill, 1960), p. 7, remarks that Conrad was born in a section of the Ukraine which, although it had been Polish from 1385 until 1793, had only about 3 percent Polish population.

THE METAPHYSICS OF DARKNESS

English Teacher's efforts to smother his Russian nature "under a wilderness of words" (XXII, 3). The rejection of his strategy represents, therefore, not only the rejection of a way of life but of a mode of art, and, on this level, *Under Western Eyes* not only maps the final journey of Conrad's adventurers, but reveals as well the final direction which the act of writing, as a version of the adventure, will take.

Under Western Eyes thus defines the last of the three major stances which Conrad adopts in his literary career. The composition of *Almayer's Folly* is an expression of Conrad's initial adoption of what is essentially a version of realism. The foundation of this realism is his assumption that language embodied in some way the actuality of the visible surface of life. Because Conrad at this point believed words did contain "things as they are," writing provided a method by which the consciousness of the artist could ground itself in the solidity of the world. By creating an image of the visible surface of life, an image into which the temperament of the artist and "things as they are" entered as equal terms, the artist could participate in the substance of the men and objects of this surface. This movement of the artist's consciousness into the visible world is the expression, in artistic terms, of a commitment to the world which constitutes one fundamental orientation of Conrad's thought.

The movement of Conrad's novels from *An Outcast of the Islands* through *Lord Jim* describes the gradual erosion of his belief in the reality of the visible world and his growing perception of the true nature of the darkness. With this erosion, the relation between the writer and the world of language changes radically. Since a language which captures this surface no longer embodies the positive reality of "things as they are" but only reflects the image of something essentially insubstantial, the possibilty of a realistic fiction—at least in Conrad's initial sense— disappears. But two new alternatives emerge. On the one hand, the writer can use language to create an illusion behind which he can hide the destructive truth of the darkness. Both Marlow in "Heart of Darkness" and Stein in *Lord Jim* adopt versions of this strategy. On the other hand, the writer can use language to create the image of the visible surface, but create it in such a way that the surface does not hide, but is rather framed against the darkness. To do so is to face directly the insubstantiality of the surface and abandon any hope of a positive commitment to life. Precisely because it does detach the writer's consciousness from the surface, however, this method seems to promise that the writer can preserve some sense of identity which will not be destroyed by his recognition of the unreality of the visible world. It is this second alternative which develops out of the investigations of "Heart of Darkness" and *Lord Jim* and culminates in the ironic detachment of *Nostromo* and *The Secret Agent*. It is an art based on the ironic juxtaposition of surface and depth that defines the attitude of detachment which is always opposed in Conrad to his desire to involve himself with the surrounding world.

Decoud's suicide in *Nostromo*, however, reveals the logical contradiction inherent in any attempt to make one's perception of the ephemerality of creation a foundation of the continuing existence of the self. Although Conrad follows *Nostromo* with *The Secret Agent*, it seems inevitable, in the light of Decoud's experience, that he will abandon the attitude, and the art, of irony. *Under Western Eyes* and the novels which follow it represent such a surrender of detachment. These novels are the expression of Conrad's desire to turn once again toward the world and to find his identity in an act of commitment to it.

This act of commitment, however, is no longer directed toward the surface of creation, but beyond it into the darkness. Razumov's story in *Under Western Eyes* is, in this light, more than an investigation of how such an act can be made. In so far as *Under Western Eyes* is an attempt to replace not only the attitude but the art of irony, the novel is an investigation, too, of how the act of writing can reach this goal. Like the English Teacher, Razumov, we recall, stands poised between West and East, detachment and the darkness, and his movement from the first to the second, from detachment and isolation to passion and Natalia can also be described in terms of his relation to language. Razumov's projected identity as a celebrated professor is predicated on a certain use of words, on the composition of a prize essay whose "neat minute handwriting" (xxii, 65) suggests the meticulous but empty formalism of the English Teacher. The "inanimate" (xxii, 288) language of the West is not, however, the only alternative

185

open to Razumov. There is the language of Russians, a language permeated by the "illogical" (XXII, 4) but vivifying force of passion. "What must remain striking to a teacher of languages," the narrator remarks, "is the Russian's extraordinary love of words ... they are always ready to pour them out ... with an enthusiasm, a sweeping abundance. ... There is a generosity in their ardour of speech which removes it as far as possible from common loquacity; and it is ever too disconnected to be classed as eloquence" (XXII, 4).

It is toward such an outpouring of passionate language that Razumov moves in the diary which is the source of much of the narrative. This movement culminates in the record of his confession to Natalia, a record which attempts "in broken sentences, full of wonder and awe" (XXII, 358) to express "the mysteriousness ... of our emotional life" (XXII, 357–58). It is this journey by Razumov from a formal, self-contained language to the language of confession which defines both the initial direction of Conrad's search for a new aesthetics of commitment and the structure of *Under Western Eyes*. The progression of the narrative consciousness of this novel, of that fundamental consciousness implicit in each word and each point of view in the work, parallels precisely the development of Razumov. This consciousness creates the perspective and the language of the English Teacher, but does so not to preserve a detached point of view. Instead, the emphasis is on its movement away from this detachment toward an involvement with Razumov. The narrative journey, too, is measured by the distance from self-protective isolation to commitment, from the English Teacher's opening attempt to bury the irrational under the weight of a dead language to a narrative which attempts to involve itself with and capture the "mystery" of the awakening of Razumov's "emotional life."

The progression from detachment to involvement characterizes not only *Under Western Eyes* but *Victory* and *The Arrow of Gold*. In each case the novel begins with the establishment of a detached consciousness which frames the action. In *Victory* this detachment is defined by the tone of the narrator who identifies himself as one of a group of onlookers who "used to laugh" (XV, 3) at Heyst; in *The Arrow of Gold* it is defined by the condescending editor whose notes open and close the novel. In each

186

case the impetus of the narrative is away from this perspective toward an identification with the protagonist during that experience of the darkness which, as we have seen, brings him to an "awakened consciousness" (xxII, 342). As in *Under Western Eyes*, the structure of these novels suggests that the act of writing is, for each narrating consciousness, an act by which they create or discover a language which, like the language of Russia, gives them access to the same experience which confers on Razumov his real life. And this movement toward identification seems to be confined in Conrad's last novel, *The Rover*. Here all vestiges of a detached perspective have disappeared. The novel is characterized by the same simplicity of point of view which underlies *Almayer's Folly*. Like the narrator of *Almayer's Folly*, the narrator of *The Rover* has the ability through successive acts of identification to move from one consciousness to another, and like the narrator of Conrad's first novel his tone is the calm, secure tone of one whose identity seems assured by these acts.

From this point of view, the later novels seem to mark Conrad's return to a point where the act of writing can ground the self positively in the source of life, but to read them in this way would be a serious mistake. Unlike Nina Almayer, Razumov's journey does not end in his discovery and acceptance of the force of passion. As we have seen its final end is not in the irrational stream of life but in the fundamental level of the darkness which lies beneath. Razumov's flight from his sterile life in Geneva is, consequently, completed not in his confession but in his death on the plains of Russia. It is his return to accept his "inheritance of space" (xxII, 33), his return to lose himself in the immensity of the darkness, which gives him his real self. In the same way that, in the logic of these novels, the new awareness which Razumov receives through his love for Natalia can only be fulfilled by the final absorption of his awareness by the darkness, so the new language which is the agency of this awareness is confirmed only when it, too, is extinguished in an immensity whose "perfect silence" (xvII, 115) is "still as death" (xxI, 114). It is because in one aspect Razumov's life is consummated in the "absolute silence" (ix, 496) of the darkness that his journey to Russia is associated with his deafening. Although Sophia Antonovna reports that Razumov still "talks well" (xxII, 379), he is clearly no longer able to converse. He can only speak to the world out of the silence of his deafness, and this situation suggests how, for Conrad, Razumov's death is in one important aspect a dying out of language.

The juxtaposition of Razumov's full journey with the movement of the narrator of *Almayer's Folly* reveals not only the distance between Conrad's initial and his final form of commitment but the real meaning implicit in the narrative progression of these last novels. If the progression draws its validity from its ⁻identification with the development of the protagonist, then the identification demands that the movement of the narrative consciousness continue to a point where it, too, gives itself to the silence of death. In this context, Conrad's rejection of the English Teacher involves more than the obvious rejection of Stein's and Marlow's retreat into a shell of language. It involves the rejection of any strategy, of any manipulation of language, which interposes words between the consciousness of the writer and the absorption of this consciousness into the darkness. The aesthetics of irony behind *The Secret Agent* had not hidden, but had recognized, the darkness. It had done so, however, in such a way that the consciousness of the artist continued to exist. It existed, of course, only as a point of view, an ironic voice, but it is precisely his existence as a voice which the artist must now sacrifice.

Under Western Eyes in this way implies a denial of both aesthetic stances which preceded it. The logic of this work, and of the novels which follow, points toward a moment when the tension between involvement and detachment will be resolved in the final extinction of consciousness in its source. It is important to see, however, that these novels can only point to the moment. Consciousness cannot transcend, and in this sense contain, the death which brings it both fulfillment and extinction. In the same way the language of the novel cannot contain the silence which is its end. The deaths of Razumov and Peyrol image, in this sense, the final movement of the narrator into the darkness and, in doing so, define an art which succeeds only in the act of transcending and negating its own existence. Like Razumov's return to the emptiness of Russia, these novels are completed at the point where the final sentence dissolves into the blankness of the margin; the narrative voice is completed in

188

the silence which follows its last words. The epigraph of *The Rover*, "Sleep after toyle, port after stormie seas,/ Ease after warre, death after life, does greatly please" (XXIV, i), suggests Conrad's acceptance of this final negation. In an article on Alphonse Daudet, written early in his career, Conrad seems, even then, to have glimpsed the final destination of his voyage, a voyage which he senses will carry him beyond the surface of life, the conversations of men, and the bounds of art to a point where, like Razumov's, his voice issues solely from the darkness, an echo whose source is already quieted:

If [Daudet] saw only the surface of things it is for the reason that most things have nothing but a surface. He did not pretend ... to see any depths in a life that is only a film of unsteady appearances stretched over regions deep indeed, but which have nothing to do with the half-truths, half-thoughts, and whole illusions of existence. The road to these distant regions does not lie through the domain of Art or the domain of Science where well-known voices quarrel noisily in a misty emptiness; it is a path of toilsome silence upon which travel men simple and unknown, with closed lips, or, may be, whispering their pain softly—only to themselves. (III, 22)

Index

Adventure: associated with voyage, ix, 1, 12; associated with writing, 43, 63; as attempt to master darkness, 12, 17; in later novels, 181–88; in *Lord Jim*, 81; as search for self, 1–2

Almayer's Folly: contrasted to *An Outcast of the Islands*, 53–54; discussed, 37–42; narrator in, 188; as realistic novel, 27; relation to later novels, 184; relation to *Under Western Eyes*, 149–56, 158

Arrow of Gold, The: discussed, 180–82, 186–87; relation to *Under Western Eyes*, 134

Baines, Jocelyn, 183*n*
Blackwood, William, 67
Bolivar, Simon, 128
Bradbrook, M. C., 24
Brooke, James, as model for Lingard, 57

Carlyle, Thomas, 28*n*

Chance: discussed, 159–79; relation to *Under Western Eyes*, 134

Chart: as image of language, 90; as image of surface, 16, 83

Consciousness: characterized by freedom, 13; negated by darkness, 14–15; as orphan, 10–12; return to source by, 180–83; source in darkness, 8–10; *see also* Taminah

Cooper, James Fenimore, 18

Cunninghame-Graham, Robert: 4, 7; Conrad's correspondence with, 22–26, 30*n*, 72, 73, 139

Darkness: Conrad's discovery of, 28; Conrad's first realization of hostility of, 54–55; in early novels, 37, 40, 41; as entombment, 100; and landscape in *Nostromo*, 109–11; as source of